TROPHY WHITETAILS

WITH PAT & NICOLE REEVE

TIPS AND TACTICS
FROM THE  *Driven* TEAM

DUNCAN DOBIE

Published by

Krause Publications a division of F+W Media, Inc.
700 East State Street • Iola, WI 54990-0001
715-445-2214 • 888-457-2873
www.krausebooks.com

To order books or other products call toll-free 1-800-258-0929
or visit us online at www.shopdeerhunting.com

Cover photography courtesy of Pat and Nicole Reeve

ISBN-13: 978-1-4402-3612-9
ISBN-10: 1-4402-3612-7

Cover Design by Al West
Designed by Sharon Bartsch
Edited by Chris Berens

Printed in China

DEDICATION

Pat and Nicole

First, we'd like to dedicate this book to our dear friends and precious family for the tremendous support you have always given us. Our schedule is so demanding, and we are gone much of the time, but you are always in our hearts. Thank you in so many ways! You are so important to us!

Secondly, we dedicate this book to two very special friends. Several years ago, while attending one of the many deer classics we go to each year, we met and became friends with a young man named Drake Taylor of Dunlap, Ill. Drake, who had been born with a rare type of dwarfism, made and sold his own jewelry. He was an extraordinary young man. We also became friends with a beautiful young girl named Emily Philip of Green Bay, Wis., at a different show. At 6 years of age in 2002, Emily had been diagnosed with a severe heart and lung condition.

Tragically, Emily passed away on Dec. 20, 2012 and Drake passed away in early 2013. Over the last few years, one of the true highlights of our entire year was looking forward to seeing these special youngsters in Illinois and Wisconsin at the shows. They touched our hearts in many ways and inspired us beyond belief. Drake and Emily loved to hunt more than anything in the world, and each had the opportunity to go on a number of memorable hunts during their all-too-short lives.

This book is respectfully dedicated to their memory. Their time on this earth was far too short but everyone who knew them was impacted in some special way. To Drake and Emily, we will never forget you!

Pat and Nicole
November 2013

CONTENTS

AUTHOR BIOGRAPHY
Duncan Dobie

Duncan Dobie has been a full-time, freelance writer and photographer for over 30 years. He has long specialized in writing about white-tailed deer. Over the years, he has earned a reputation as being one of the nation's top whitetail writers. He has written hundreds of magazine articles and sold hundreds of photos to numerous outdoor publications.

Duncan has written nine books, contributed to a number of others, and helped edit and produce several books for other writers. Among his most recent books are *Hunting Mature Whitetails the Lakosky Way* published in 2011, and *Legendary Whitetails III* published in 2012, both with Krause Publications.

Duncan was very excited to have the opportunity to work with Pat and Nicole on this very special book!

ACKNOWLEDGEMENTS

Sincerest thanks to all of our family, special friends and sponsors who have helped us so much over the years. Without their support, this book would not have been possible. We owe so much to so many!

PAT AND NICOLE'S CHILDREN

Olivia, Cole, Carson and Isabel

NICOLE'S PARENTS

James and Susan Jones

PAT'S PARENTS

Keith Reeve, Mikael and Carol Newman

A special thank you to all of the outfitters that have become close friends over the years. Without each and every one of you we would not be where we are today!

SPECIAL FRIENDS

Adam Helwig
Bryan Lemke
Grant Kuypers
Dean Kuypers
Brandon Schreiber
Gene Bidlespacher
Dave Boland
Paul Brazil
Bill Konway Photography
Garry Donald, *Big Buck Magazine*
Dave and Carman Forbes
Donnie Hansen
Ron and Kent Hurlburt
Laurie and Tom Indrebo
Shane Indrebo
Mike Jahnke
Myles Keller
Ken Kemper
Mitch Hagen

Mike Law
Brian Lovett
Darren and Sherri Martin
Jim Musil
Chad and Jen Nolte
Steve Puppe
Cody and Kelsey Robbins, *Live 2 Hunt*
Dan Schmidt
Steve and Micki Snow
Dennis and Janet Williams
Mark and Karen Wimpy
Wes Good's Wildlife Studios
Klaus Lebrecht, Antlers by Klaus
Mark Rigotti, Viola Taxidermy

SPONSORS

Barnett Crossbows
Big Game Treestands
BogPod Shooting Systems
Campbell Cameras
CanCooker
Dick's Sporting Goods

Evolved Harvest
Field Logic
Eyecon Trail Cameras
Lumenok
Markquart Motors
Mathews
Mossy Oak

Muzzy
Nikon
Otis Gun Cleaning Systems
Outdoor Edge
Polaris
Primos

Ripcord
ScentBlocker
TruFire Releases
Thompson Center Arms
Wildgame Innovations
Yeti Coolers

INTRODUCTION

By Duncan Dobie

As soon as I found out I was going to have the opportunity to work on a book with Pat and Nicole, I was excited to say the least. When it comes to successfully hunting mature whitetails with a bow, this enterprising couple has few peers. Pat and Nicole are phenomenal bow-hunters. More importantly, they are extraordinary human beings.

I first met Pat back in the summer of 2004 and we became immediate friends. I had just become editor of *North American Whitetail* magazine. Pat had been hired some months earlier to co-host and produce the brand-new *North American Whitetail Television* series on Outdoor Channel. It was an exciting time. I had known of Pat through several groundbreaking videos he had produced for Hunter's Specialties with the *Prime Time Bucks* series. When I finally met him in

Not only do they make sure their own children spend plenty of time outdoors, but Pat and Nicole go out of their way to share their love for the outdoors with young audiences whenever possible. "Today's kids are spending more and more time playing video games, and we encourage and try to nurture a love for nature whenever we can," Pat says.

Pat's intense passion for deer hunting started at an early age, and has catapulted him into an unbelievable career and lifestyle filled with great family, friends and never-ending adventure.

person, I was deeply impressed.

Over the next year while he was filming for *North American Whitetail Television*, I never ceased to be amazed at his incredible talent. Not only was he a gifted hunter, he was also an amazing photographer, videographer and TV producer. He sent me outstanding photos and helped me get stories for the magazine. He was a huge asset to both the TV show and the magazine and I was in awe of his ability. I still am today. I met Nicole for the first time in early 2005 and was equally impressed with her charm, beauty and knowledge of whitetail hunting. Who in the world would have thought that they would get together and become soul mates a few years later!

Pat and Nicole are two of my favorite people in the hunting industry. They are tremendous role models for hunters of all ages, and they are so good at what they do they make it look easy. But nothing in life is easy, and they have certainly paid their dues by overcoming more than their share of tough challenges over the years.

Pat and Nicole talk a lot about "making memories." Their motto is "make life an adventure and follow your dreams," and they've inspired countless people through their TV show and personal appearances at hunting shows to do just that. Their lives together have been filled with excitement, and they have traveled the world sharing many heart-stopping adventures making many special memories together. They have accomplished a great deal in a very short period of time.

Whenever Pat and Nicole go somewhere to hunt mature whitetails, they set the bar so high that the difficulty factor is double or triple what most whitetail

Pat and Nicole believe that every day should be an adventure and that every individual should try to follow his or her dreams. Their lifestyle inspires countless people through television and numerous personal appearances throughout the year.

The title of their TV show suits Pat and Nicole to a 'T' because few people in the outdoor industry strive for excellence the way this hardworking couple does every day of the year.

Pat is constantly thinking and scheming about new ways to make each television production a true work of art.

Whether it's hunting, planting food plots or looking for sheds, the quest for trophy whitetails is a year-round family affair for the entire Reeve clan, and they tackle it with much energy and passion.

Pat couldn't be prouder of sons Carson and Cole, who each in their own way share his passion for the outdoors.

has become a wonderful surrogate mom to those special children. Getting their children involved in the outdoors is what truly drives them to do what they do. In fact, they are constantly encouraging everyone they know to get *all* young people involved with nature and the great outdoors.

I feel tremendously privileged to have had a small part in telling the amazing story about Pat and Nicole. I sincerely hope you enjoy reading this book as much as I enjoyed working on it.

Scan the QR codes throughout this book with your smartphone to view bonus video footage.

CHAPTER 1

PAT'S BIGGEST BUCK EVER

A 200-Inch Illinois Megabuck by Bow

When Pat traveled to Schuyler County, Ill., in mid-November 2005 to hunt with Sugar Creek Outfitters, he was operating on hope, faith and a shoestring budget. Never in his wildest dreams did he expect to arrow this 200-inch monster! But he did, and this great buck turned his life around by ensuring that his new TV show on the Men's Channel would get off the ground with a big bang.

A DOLLAR AND A PRAYER

"During the summer of 2005, I lost my job as co-host and producer of *North American Whitetail Television*. It was an unexpected blow to me and my family to say the least. I no longer had a steady paycheck coming in and things were looking bleak. My family was literally living on macaroni and cheese. Because of the popularity of *North American Whitetail Television*, I was determined to start a new show equally as successful – and I knew I didn't have any time to waste.

"My plan was to produce 13 original episodes and call my new show *Driven 24/7*. The name seemed appropriate because I was so passionate about hunting and filming big whitetails. The new show would air on the Men's Channel in 2006. But, there was one big drawback. In outdoor television, sponsors' dollars don't start coming in until after the shows air, so I had to make it through the next 10 months on almost no income.

"Intermedia Outdoors, owner of *North American Whitetail Television,* terminated my employment in August 2005. Before that happened, I had planned an early season September hunt in Kansas, so I decided to film that hunt for my new show. At the time, I had a brand-new pickup truck sitting in the garage. Even though I owned the truck, I wasn't about to take it on a road trip because the entire body was painted with my old employer's logos and I didn't want anybody to see me driving it. I certainly didn't want to give them any exposure. There was another reason as well. I couldn't afford to put gas in it.

"So I went out and bought myself a $400 clunker, an old, beat-up Cutlass Supreme that we later dubbed the 'Red Rocket,' and headed to Kansas. While there, I shot

By the fall of 2005, Pat's close friend Tom Indrebo of Bluff Country Outfitters in Buffalo County, Wis., had captured numerous trail camera photos of a huge buck one of his hunting guides had named Moses. Both Pat and Tom had been following this buck for several years, and Pat drove his old clunker over to Buffalo County in October 2005 to bow-hunt the big buck as soon as archery season opened. (See Chapter 4 for the complete story of Moses.)

A beaming Pat Reeve sits behind the wheel of the famed "red rocket," a $400 clunker he bought at the beginning of the 2005 season for basic transportation to and from several of his hunting destinations in various states. That same year Pat also conducted a Driven "camera school" at Tom Indrebo's lodge in Buffalo County, Wis. Attended by a number of cameramen that were filming for him as well as other budding young outdoorsmen who wanted to learn some of his techniques, the school was a great success!

a nice buck with my muzzleloader in late September. Then as soon as bow season opened in Wisconsin, I drove my old clunker over to Buffalo County to hunt a big non-typical buck named Moses that I had been following on property belonging to my good friend Tom Indrebo of Bluff Country Outfitters. (See Chapter 4 for the complete story of Moses.) I'd hunted Moses the year before at Tom's place and I felt confident I could kill him under the right conditions. Moses was a special deer to me and I felt like we pretty well had him figured out.

"I set up a treestand in the area where I felt sure to see Moses. While in the stand, a smaller buck came along and offered me a shot. Suddenly all of the pressures of trying to produce a brand-new TV show with limited resources started pouring through my mind. In a moment of weakness, I shot the smaller buck. The minute I released my arrow, I regretted doing it. My cameraman was shocked. 'I thought we were hunting Moses,' he said.

"I didn't have a good answer for him. The pressure had simply gotten to me. If any good came out of the lapse in judgment that day, it was the fact that I was so mad at myself that I vowed to never let something like that happen again. For the next few weeks I felt terrible about what I had done, but knew I had to move on. Plus, I knew I couldn't hunt Moses again for another whole year – *if* he survived the season.

"My next out-of-state hunt was scheduled for Illinois. While still employed by *North American Whitetail*, I had also made arrangements to hunt in mid-November at Sugar Creek Outfitters in Schulyer County. Now that I was no longer working for a prominent TV show however, I wasn't sure if the outfitter would still want me to come. I called up the manager, Chad John, and explained the situation, not knowing what he might say. Chad said, 'Come on! We'd love to have you!' I'll never forget Chad's generosity.

"With a tremendous sense of relief, I headed to Illinois in my wonderful old maroon clunker, leaky gas tank and all. I had done some scouting at Sugar Creek during the previous summer, and knew there were some nice bucks on the farm where I planned to hunt. But never in my wildest dreams did I envision shooting a 200-inch typical megabuck!"

A BUCK FOR THE AGES

The date was November 14, 2005 – prime time in west-central Illinois. It was the second morning that Pat and cameraman Jim Musil were hunting a promising farm in Schulyer County. Pat had set up several stands in different locations on the farm owned by Sugar Creek Outfitters, but he and Jim had zeroed in on one spot in particular that held much promise. One "double-set" treestand (for a cameraman and a hunter) had been placed in a wooded draw that was full of big buck sign, and another at the top of the ridge that led down to the draw.

Pat examines a series of well-used trails on the ridge where his 200-inch buck was taken.

"This man-size rub is the reason I shot my big buck," Pat said. After seeing the sign his buck was leaving in the area, Pat felt confident that a very large buck was responsible.

As the 200-inch giant was approaching his stand, Pat waited patiently for the buck to step into a 20-yard shooting lane before drawing his Mathews bow and sealing the deal.

However, the wind had not cooperated on the first day of hunting, so he and Jim had been forced to go elsewhere. Now, in the predawn darkness on the second day, the wind seemed just right to hunt the draw. They were in the double-set treestand well before daylight. The rut was in full swing, and Pat had hopes of connecting with one of the thick-antlered trophy bucks that Illinois is so famous for producing.

Shortly after daylight, a small buck appeared in a CRP field chasing a doe. About an hour later, Pat saw several does across the ridge. Watching them through his binoculars, he noticed they were acting strangely. *Could there be a big buck in the area?* Pat wondered. *After all, what else would make a group*

of does act this way?

He made several tending grunts with his Hunter's Specialties can call. Nothing happened for another hour. Disappointed, he started second-guessing his stand location. Should they have gone to the top of the ridge instead of near the bottom?

That question was answered moments later when Pat heard the unmistakable deep, guttural grunt of a mature buck in the heavy brush about 80 yards away. By now, it was about 9:30 a.m. when a doe suddenly came running out of the thicket and stopped. Pat knew that a buck was following and told Jim to get ready with the camera. He heard another deep grunt but a large tree blocked his view of the buck as it stepped out of the thicket.

Jim spotted the buck first and instinctively whispered, "Shooter!" Then he did a double-take. This was no ordinary whitetail. The buck was huge! Jim corrected himself and whispered, "Monster!"

As the buck emerged into Pat's view, he was not prepared for what he saw. Out stepped a massive 5-by-5, easily the biggest buck he had ever seen in the woods while hunting. He knew immediately that this deer was a record-book contender. What he didn't know was that the deer was about to change his life forever. Pat was immediately struck with a severe case of buck fever, something that didn't happen often.

"He was still about 60 yards away walking toward us," Pat said. "Then he started walking toward the doe. She was off to our left in a thick spot where I knew I couldn't get a shot. The buck was walking in a stiff-legged fashion like big bucks often do. For a moment, it looked like he was actually going to try and corral her in that thicket. I knew if he did my chances of getting a shot would be slim to none."

Pat also knew he was in danger of being winded. If the buck continued on its present course, it would almost certainly walk right into their scent stream. Pat said a little prayer and tried to envision every possible scenario that might occur so he would be ready to react. All of a sudden, the doe darted around the buck and ran straight toward Pat's tree. His prayer was answered.

The doe stopped right under the tree and the buck followed in her footsteps. Trying to control his excitement and moving extremely slowly so that the doe wouldn't see him, Pat focused on a shooting lane 30 yards out in front of the tree. But in the blink of an eye, the buck stepped through that shooting lane without offering a shot.

Now Pat focused all of his attention on the next shooting lane – located just 20 yards from the tree. He quickly made sure Jim was on the deer with the camera,

Certificate of Aging™

We hereby certify that the **Whitetail Buck Deer** harvested by **Pat Reeve** on **November 14, 2005** in **Schuyler County, Illinois** was **five and one half (5 1/2)** years old based on the specimen submitted to us and analyzed in our laboratory by forensic cementum annuli aging. It was reported to us that it was **Typical**, had **11 points**, a **gross score of 200"**, a **net score of 192 3/8"**, weighed **220 lbs** and was harvested with a **bow**.

Henry Chidgey
Founder
Wildlife Analytical Laboratories

Pat and Don Barry, owner of Sugar Creek Outfitters, proudly show off Pat's incredible buck after it was brought in. Wanting to know the exact age of his Illinois trophy, Pat later sent a tooth sample to Wildlife Analytical Laboratories for verification. The buck was found to be 5½ years old.

then as soon as the buck stepped into the next opening, Pat voice-grunted and the buck stopped, offering a perfect broadside shot. Pat settled his 20-yard pin right behind the buck's shoulder and released his arrow.

"I knew it was a good shot," Pat said.

The buck ran only about 10 yards while the doe ran off for parts unknown. The buck was stamping his feet and looking around as if nothing had happened, then slowly started to walk away. Watching the deer with his binoculars, Pat could see blood trickling down the buck's shoulder. A few seconds later the huge whitetail toppled over. Jim had not missed one second of the drama with the camera, so it was all there on video for the world to see! They both knew the buck was absolutely enormous, but had no idea its rack would gross score 200 typical inches.

"When I reached his side, I realized that he was much larger than I had originally thought," Pat said. "I didn't know what he would score, but I knew he was a 190-class typical. I knew he was my lifetime buck and I'd probably never top him. I had seen a lot of world-class whitetails at shows and other events, and now for the first time I realized that I had been given the chance to take one. I can't begin to describe the feeling. It was overwhelming. I was in a state of shock for a long time. God was really looking out for me on that one!"

A GIFT FROM HEAVEN

"When Jim and I returned to the lodge, no one was there. Everyone was still out in the field except for one of the hired hands. When he saw us come in he said, 'Well did you get one?'

"'Yes, I got one.'

"'Is it a pretty good one?'

"'Yeah, it's a pretty good one.'

"He walked outside with us to see the deer in the back of Jim's Toyota 4Runner. When we opened up the back, his eyes got huge and he almost fell over. 'A good one?' he said with a startled look. 'Hell, that's a monster!'

"Later on the owners of Sugar Creek, Don Barry and Don Barry Jr., returned to the lodge from hunting with manager Chad John. I had never met the Barrys before. When they saw the deer their jaws hit the floor. They were stunned. 'Where did *that* come from?' the elder Barry asked. 'You actually shot that deer on our property?' They couldn't believe it.

"Everyone seemed genuinely happy that I had shot that deer. The Barrys couldn't have been nicer. There was no jealousy whatsoever from any of the other hunters in the lodge and that meant so much to me. We did some celebrating and everyone wanted to know what the deer would score. One of the guys who had been filming the Barrys said he'd had a lot of experience measuring deer, so we found a tape and he started scoring the antlers. While we waited, everyone was guessing what the total would be. I thought it might gross around 190 inches, but I was off by 10. When he added up all the numbers, we were astounded. I learned for the first time that I had just shot a 200-inch typical whitetail!

"The next day, Jim Musil and I spent the entire day photographing my deer. We got some outstanding photos. The deer weighed 200 pounds field dressed. I later sent a tooth sample to a company in Texas for aging and found out he was 5½ years old. I caped out the entire hide myself because I planned to have him

mounted life-size. I also butchered the meat myself; Nicole and I are fanatics about dressing and butchering our own meat.

"I had the biggest buck of my life in the cooler and still had a couple of days until the first Illinois firearms season opened on Friday. I had planned all along to hunt both seasons, and had tags for both. That way, if things hadn't worked out during my bow-hunt, I could still hunt with my muzzle-loader during the three-day firearms season and hopefully still end up with a TV show. When you're filming for TV, you learn to take advantage of every hunting opportunity available. You can't afford not to because deer season only lasts a few months. Chad John had graciously invited me to hunt both seasons and I'd purchased two separate tags with plans to do just that.

"In Illinois, you can buy an archery tag to hunt anywhere in the state. You can also buy a county specific firearms tag. So that's what I had done. After killing my big buck however, I certainly didn't want to take advantage of Sugar Creek in any way by continuing to hunt. But, Don Barry immediately put me at ease when he said, "Maybe you'll get another big one during gun season." I was floored. He wanted me to stay and shoot another buck! I'll always be indebted to the Barry family for their incredible generosity.

"After you shoot an outstanding buck like I had, you're on a roll and you

Watch the incredible footage of Pat shooting his 200" Illinois Megabuck – the largest typical whitetail ever taken on video!

want it to continue. You figure luck is on your side. I definitely had the feeling that I was going to shoot another good buck. On the second morning of gun season, Jim Musil and I were sitting in a treestand in a very good spot overlooking a field. Later in the morning, the battery in the video camera suddenly went dead. Both of us were very distracted with the camera as we tinkered around with replacing the battery.

"Suddenly, we heard a deer blow from very close by. We looked down just in time to see a massive buck with probably a 180-class rack bounding off for parts unknown. He ran into the timber and I couldn't get a shot. He had walked 60 or 70 yards across the open field right up under our tree while we weren't paying attention and caught us with our pants down. I vowed to never make that mistake again. We learned that whenever filming, always replace a low battery before it dies. As a result of our mistake, we missed out on the opportunity to shoot another unbelievable buck.

"The first three-day firearms season ended without further incident. I returned two weeks later to hunt the second firearms season in early December with Chad

Ranked within the top 20 typical whitetails ever taken with a bow, Pat's Illinois monster is one of the highest scoring typical whitetails ever taken on camera.

Pat's good friend Jim Musil offered to travel to Illinois with him to film his bow-hunt in November. Neither man had any idea it would become such a historic event.

After shooting the enormous buck, Pat knew he had taken a deer that would probably make B&C, but he had no idea the massive whitetail would score 200 inches.

Nolte, a good friend and one of my pro-staffers for the new TV show. On the last day of the hunt, the weather turned bitter and nasty with a cold wind and spitting snow. During the last five minutes of shooting light on the last afternoon, I made an unusually long shot on a beautiful 155-inch 10-pointer with my Thompson/Center muzzleloader. He went right down. What a way to end my 2005 season in Illinois. What more could I have asked for?

"Just three weeks earlier, as I drove from my home in Minnesota down to Illinois in my old clunker with a leaking gas tank and almost no brakes, my future had looked pretty shaky. Now, I had taken two great bucks from Illinois. It just goes to show: Sometimes when things look their worst, life has a way of turning everything around if you just hang in there!

"Riding home to Minnesota in that old clunker, with my 200-inch rack lying in the front seat next to me where I could put my hand on it, I knew I was going to make it with my new TV show and career. After

Pat was thrilled to be invited back to Sugar Creek Outfitters by owner Don Barry for the 2005 firearms season. During the second firearms season in early December, he shot yet another trophy buck using a T/C muzzleloader. The outstanding 10-point brute tallied up 155 inches.

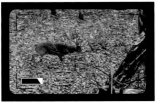

going through the humiliation of being fired from my former job as co-host and producer of *North American Whitetail Television*, the trip to Illinois had been the shot in the arm I needed to keep going. That big buck changed everything and truly was a gift from heaven. I had a new lease on life and a new boost of energy. I was ready for anything."

THE REST OF THE STORY

"The farm where I killed my big buck was one of many owned by Sugar Creek Outfitters in a several-county area. As far as I had been able to find out, no one had ever seen the deer before. I later found out from his shed antlers that he had been almost the same size the year before, and a buck like that certainly wouldn't have gone unnoticed if he had been seen by anyone at Sugar Creek. If any others hunters in the neighborhood had known about him, they certainly had been very tight-lipped about it.

"The following spring, Mark Wimpy, a good friend and another pro-staffer for *Driven 24/7* from Illinois, called one day. 'Hey, I think I know about a guy who might have the sheds from your buck,' he told me. Mark put me in touch with a young man named Lucas

Pat called on good friend Dave Boland of Chatfield, Minn., to officially score the huge rack. Dave is a nationally-known measurer who has scored numerous world-class racks during his distinguished career. The massive 11-point rack grossed 200 typical inches and netted 192⅜.

Barbie that had found a huge set of sheds in Schuyler County. If they were from my buck, I certainly wanted to see them and perhaps offer to buy them. We set up a time to meet in March 2006. Oddly enough, we met late at night along the highway while I was en route to the Illinois Deer Classic in Bloomington. The moment I saw the antlers, I knew they were from the buck.

"Lucas told me he'd found both antlers in the same general vicinity of where I had shot the buck on an adjacent piece of property. He had found them in the spring of 2005 lying together, side by side in a picked cornfield. It was his first time shed hunting and the first set of shed antlers he'd ever picked up. What a find! I told him I would love to own them but he said he didn't want to part with them. So I told him I would stay in touch.

"The sheds grossed in the high 190s (given the same 21³/₈-inch inside spread), only several inches less than the original rack. The G-4 on the right side was slightly shorter, but both sheds had almost the exact same beam length – right at 30 inches. The rack really hadn't changed much from 2004 to 2005. It had just put on a little more tine length in 2005 so the score was slightly higher.

"Over the next few years, I bumped into Lucas at the Illinois Deer Classic and always asked him if he wanted to sell the sheds, and he would always say, 'No, not right now.' About five years went by when one day Matt Beard, a well-known shed antler collector in Missouri, called and told me that Lucas had called him to ask what the sheds were worth. Apparently he was finally ready to do something. I contacted Lucas as soon

First-time shed hunter Lucas Barbie found both shed antlers from Pat's buck in the spring of 2005. They were lying side-by-side on the edge of a cornfield only a few hundred yards from the spot where Pat eventually arrowed the deer. Pat later acquired the massive sheds from Lucas.

Pat's awesome trophy caused quite a stir when he returned to the Sugar Creek lodge shortly after dark, after taking photos all day long. Pictured left to right are: Chad John, manager of Sugar Creek Outfitters; Don Barry, owner; Ty, one of the hunting guides; Pat; and Don Barry Jr.

Pat's incredible Illinois giant soon became a national sensation. Photos later appeared on the cover of Buckmasters and Big Buck magazines.

as I could and we worked out a trade that included him getting a beautiful set of replicas made by Klaus Le-Brecht, owner of Antlers by Klaus, probably the best-known antler replicator in the country.

"I was thrilled to get the sheds from my big buck – as any hunter would be. Even with over 2,000 shed antlers in my collection, this set definitely means the most. I had several sets of replicas made. Later on I mounted the shed replicas, along with a mounted replica of the original rack, and put them in a beautiful revolving display so that both sets of antlers could be seen from all angles.

"Up until the time I killed my big buck in 2005, I'd never had a set of antlers scored for the record book. Like many people, Nicole and I like to gross score our deer as a gauge to see how big they are in total antler inches, but we'd never entered any animals in either Boone and Crockett or Pope and Young. But this time was different. I called Dave Boland, a master B&C scorer from Minnesota, and asked him to score my deer. With a total of 13 points the rack grossed 200 typical inches and netted 192. The Buckmasters BTR score was 182 typical. In the fall of 2006, my buck appeared on the covers of *Buckmasters* and *Big Buck* magazines and I couldn't have been more proud.

"As far as I know, my Illinois giant is still the largest typical whitetail ever shot on video. It's extremely difficult to shoot a 200-class typical whitetail under any circumstances, because most mature bucks tend to grow abnormal points as they get older and eventually they have to be scored as non-typicals. So a 200-inch typical whitetail is rare indeed.

"It also was the largest typical buck taken by a bow in North America in 2005. It ranks within the top 20 typical whitetails ever taken by bow in North America, and within the top five typical whitetails ever taken by bow in Illinois. But the record that means the most to me is the video record. A number of 230-inch-plus non-typicals have been taken on camera, but never a 200-inch typical. For that, I'll always be extremely proud!"

CHAPTER 2

NICOLE'S NORTH COUNTRY GIANT

Pat fell in love with hunting whitetails in Canada early in his deer hunting career. During his *North American Whitetail* days, he hunted both Alberta and Saskatchewan several times. But he had never been able to find the right situation where he could go back year after year to the same spot, especially in Saskatchewan. Now that he and Nicole were filming together for *Driven 24/7*, he became more determined than ever to find the ideal situation where they could hunt together.

While on an Alaskan brown bear hunt in the spring of 2007, Pat's guide Doug Klunder told him about a spot in Saskatchewan where he said the top-end potential for trophy whitetails was excellent. Upon Doug's recommendation, Pat contacted an outfitting service, named Baitmasters, in 2007 and booked a whitetail hunt for Nicole and himself. Nicole would be bow-hunting for *Driven 24/7*, while Pat would be bow-hunting for *Winchester Whitetail Revolution*, a show produced by Orion Multimedia that aired on the Versus Channel. (The Versus Channel was combined with the NBC Sports Channel in 2012.)

Interestingly enough, the format of *Winchester Whitetail Revolution* called for Pat to hunt from the ground without the use of any type of blind or manufactured stand. Everything had to be natural. This was fine with him. He loved the idea of hunting on the ground. In order to do that successfully, however, he knew he'd have to find a place with lots of bucks and some good cover on the ground in which to hide. He would also have to play the wind perfectly.

Pat did just that. He and his cameraman found a large spruce tree near the spot they wanted to hunt. They trimmed just enough limbs so that they could tuck themselves back into the dark foliage and set up the camera. They then placed some of the cut limbs in front of them, and they were all set in their natural ground blind.

Pat ended up shooting a beautiful 157-inch bruiser with lots of character. The deer was a heavy-horned 5-by-5 with some extra stickers and very tall brow tines. During the summer of the following year, he talked to the same outfitter about returning in the fall of 2008 for another whitetail hunt. As of that time, the TV show filmed in 2007

After Nicole arrowed her unbelievable 181⅞-inch bruiser on the second day of their 2007 Saskatchewan hunt (left), Pat brought down this long-tined 157-inch main-frame 5-by-5 while hunting on the ground from a makeshift brush blind fashioned out of cedar limbs (above).

had not yet aired, and the outfitter was reluctant to make a commitment because he didn't know what kind of response his business would get from the show. So Pat ended up making plans to hunt with another well-known outfitter just across the lake – Buck Paradise Outfitters operated by Grant Kuypers. As luck would have it, Pat and Nicole at last found the situation that Pat had always hoped to find. Hunting with Buck Paradise in 2008 marked the beginning of a great long-term relationship – for whitetails in the fall and black bears in the spring – that has continued to this day.

NICOLE'S 2007 SASKATCHEWAN MONSTER

"Looking back, 2007 was truly my breakout year as far as my deer hunting was concerned," Nicole remembers. "It was my debut year of filming with Pat for the TV show and things had been going incredibly well. So far, it had been a whirlwind of nonstop action. We had been to North Dakota in early September where I had taken a magnificent velvet buck. Then I had turned right around and taken another great buck in Minnesota. Pat kept telling me, 'This is not how it usually goes. It's not that easy to shoot a big buck in front of the camera.' But I was still very naive and it would take me awhile to fully understand what he was talking about.

"And now we were on our way to Saskatchewan. This was my very first trip out of the country and I was both excited and a little overwhelmed. I had cut my teeth hunting Illinois whitetails with my dad and two older brothers, Zack and Jared, and deer hunting had been a way of life for our family back home. As I headed to Saskatchewan my dad kept telling me, 'Make you sure you pack some warm clothes. It's really going to be cold up there.'

"Although I had been deer hunting all of my life, I had never watched any outdoor television and I didn't have any expectations for shooting a giant buck. I had no idea there was such a striking difference in the antler and body size of Canadian deer compared to the deer I was used to hunting in Illinois. That's how naive I was. I was more focused on packing warm clothes and enjoying the adventure than trying to shoot a giant buck. Don't get me wrong – I wanted to shoot a good buck for the TV show and I wanted to please Pat, but I had no idea what I might encounter north of the border.

"Since Pat and I were hunting separately, we brought two cameramen with us. Our friend Doug Klunder would be filming me, and Mike Law would be filming Pat. Up to that point, I had never been in a treestand with anyone else besides my dad and Pat. That in itself was very

From an early age, Nicole (above) was hooked on deer hunting with her dad. Jim Jones quickly learned that he could not go to the deer woods without taking his daughter. (Below) Nicole enjoys a pleasant meal with her Saskatchewan outfitter. Mike Law, Pat's cameraman, sits at the end of the table on the right while Nicole's cameraman Doug Klunder, wearing a black T-shirt, sits next to Mike.

Nicole found the Saskatchewan sunrises and sunsets to be breathtaking, but she worried about being able to sit in a stand all day long and withstand the cold. As things turned out, she persevered and her fears were unfounded.

strange, and the entire experience was a huge learning curve for me. Doug had only filmed Pat once before and did not have much experience as a cameraman. So here we were, hunting in the land of giants, and in a way we were both complete novices. But Doug was a great, hard working guy.

"On the first morning out, I was more worried about staying warm than anything else. Back in camp Doug told me, 'If you get really cold, it's all right to get out of the tree and build a fire. It won't spook the deer at all.' I'd never heard of such a thing. I thought, *How can anybody do that without alarming the deer?* In all my years of hunting with my dad in Illinois, that's something we never would have done. But I knew Doug was just trying to look out for me.

"As we got ready to leave camp in the predawn darkness, our outfitter pulled up in front of the lodge in a Polaris four-wheeler pulling an old-fashioned trailer. Pat, Doug and I piled onto the four-wheeler and Mike got in the trailer. Soon we were headed for parts unknown, bouncing along in the darkness. The outfitter was going to drop off Doug and I at our stand first, then drop off Pat and Mike. So we were cruising along, holding on for dear life, when all of a sudden the quad hit a huge bump. The trailer came unhitched and the four-wheeler went down one trail while Mike and the trailer went down another!

"It was hilarious and we tried to contain our laughter because we didn't want to spook any deer. But the outfitter just said, 'Ah, it's okay to laugh. It doesn't matter.' Again, hunting with my dad in Illinois, we never would have made any noise like that out in our woods. So here I was thinking, *I have a lot to learn about hunting in Canada.* I also questioned the fact that the outfitter was going to drop us off at our stand. I knew my dad would have never done that in a million years. He would always park the truck hundreds of yards away and carefully tip-toe to his stand on foot.

"The outfitter said, 'It's good for the deer to hear the four-wheeler. They're actually attracted to the noise.'

"Doug and I climbed into our stand that first day and sat all day long. I remember thanking God that the sun was shining because it was cold enough as it was – if it had been overcast or snowing I would've been miserable. But, we had action all day long. In Canada baiting is legal, and we were hunting over a bait pile.

(Left) A very photogenic Nicole Jones, probably around 13 at the time, proudly shows off a great Illinois buck that her dad Jim shot. (Right) A beaming 13-year-old Nicole poses with a doe she shot during the Illinois shotgun season.

During the seven seasons they've been hunting together, Pat and Nicole have become a formidable whitetail hunting team. Pat often films Nicole, and she often films him. Together they have a knack for shooting big bucks, producing spectacular footage and living their dream!

In this vast country it's really the only way to draw deer out of the thick bush and into a particular area so that you can see them. Otherwise we would have been lucky to see maybe one deer all day long. Since I was bow-hunting, it was the only way to bring the deer in close enough for a shot. I don't think there was a five-minute span during the entire day when we didn't see deer. In all, we probably saw around 15 deer that day. That was totally unlike anything I had ever witnessed in Illinois.

"One particular buck kept coming in and leaving throughout the day. He was a beautiful 140-class 10-pointer, and I tried every way I could to talk Doug into letting me shoot him. Doug just kept saying, 'I promise there are much bigger bucks than this around here.' The buck would leave, then come back 30 minutes later, and we'd go through the same routine again. He kept assuring me that this was not the deer I had come all the way to Canada to shoot.

"The next day we went to a different location. We hunted out of an extremely uncomfortable ladder stand that was only a couple of hundred yards off of the highway. I thought that was strange. The outfitter said that some of the local neighbors had been seeing a really big buck crossing the highway in the same spot on a regular basis. He never would tell us just how big this buck was – only that he was a really nice deer. Once we were in there and set up I thought, *how good is this going to be?* We sat there all day long and saw a couple of 120-class bucks, and we actually heard a moose back in the woods behind us. That was a neat experience for me because I had never been close to a moose before.

"Just before dark, I heard something back in the woods behind me to the right. I looked back and saw a couple of deer. I pulled up my Nikons and almost fell off the ladder! I had never seen anything like that in my life. It was an old, mature buck with a neck like a bull and a huge body to match. He seemed to be at least twice as big as any other whitetail I had ever seen. I whispered, 'Here he comes, Doug.'

"Doug was on him with the camera in an instant. He kept saying, 'That's a monster buck, Nicole! That's a monster buck!' and he was really breathing hard. He was more excited than I was. I told him, 'Calm down. Take a breath.'

"The buck skirted around us about 40 yards out in thick brush and I couldn't get a shot. He walked out away from us at about 50 yards, stopped and started making a scrape as he faced away from us. It was beginning to get dark and we were rapidly losing camera light. When you're in thick cedars and pine trees like we were in, you lose the light a lot faster. I kept asking Doug, 'Do we still have enough light?' and he kept saying, 'Yes, we're good.'

"Finally the buck decided to come in. The moment he started coming in, the other deer feeding in front of us immediately dispersed out into the surrounding woods. They wanted nothing to do with him. It was plain to see that he was the bull of the woods. Doug kept whispering, 'Shoot him if you can; we've still got pretty good light.' All the while I was thinking, *Pat will kill me if I shoot a buck without enough light to film.*

"The buck kept getting closer and Doug kept reassuring me. Finally I put my 20-yard pin on the deer and released my arrow. It looked liked a good hit, but as the deer ran off we could see the arrow in his shoulder. My heart sank for a quick second because I knew my arrow hadn't gotten the kind of deep penetration you always hope for. Both of my arrows had completely passed through the two bucks I had shot earlier in the season with the same bow, but this time the arrow was still visible. Doug whispered, 'You're okay because you made a good shot right behind the shoulder. It was perfect all the way and you have to remember the size of these deer – they're huge!'

"After the shot, Doug and I were freaking out in that stand together. I was so excited. I was crying one minute and laughing the next. I tried to call Pat but his cell phone was off. So I called the outfitter on the radio and told him we'd shot a big buck. He said he'd go and get Pat and Mike and be there as soon as possible. Then I called my dad. In the excitement of the moment, my mind was suddenly flooded with all the memories of my dad and I hunting together when I was younger – shooting deer, following blood trails and dragging deer out together. Dad had always been there for most of my deer.

"My mom answered the phone and I started crying and she immediately thought something terrible had happened. 'What's wrong?' She asked frantically. 'Are you alright?'

"'I just shot a big buck,' I told her. 'Is Dad there?'

"'Yes,' she answered, 'but are you alright?'

After reassuring her that I was fine, she put Dad on the speakerphone. The moment I heard his voice I lost it again. Finally I was able to stutter out that I had just shot a huge buck.

"'Well why in the world are you crying then?' he asked.

"I knew this was the biggest deer of my life and to be able to share that moment with my dad was special. After I got off the phone with my parents, Doug looked over and said, 'Let's play a joke on Pat. When we get him on the radio let's tell him you shot a 140.'

"We knew my buck was a giant but we had no idea just how big he was. Talking to my parents was

By the time she and Pat headed to Saskatchewan in mid-October 2007, Nicole's first year of hunting with Driven TV had already been extraordinary. In two previous hunts, she had arrowed two fine bucks. On the second day of her Canadian hunt she arrowed this North Woods giant. The massive main-frame 5-by-5 grossed 181⅛ inches. The massive buck easily weighed in excess of 300 pounds.

special but I couldn't wait to share the news with Pat. I knew he'd be both happy and proud. When you shoot a deer like that – or any good deer for that matter – you naturally want to share it with the person closest to you. That season, Pat and I had been together on every hunt up to that point and I was used to sharing my successes with him. We'd shared almost every second together. So I was going crazy waiting for him to pick up his radio so I could tell him the news. 'Come on, pick up your radio! Turn it on so I can talk to you!'

"Finally I got Pat on the radio and told him we had shot a deer. 'Yes, the outfitter just told me,' Pat said. 'We're on our way.' When they pulled up I tried to contain my excitement as much as possible. Pat was all excited for me and he asked, 'Well, what'd you shoot?'

"'Oh, I don't know, I think he'll go 130 or 140 maybe.'

"He was excited for me but he didn't say much. In truth, I think he was probably a little disappointed although deep down inside I think he knew I was trying to pull one over on him. The deer hadn't run but 30 or 40 yards from where I had shot him. I wish you could have seen Pat's face when we walked up on that buck. He was almost speechless. Then he said, 'I knew you wouldn't have shot a 130 or a 140! You were trying to pull my leg!'

"The rack of my huge buck was a basic 5-by-5 with split G-2s. Pat the

Don't miss Nicole's heart-stopping hunt for a true Canadian giant. View this incredible video footage now!

By age three, Nicole was enthralled with every buck her dad Jim brought home.

hunter now changed gears and immediately went into overdrive as Pat the videographer and TV producer. Maybe I didn't realize what we had at that moment in time – but he certainly did! He wanted to make sure we filmed a great recovery. I knew we might film it 10 different ways before he'd be satisfied. I told him everything that had happened regarding the hunt.

"The one cardinal rule of outdoor filming is that you never rewind the tape and watch the replay of a hunt while you are still out in the field for fear of taping over or somehow ruining the kill footage. That is a rule we adamantly adhere to. You always wait until you get back to camp and make sure you have the kill shot copied or recorded somewhere else before you start reviewing it.

"Pat knew we had a lot of work to do in order to recreate all of the various aspects of the hunt, from being in the treestand and making the shot, to the actual recovery. He was determined to do as much as we could right then and there. He was not going to leave those woods until we had all of the footage we needed. That meant shooting every scene from several different angles and also taking some good still photos of my deer. Not only did my buck have a huge rack, he also

Not to be outdone by Pat, who had appeared on the cover of Big Buck magazine in the fall 2006 edition with his Illinois record-breaker from the previous year, Nicole garnered the coveted cover position with her incredible North Country giant in 2008.

had a huge body. He easily weighed over 300 pounds.

"So here we were trying to get all of this done with my buck of a lifetime while the outfitter kept saying, 'We need to get back to the lodge because dinner is on the table and it might get cold.' We were incredulous. Pat and I were both thinking, *we just shot one of your biggest deer and all you're worried about is going back and eating dinner?* In all fairness to him, however, this was probably his first experience filming for TV, and he didn't understand that there was much more involved in filming a hunt than simply making the shot.

"But Pat made it quite clear. He said, 'We're not moving this buck from the spot where he died until I get everything I need on film.' And we didn't! Based on the caliber of the animal we were dealing with, I knew Pat would leave no stone unturned in doing it the right way, and making the best video he could possibly make. That's what being driven to achieve excellence is all about.

"It was well after midnight before we got everything done and headed back to the lodge. It took all five of us to get the huge buck loaded into the little trailer behind the quad. On the way back, I sat in the trailer with the deer's head in my lap with my hands wrapped around his head, so that his antlers wouldn't rub on anything or get damaged in any way.

"When we got back to the lodge, I called my mom and dad again. I also called both of my brothers and all of our pro staff team members to share my story. All of the team members were very happy for me. Since they were all veteran hunters with years of experience under their belts, they were also realists. They were very supportive and genuinely happy for me, but just as Pat had done, they also tried to let me know in a nice way that this was not how things normally went when you were trying to film for TV. They told me, 'We understand you're on cloud nine this year with all of the bucks you've killed so far, but it won't always be this way.' Here I was filming my first year for *Driven 24/7,* it was only mid-October, and I had three big bucks on the ground including one that was absolutely gigantic. But ignorance is bliss – I had no idea what they were talking about.

"The next morning Pat carefully measured the rack. My buck gross-scored $181\frac{7}{8}$ inches. We spent most of the next day taking photos, and the outfitter thought we were totally out of our minds. Months later after he viewed our TV show, I'm sure he realized why we had spent so much time filming various scenes and taking so many pictures."

THE COUNTRY GIRL GROWS UP

"Slowly but surely the magnitude of what I was involved in began to sink in and I knew I had big shoes to fill. For a girl from southern Illinois, it was a little intimidating to think that I could hunt with Pat on the show and experience the sort of success he was used to having. I knew he set the bar higher than anyone else in the industry and that he also expected the same from me. But, just because he expected it didn't mean I could live up to it.

"I'd been hunting with my dad since I was old enough to walk, but back then deer hunting was a hobby and a passion. We did it because we loved it, and not because I ever considered turning it into some type of career path later on. I never bow-hunted until I was in high school, because I couldn't pull back the legal poundage required until I was almost full grown. My family always hunted shotgun season in Illinois, as it was an annual ritual as important as Christmas. I always looked forward to shotgun season in November because I knew I would be able to miss a Friday of school. Being able to miss a day of school was a really big deal!

"I never felt out of place or different. My dad's friends were always so good to me. They made me feel right at home. Our deer camp was a tiny cabin in the woods with no running water and no electricity. It was very rustic and that's the way we wanted it. My dad had hunted there with his friends for 20 years.

"I shot my first deer at an early age sitting between my dad's legs. He helped me hold my gun up and I was hooked. From that point on, he really gave up his own personal hunting. Between my two older brothers Zack and Jared, and me, all he had time to do was take us hunting. It was something he obviously loved doing, but it had to be a huge sacrifice for him because he loved to hunt so much himself. I vividly remember him saying to me, 'Someday you'll be doing the same thing for your kids.'

"He was so right. It's funny how everything seems to come full circle. Right up until the time I graduated from high school going to deer camp was my life. It's all I ever wanted to do. I didn't know anything different. My dad loves to tell the story about the first time he took my brothers hunting without taking me along. That was one mistake he'd never make again. When he returned home with my brothers after the weekend hunt my mom told him, 'You'll never leave here again without taking Nicole because all she did was cry and carry on the entire time you were gone.'

"Never again did he go without me. My dad's

good friends Jack and Gary Crowell, Gary Crow and Phil Bullar also had a major impact on me as I was growing up. They always told dad, 'if you can't watch her we'll be glad to.' They'd go walking through the woods with me on their shoulders when I was only two or three years old. They didn't care whether they shot a deer or not and just because I was a little girl didn't mean that I couldn't be out there as well. To them that's what hunting was all about. I'll never forget their kindness.

"We had an old Coleman propane stove that my dad would fire up outside because the fumes were so bad. Then, after some of the heavy fumes died down, he'd bring it inside and cook fried spam for lunch. That was a real delicacy to us; fried spam and noodles or macaroni and cheese. We had donuts or oatmeal for breakfast, and the men drank strong coffee.

"Instead of regular chairs inside the cabin we used an old front seat out of a truck to sit on. The mice had eaten half of the stuffing out of it but that didn't bother us one bit. That was the essence of deer camp. It was nothing fancy, but we cherished everything about it and had so many special memories.

"My mom didn't hunt, but she loved the outdoors and sometimes she would come to visit camp and bring us some home-cooked food. She hated mice and snakes and I guess that's where I got my phobia about mice from (more on that later). She'd sit out in the car and dad would say, 'Come on in and stay for a while.' But she didn't want to come into the cabin because she was afraid she'd see a mouse. Just because she didn't hunt with us didn't mean that she wasn't part of our deer camp. It was a family thing that we all shared together.

"One time we were all out hunting and one of dad's friends, Bryce Cramer, was hunting just a short distance from camp when he heard a blood curdling scream down by the river. My mom had gone down to the river to get a canteen of water to put out the fire, because it was Sunday afternoon and we were all leaving camp after the evening hunt was over. She had fallen into the river! The bank had given way and she went right into the frigid water. Bryce found her, brought her back to camp, helped her warm up, and

Pictured with Nicole's dad Jim (left) are two of Jim's favorite hunting friends – Jack and Gary Crowell (middle and right) – who loved to put little Nicole on their shoulders and carry her through the fall woods. Sadly both men are no longer with us.

she was fine.

"Whenever I hunted with my dad in November during shotgun season, I wore all of my brothers' hand-me-down clothes. I'd put on whatever it took to stay warm. My dad would hang two lock-on stands in the same tree for us to hunt out of. He'd hang one on one side of the tree and one on the other and say, 'You watch from your side of the tree from daylight to 2 p.m. and I'll watch from my side.' There was no such thing as two-man ladder stands in those days.

"The first time he ever let me go sit in a stand by myself I think it was harder on him than it was on me. He said, 'Are you sure you can do it? Are you

Nicole's first-ever hunt to Saskatchewan in 2007 turned out to be a memorable experience in more ways than one. Who would have thought that the country girl from Illinois would arrow such a magnificent buck on her first trip north of the border? Pat didn't do too bad either!

sure you'll be alright?' He gave me my shotgun and a pocketful of shells and helped me get up in my stand that morning. 'I'll only be a few hundred yards away from you and if I hear you shoot I'll come right over,' he said.

"A little while later, a small four-point buck came in. I shot twice and missed him with both shots. Dad got out of his tree, walked all the way over to my stand and asked, 'Did you get one?'

"'No, I missed.'

"No sooner had he gone back to his tree then another deer came by and I shot two or three more times and missed again. Dad came all the way back for a second time. When he found out I had missed again, he took all of my remaining shells except for one. Then he said, 'Nicole, you're going to have to make this one shell count because I only plan to walk over here one more time today.' As luck would have it I shot a deer with that one shell later that day, and he was very proud of me.

"All of these memories are what help you remember your childhood and cherish those special times with your family. I was very lucky to have such loving parents. Now here I was in Saskatchewan, thousands of miles away from my childhood home in southern Illinois. I was just able to enjoy shooting my biggest buck even more because of all that my dad had done for me so many years earlier. It's awesome to be able to have those memories. On the first day of hunting in Saskatchewan, before I shot my big buck, I told Pat,

'Canada is absolutely awesome! Mark my words: one of these days when we can afford it I'm going to bring my dad up here to hunt with us.' And I did – four years later in 2011!

"In many ways, having had such a great season in 2007 and shooting the biggest deer of my life in Saskatchewan really did take some time to sink in. I was naive about so many aspects of the hunting industry. The entire experience was surreal. I had just shot the biggest deer of my life and was definitely on cloud nine. But I had not grown up watching much hunting TV and really didn't have a grasp on how much that buck would impact our TV show, or increase my stature as a hunter in the eyes of others.

"I hadn't even thought about those things. I wanted to work hard and make Pat happy. I wanted to do my part for the TV show and felt extremely fortunate to be hunting with Pat. I loved everything about what I was doing but it honestly took me awhile to realize how lucky I was. The guys on the prostaff were right. It doesn't always happen that way. In the coming seasons, when I sometimes struggled to shoot a buck for months at a time, I would come to understand exactly what they were talking about.

"But for now I intended to savor my good fortune. I might have been a small-town girl from southern Illinois who still had a tremendous amount to learn, but one thing was certain – I knew I had the desire and energy to do whatever it took. Like Pat, I was hopelessly driven!"

CHAPTER 3

AN OUTDOORSMAN IS BORN Pat's Early Life

A young Pat Reeve smiles broadly as his dad Keith poses with one of the many bucks he brought home over the years. Like Nicole, Pat was fascinated with deer and antlers at an early age.

Born in 1969, some of Pat's most vivid memories of early boyhood revolve around tagging along behind his dad at deer camp. The sights, sounds and smells were magical and had a profound impact on the 4-year-old. Growing up near the small farming community of Plainview in southeastern Minnesota afforded the budding outdoorsman many opportunities to hunt and fish with his dad and granddad. He cherished those times. He lived to be outdoors.

"It was an old-fashioned deer camp where about a dozen men got together every year," Pat remembers. "I loved listening to the stories about the big ones that got away. Opening weekend was always a big deal. We would usually hunt for three days – Saturday, Sunday and Monday – and then go home. Dad was strictly a meat hunter, anything that had antlers was a trophy but it was more important to shoot does for venison.

"When I was about 7, I would sit in the stand with dad and wear his clothing to stay warm. We wore electric socks that never worked and we had butane hand warmers that always gave off a strong odor. We always had a thermos of hot coffee or hot chocolate.

"In Minnesota, you have to be 12 years old to get a deer license, so my 12th year was a milestone in my hunting career. That year, I shot my first deer ever – a doe that I shot with my grandfather's Remington 12-gauge pump. On opening day, we would always sit for a few hours in the morning and then we'd start driving the hills. Being one of the youngest hunters, I was always a driver. It didn't take long for me to figure out that sneaking along the outside edge of the drive without making any noise was much better than storming through the

Pat, Dad & Grandpa Reeve – 3 Generations all hunting together

Posed with his Grandpa Reeve and dad (top photo), Pat (right) was bitten by the deer hunting bug early on. Although he started out hunting in Minnesota with a shotgun on family hunts, he became fascinated with bow-hunting during his teenage years. His first bow was a Bear Whitetail.

woods making as much noise as possible. I shot a lot of deer being a driver.

"I never missed an opening weekend with my family until I was in college. When I reached high school, I became very interested in bow-hunting and talked my dad into getting us each a bow. My first big buck with a bow was taken on the same farm where my dad had killed his first buck. It made Pope and Young. I was thrilled. Each year deer hunting became more and more important in my life."

THE CALL OF THE WILD

By the time he reached high school, Pat knew that seeking a "normal" nine to five job was not for him. So he attended Mankato State University in the late 1980s where he earned a degree in criminal justice. His plan was to go to work for the Department of Natural Resources as a game warden because he knew that career would definitely keep him in the woods. Unfortunately, the long, misdirected arm of affirmative action prevented him from getting a job with the state.

While attending college, Pat had lucked into a job

trapping wild turkeys in Minnesota. The program was sponsored by the National Wild Turkey Federation and was carried out by the Minnesota Department of Natural Resources. The DNR wanted to reestablish turkeys across the southern half of the state. At the time, it was thought the climate was too harsh in northern Minnesota to support wild turkeys, but that theory was soon dispelled and turkeys eventually spread northward.

Pat trapped turkeys on a seasonal basis during the spring and summer for three years while attending college in the fall. He came to love the big birds and savored every moment working with them. "We baited the turkeys and used rocket-propelled nets to capture them," Pat remembered. "We sometimes sat in a tiny, cramped, wooden blind for hours at a time before they would come in to the bait, but I loved every minute of it. It was great training for later on sitting in a treestand all day long."

One of Pat's most memorable moments was releasing several birds near the area where he had grown up in southeastern Minnesota. Today, whenever he sees a flock of turkeys on his 35 acres near Plainview, he smiles broadly and thinks back to those special days working with the DNR. Thanks to the hard work of Pat and people like him, turkeys are now plentiful across the southern half of Minnesota and are a much sought after game bird.

Releasing turkeys in his boyhood stomping grounds was special, but Pat's three-year stint working outside did something else. "It made me realize that it was

One of Pat's proudest achievements was trapping turkeys for the Minnesota DNR for three years on a seasonal basis while he was attending college. This experience crystallized his desire to follow a career path geared toward wildlife, nature and the outdoor industry.

Pat, the budding deerslayer, poses with two nice Minnesota does that no doubt made some fine eating for the Reeve family. In those early days, shooting any deer for the freezer was cool, but displaying them on the hood of the car was way cool!

Pat Reeve is not only an expert hunter who knows his quarry, but he is also an artist with a camera — each hunt and each situation during a hunt represents a special challenge as to how the story can best be told on film. His cameras always tell each story with exciting visual effects and heart-thumping action that few others in the outdoor industry can match. No Hollywood producer has ever strived for excellence harder or longer than Pat Reeve. This is what sets him apart in the hunting industry. This is why he is driven.

Pat, at age 13, stands next to a mounted trophy at the first ever Minnesota Deer Classic held in Minneapolis/ St. Paul in 1983. Pat was enthralled with the incredible array of trophy antlers on display.

possible to pursue a career working outdoors," he said. "At the time, I still had plenty of self-doubts, and people were advising me to do all sorts of other things, but I knew in my heart I wanted to dedicate my life to working outdoors in the wildlife field."

Pat's outdoor interests were always multi-layered and went far beyond being just a hobby. Spawned by the early childhood hunts with his father, during his late teens he developed a burning passion for hunting whitetails, especially with a bow. He also developed a deep love for turkeys and turkey hunting as a result of his trapping days. In truth, he loved all wildlife, and had a deep desire to learn as much as

Pats 1st Buck w/ —
Bow 6 pointer 1984

Pat poses with his first bow buck, a hefty
Minnesota 6-pointer taken in 1984.

One year later on opening day 1985, Pat took an even larger
buck with his bow while hunting from a homemade platform
stand perched in a tree.

he could about every facet of nature. For a time after college he worked for the DNR as a naturalist.

During his high school years, Pat also developed a deep interest in photography. One year the Minnesota Deer Hunters Association sponsored a photo contest. A friend of Pat's had acquired a very young fawn, and Pat thought it would be neat to take some pictures of it. Since he didn't own a good camera, he borrowed a 35mm camera from his stepfather Mikael Newman. Pat took some photographs of the fawn and submitted one to the photo contest. To his utter surprise, he won the contest and some nice prizes!

But along with his prize-winning photo came some animosity and jealousy from several local people. "Anybody can take a picture of a tame deer," someone commented. "But it's a little different with wild deer."

Pat had not tried to deceive anyone. He had simply taken some pictures of a beautiful little creature. But now, as far as he was concerned, the proverbial gauntlet had been thrown down. He was determined to show his critics that he could take pictures of wild deer as well. More than anything else, though, he wanted to prove to himself that he could do it since he also prided himself on being a deer hunter. The 27,000-acre Whitewater Wildlife Management Area was located only 10 minutes from Pat's house. The park teemed with mature whitetails and inside the boundaries of the WMA was a 2,700 acre state game refuge where no hunting was allowed. Not surprisingly, smart

During Pat's last year of high school, a friend acquired
a young fawn, and Pat took several photos of the tiny
animal. He later entered his pictures in a photo contest
sponsored by the Minnesota Deer Hunters Association.
To his surprise, he won the contest and his photo appeared on the cover of Whitetales, the Minnesota Deer
Hunters Association magazine!

Pat's photo of Garth appeared on the cover of Monarch Valley, Tom Indrebo's first video in what would later become a trilogy. It was the first photo Pat ever sold.

As his interest in wildlife photography blossomed, Pat started taking photos of wild bucks in a nearby refuge and WMA. This wide-spreading brute earned the name "Garth" – because its rack was so wide it resembled country music star Garth Brooks' hat! As a result of Pat's photos, Garth became widely known in the local community, and this notoriety gave a boost to Pat's budding photography career.

bucks from surrounding areas swarmed into the park during hunting season.

With his borrowed 35mm camera, Pat went out and started stalking some of the big bucks in the refuge. He got lucky right away and took some amazing photos of several mature bucks. It didn't take him long to see that he needed a telephoto lens for his borrowed camera, so he saved up $350 and bought a Sigma 400mm lens. He continued to get decent photos, but the perfectionist in Pat quickly made him realize that he couldn't shoot the magazine-quality photos he desired unless he bought some very expensive camera equipment.

During the summer, most of the big bucks left the state park, so Pat went out into mosquito infested swamps of the WMA and began to get images of several large bucks in velvet that he saw on a regular basis. One he named "Garth" after Garth Brooks. The country legend was very popular at the time, and Pat named the buck Garth because the big deer had a "cowboy-hat-style" set of antlers resting on top of his head. Garth was a wide 8-pointer that actually became quite well known in the area after some of Pat's photos started circulating around. Pat also snapped photos of a buck he called "Elvis" and one he called "Hank."

Soon he was framing some of his photos and selling them in Mauer's Tavern, a local gathering place where Pat and his friends often got together. That fall, Pat shot a nice

Pat's striking silhouette shot appeared on the back cover of a popular whitetail video – Monarch Valley – produced by his good friend Tom Indrebo of Buffalo County, Wis.

During his junior and senior years in high school, Pat photographed some outstanding bucks in a game refuge not far from his house including this buck he named "Hank." Pat was using a borrowed 35mm camera owned by his step-dad Mikael Newman.

Hank was later killed during firearms season by a local hunter named Terry Gates. This photo was taken by Pat and won the "best buck photo" in a contest sponsored by Minnesota Outdoor News.

buck with his bow on the first weekend of the season while hunting with his dad. Since his buck tag was filled, he decided to spend the remainder of the season in the state game refuge photographing bucks. "It was just like hunting them with a bow," Pat remembered. "I had so much fun that fall taking pictures and I got some really neat photos." When the time came for him to return his borrowed camera, he was left with a lens and no camera.

About that same time, a newspaper reporter for the *Rochester Post Bulletin* came out to interview Pat about how he was able to get so many good pictures of wild bucks. "He wanted to know what kind of camera I was using and I didn't even own one at the time," Pat remembers. "It was quite embarrassing."

A SPECIAL FRIEND

The following winter, Pat attended a local deer show in Eau Claire, Wis. There he bumped into Tom Indrebo, a fellow whitetail enthusiast from Buffalo County, Wis. Although Pat was in his early 20s and Tom was in his mid-40s, the two men hit it off right away because of their shared passion for hunting and photographing whitetails.

"We became buddies instantly," Pat said. "That spring we did some shed hunting together, and by the following fall we were ready to hit the woods with our cameras. Tom owned a video camera, and he introduced me to the exciting world of whitetail videography. Now, instead of taking only still images, I could follow the deer, zoom in on them and get plenty of live action. About that same time, Tom started to develop a video that he called *Bucks of the Buffalo*. I helped him by doing a little bit of the filming and we combined the story lines of several bucks we had each been following."

Tom produced and sold a few copies of his video to various local individuals. It became very popular. He had included information about quality deer management in the video, and eventually the Quality Deer Management Association saw it and encouraged him to take the video to a more professional level. So Tom

Pat often stalked bucks with his camera in a state game refuge where no hunting was allowed. Bucks would pour into the park from surrounding areas as soon as the Minnesota firearms season opened.

Pat and his longtime friend Tom Indrebo started videotaping deer and hunting together on a regular basis in the early 1990s.

Pat poses with his camera during his first bona fide video assignment in Canada where he filmed bow-hunting legend Myles Keller on a black bear hunt.

reworked the original video and named it *Monarch Valley*. He used Pat's photo of Garth on the front cover, and on the back cover he used one of Pat's silhouette shots. Pat was excited because Tom actually paid him for the use of his photos. That was the first time anyone ever paid him for any of his photos and he thought, *Wow, maybe I can make a living doing this.*

During that fall of 1990, Pat decided to forego the Minnesota gun season and spend the entire season filming with a video camera instead. He had never missed an opening day with his dad and family, and it was a tough decision to make. But he had such a burning passion to film big bucks in the refuge that he was willing to sacrifice his hunting season to make it happen.

"We were having so much fun filming in the game refuge," Pat said. "By that time there were actually four of us working together: a great guy named Duane Boehm, who has since passed away, Tom's brother-in-law Monty Nichols, Tom and I. We spent the entire weekend in that game refuge during gun season and the deer would come pouring in there to get away from the hunting pressure in the surrounding areas. We had a contest to see who could get the best footage. Tom loaned me a video camera, and we did little deer drives and came up with all sorts of ways to get footage. 'Good footage' to us was anything we could get.

Hunting legend Myles Keller (right) and the late outdoor writer Jeff Murray (far left) pose with other hunters in bear camp in Canada. This was Pat's first official job as a cameraman and the hunt was a disaster. Keller became sick and no bears were even seen.

Unlike many photographers who would have left the woods at sunset due to failing light, Pat the artist often waited for darkness to fall in order to catch special lighting situations for some spectacular images. The buck pictured here is Garth.

The quality of the video we shot back then was primitive compared to what it is today, but we never knew the difference. We were in hog heaven and were having a blast!

"First prize for the best footage was a beer at Mauer's Tavern. Duane, who was a real character, proclaimed that he was the contest winner. So we all waited expectantly as he turned on his camera to show us what he had. As we watched, we got a very brief glimpse of an out-of-focus deer's tail and that was it. The entire clip was about three seconds long. That was all Duane had filmed all day long. While the rest of us had all kinds of great footage of different bucks, Duane had almost nothing. We all got a big laugh out of that one. Tom and I still laugh about that to this day!

"At that point, our filming was strictly a hobby. Later in the year, we found out about a company that was selling some expensive Canon Hi-8 video cameras that had been used in a recent Olympic Games. Tom and I each bought one. I had to take out a loan for mine. We thought we had hit the big time!"

Monarch Valley was very popular by this time and Tom was now working on his second video called *Legend Lane*. People loved watching these videos because of the big deer images in the wild and story lines about specific bucks. Little did Pat know that this filming experience would become invaluable to him in the years ahead.

The next summer, Pat graduated from college and was raring to go with his new video camera. July 4 was always the magical date to start filming because

by that time of the summer the velvet antlers on the deer were large enough to be impressive. Also around that same time, Pat met local resident and bow-hunting legend Myles Keller at Mauer's Tavern. In those days, Myles was known far and wide as the man who had shot more Pope and Young class bucks than anyone else in the country (at that time around 20 including one or two bucks that also qualified for Boone & Crockett). Myles liked Pat's work and took an interest in the budding young photographer. He asked Pat to be his cameraman on an upcoming bear hunting trip to Canada. Myles planned to produce a video, and he offered to split any future profits with Pat. Although the job didn't pay anything up front, Pat felt like he'd just won the lottery!

FOLLOWING THE DREAM

Myles bought a state-of-the-art, professional grade Sony video camera for the trip. Pat took one look at the boom-box-size camera and realized the only thing he knew how to do with it was turn it on and off. Undaunted, he was determined to learn everything he could about using this ultra-sophisticated production camera. Off to Canada they went.

"As soon as we got there, Myles came down with a severe case of pneumonia," Pat remembered. "He was deathly sick for about a week. So I filmed several other hunters in camp. Finally Myles recovered enough to start hunting. On our first day out, the outfitter took us out to a bait site, pointed to a huge white pine tree and said, 'There's your tree stand.' I looked up in that tree and I swear it was all I could do to spot the stand. It was the highest stand I had ever seen. It must have been over 40 feet high.

We got up in that tree and I was scared to death. We were so high up that I was sure I could see all the way back to Minnesota. In those days, no one used safety belts. I had this huge, heavy expensive camera hanging around my neck, almost pulling me out of the tree, my knees were knocking, and I was hanging on to the tree for dear life. Myles looked at me and said, 'Is there a problem?' The last thing I wanted to do was let him know how scared I was. All I could think of was, *Don't fall and don't drop this expensive camera.* Myles never did get a bear. In all, we were there for about a month."

Even though the trip had been an adventure and a learning experience, Pat's first job as a professional cameraman didn't buy any groceries or put any money in the bank. But during their time together, Myles had given Pat some invaluable insights and advice about how the hunting industry worked. Among the sage advice he gave Pat was, "If you really want to be successful in this business as a cameraman, don't get married. Being gone so much really affects your family life." Pat was married a few months later. In the meantime, he went home and out of necessity got a day job working for Uni-Patch, a company that manufactured medical supplies.

While in bear camp, Pat had also met outdoor writer Jeff Murray (who has since passed away). Jeff was a friend of Myles, and had written a number of stories about him. One day out of the clear blue, Jeff called Pat and asked him if he would accompany him as cameraman on an elk hunting odyssey he planned to make to Alberta and Colorado. With the promise of being paid for his work, Pat couldn't say yes fast enough.

"I'll never forget the day I walked into the HR person's office at Uni-Patch and quit my job," Pat said. "I told the lady that I wanted to pursue my dream of outdoor filming and she looked at me like I was crazy. I knew what she was thinking: *You'll be back in two weeks with your tail between your legs.*"

Once again Pat was off to Canada and once again the trip was a near disaster. The moment he arrived in Alberta, the video camera stopped functioning. In a panic, Pat called his friend Tom Indrebo. "Tom, I'm up in Alberta," he explained. "I need you to ship me your Olympic camera as soon as possible." Without hesitation, Tom crated up his expensive camera and express mailed it to Calgary. Pat never forgot that incredible gesture of friendship.

After an ill-fated month of unproductive hunting in Alberta and Colorado, Jeff Murray gave up the ghost on trying to produce a video. Pat returned home with no compensation for his time. The trip had been an unforgettable adventure for Pat, but once again, it failed to put any groceries on the table. By now, Pat was married and his wife was understandably frustrated. "You're going to have to get a real job and stop going on these wild-goose chases," she insisted.

Fortunately, not long after he returned from that trip several important things happened that would greatly influence Pat's future. Tom Indrebo was in the process of producing his third video, *Monster Alley.* He also bought a 300-acre farm in Buffalo County, Wis. He called Pat and told him he was thinking about starting an outfitting business and naming it Bluff Country Outfitters. He offered Pat a job as a guide for the fall hunting season. Pat energetically accepted and went to work helping Tom turn his beautiful farm into a viable outfitting business.

DOORS BEGIN TO OPEN

During the second year of Tom's outfitting operation, Jackie Bushman of Buckmasters came to Buffalo County and filmed a TV show with Bluff Country Outfitters. Pat was afforded the opportunity to meet Gene Bidlespacher, Jackie's cameraman. Gene was an iconic figure to Pat because he'd had a hand in producing the classic video, *Bowhunting October Whitetails,* in the mid-1980s. The video featured well-

As co-host for North American Whitetail TV in 2004, Pat made several hunts with his mentor Gene Bidlespacher, a legendary cameraman who worked for many years filming for Buckmasters. This photo was taken on a very cold day in North Dakota. Bidlespacher is generally recognized as one of the great cameramen of his era.

This Deer and Deer Hunting article was one of several that helped put Tom Indrebo's Bluff Country Outfitters in Buffalo County, Wis., on the map. (Pictured left to right) Tom Indrebo, owner and guide; Dan DeFauw of Michigan, a lucky sweepstakes winner; outdoor writer Greg Miller; and Patrick Durkin, then editor of Deer and Deer Hunting.

known bow-hunters Gene and Barry Wensel, and is still considered one of the best whitetail bow-hunting videos ever made.

Pat talked to Gene about various aspects of the outdoor video business. Recognizing Pat's passion and creative eye, he told the budding young photographer, "You ought to take your hobby to a higher level and consider becoming a cameraman for an outdoor TV show. There's always a demand in our industry for a good cameraman."

Because of the exposure Bluff Country Outfitters got on Jackie Bushman's TV show, in addition to a feature story written in *Deer and Deer Hunting* by then editor Patrick Durkin, Bluff Country Outfitters became a popular destination for many out-of-state deer hunters. Among those hunters was Steve Puppy, an old acquaintance of Pat's. Steve had once lived in southeast Minnesota and now worked full time for Hunter's Specialties in Cedar Rapids, Iowa. He called Pat and told him he was planning to hunt with Bluff Country Outfitters that fall, and asked Pat if he'd be interested in filming him. "I'd love to!" Pat told him enthusiastically.

Steve came up and hunted that fall as planned. While there, he told Pat that Hunter's Specialties was putting together a team of hunters and cameramen to do a series of whitetail hunting videos to be called *Prime Time Bucks*. He invited Pat to be a part of the team. Pat attended a meeting at company headquarters in Cedar Rapids and was asked to film Steve on a late-season muzzleloader hunt in Iowa. Pat was very

excited to know that finally he was going to get paid to film an actual hunt. At the last minute, unfortunately, the hunt was canceled due to budget constraints and Pat was devastated.

But, Steve was able to borrow one of the company's brand-new, state-of-the-art Beta cameras, and he told Pat that they could still go and hunt in Iowa on their own. There was one drawback – Pat would not get paid for his services. So there he was again, in the same situation he had faced in Canada and Colorado, being offered a trip without pay. Pat agreed to go anyway. If he got good footage, he reasoned, it might open some doors with Hunter's Specialties in the future. Pat actually filmed a nice buck even though Steve was not able to shoot it. Later on the footage Pat had filmed was used in the company's first in-house video, *Prime Time Bucks II*, and it did in fact open some doors. Note: *Prime Time Bucks I* was not produced in-house by Hunter's Specialties so the company actually started its series with *Prime Time Bucks II*.

That same year, Pat did some filming for well-known TV hunting personality Tom Miranda and his show on ESPN. Tom liked Pat's work and invited him to work as a contract cameraman. When Hunter's Specialties found out that Pat would not be available to film for the next *Prime Time Bucks* video, the company hired him as a full-time pro staff member and cameraman. Pat's job description included doing seminars at stores and shows as well as filming some of the other pro staff hunters for the video series.

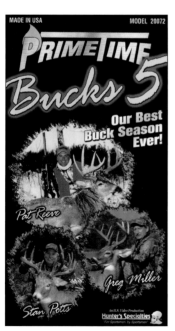

Pat shot this outstanding 182-incher in Greene County, Ill., with his Thompson/Center muzzleloader during his first year as co-host of North American Whitetail TV (2004).

While working as a freelance cameraman in the early 2000s, Pat filmed a turkey hunt in Florida with Tom Miranda (left) for his popular TV show on ESPN. Hunter's Specialties pro staffer Alex Rutledge (center) shows off a great Osceola gobbler, while Pat the beaming cameraman looks on (right).

Pat's photo appeared on the cover of Prime Time Bucks 5 with this outstanding 160-inch trophy. In addition to doing much of the film work, Prime Time Bucks 6 marked Pat's first involvement with video production. Thanks in part to Pat's vision and skill, the Prime Time series was enormously popular.

As a pro staffer for Hunter's Specialties, Pat proudly shows off his first on-camera buck to his good friend Tom Indrebo, owner of Bluff Country Outfitters.

While filming for the Hunter's Specialties Prime Time Bucks video series, Pat videotaped a whitetail hunt in Illinois with good friend Bob Foulkrod, a well-known professional hunter.

While filming in Kansas for Hunter's Specialties, Pat shot this beautiful 150-inch buck. Posed with him is cameraman Rick White.

That first year, Pat ran the camera and contributed quite a lot of footage to *Prime Time Bucks III*. A year later, as *Prime Time Bucks IV* was being produced, the company allowed Pat to have one hunt in which he could be in front of the camera. So he chose to hunt in Buffalo County where he was confident he could shoot a nice deer on camera with his bow. Pat did just that – he shot an outstanding 9-pointer on camera. "The footage was not the best, because my cameraman was a trainee," he said. "But at least we got it on film. I still have that deer hanging in my house and I look at it every day. It means a lot to me."

When it was time to produce *Prime Time Bucks V* the following year in 2000, Pat wanted to have a little more input into the production and content of the video. He again hunted in front of the camera in Buffalo County – this time with a muzzleloader – and shot a beautiful 160-class 10-pointer that appeared on the cover of *Prime Time Bucks V*. During this same time period, he produced a video called *Operation Predator*, featuring well-known predator hunter Ed Wimberly. Although whitetails were always his passion, Pat also filmed a number of turkey hunts, several elk hunts in New Mexico with Wayne Carlton, and hunts for numerous other species.

"I felt like I had a real stake in the *Prime Time Bucks* video series because I wanted those videos to be the best they could be," Pat said. "My goal for *Prime Time Bucks VI* was to bring some unique stories

During the late 1990s, Pat's dad Keith managed to get in a successful elk hunt while Pat was videotaping a segment for Hunter's Specialties at the famed Three Forks Ranch in northwestern Colorado.

to the table and do things that our competition wasn't doing. I killed a couple of nice deer for the video but the real highlight that year was when Stan Potts shot a giant 220-inch non-typical in Illinois on camera. At the time, it was the largest non-typical ever captured on video, and I happened to be the one filming him. But because he shot it straight on with a bow, the buck was somewhat controversial.

"Another groundbreaking story we featured in *Prime Time Bucks VI* in 2001 was about a massive Iowa non-typical that Ron Willmore captured live on video. A story later appeared in North American Whitetail magazine that referred to this buck as 'a

Three Forks Mountain in Colorado looms up behind Pat as he poses from the lodge during the filming of an elk hunt with Stan Potts (right) for Hunter's Specialties, in the late 1990s.

Pat was behind the camera when Stan Potts (left) arrowed this 220-inch megabuck in Illinois in 2001. At the time, this was the largest whitetail ever captured on video.

walking world record.' In 2003, the buck was killed by 15-year-old Tony Luvstuen. With a score of 307⅝ non-typical points, the buck ended up being the largest non-typical ever taken by a hunter. So it had, in fact, been a walking world record."

After the success of *Prime Time Bucks VI* due to its amazing whitetail content, Pat was energized. He knew in his heart that his real passion, as well as his future lay in filming and producing top quality television

Several members of the North American Whitetail TV crew pose for a photo while hunting in Wyoming with outfitter Mike Watkins of Trophies Plus Outfitters. Pictured from left to right are: Rob Scott, Stan Potts, Jeff McHugh, Pat Reeve and Greg Miller.

about whitetails. Since his job at Hunter's Specialties involved having to film many other species, he decided to leave the company so that he could follow his dream of trying to produce an exclusive, all-whitetail TV show. He had no idea how he was going to do it, but somehow, he believed he could make it happen.

LIVING THE DREAM – NORTH AMERICAN WHITETAIL TELEVISION

Pat talked to Stan Potts and Greg Miller who had both filmed with Hunter's Specialties on a freelance basis. Since they were free to do video work with anyone in the industry, they expressed an interest in being a part of a new venture. "My first thought was to go the best name in the whitetail industry – *North American Whitetail* magazine," Pat said. "I had grown up reading *North American Whitetail* and it was the standard by which everyone else in the industry went by."

Ironically, the magazine had recently been sold to Primedia, a New York conglomerate, and the new owners were interested in starting a TV show with the *North American Whitetail* brand. It seemed like the perfect fit. Pat was hired as an employee of the company to produce the show and be one of five team members that included Stan Potts, Greg Miller, long-time *North American Whitetail* editor Gordon Whittington and Texas biologist Dr. James Kroll.

Because *North American Whitetail* was thought of

In January 2005, North American Whitetail TV won a prestigious Golden Moose Award at the SHOT Show in Las Vegas for "best opening montage." Pat, standing in back with the show's four other co-hosts – Greg Miller, Stan Potts, Gordon Whittington and James Kroll – was very proud of the part he had played in producing such a popular TV series. Pictured on the far left is North American Whitetail editorial director Ken Dunwoody and magazine Publisher Jimmy Stewart. Pictured on the far right is advertising director Darren Shepard.

as the "bible" of the whitetail world, expectations for a top-rated show were high, and Pat wanted to produce the best whitetail show on cable TV. Right off the bat, as the man leading the charge, he was faced with significant challenges during the first year of production: Hunts had to be booked for each hunter; camera equipment had to be lined up; cameramen had to be retained; and sponsors and sponsor equipment had to be procured and distributed to the team members. It was no small task but Pat eagerly took on the challenge.

Everything fell into place and the first year was an overwhelming success. A number of good bucks were taken by the five team members. Pat achieved his goal of filming several outstanding segments in which special interest stories were woven into a section called *Muzzy Moments*. Those segments gave the show that extra flare Pat had been looking for. The show was off and running!

Pat spent many weeks in the spring of 2004 editing the first 13 shows with Ken Kemper of Twisted Pair of Posts, a production company in Iowa. Late in the summer of 2004, *North American Whitetail Television* premiered on Outdoor Channel to rave reviews. Nominated for several awards on Outdoor Channel, the show later won a prestigious Golden Moose Award for the best opening montage. The show quickly became regarded as one of the best whitetail shows on cable TV. Pat had achieved his goal!

Life was good. At last Pat was living his dream. Not only was he doing what he wanted to do, he was finally getting paid to do it! He strived to produce an even better show the second year. Ironically, that year Pat was introduced to Nicole Jones by a fellow bow-hunter in Illinois. Taken by her good looks and charm, Pat came up with the idea of using Nicole in the opener of the second season of the show. The idea was to let Nicole be sort of a "Daisy Duke" type figure in a high-energy truck race involving Pat, Stan and Greg. After that, Pat didn't see Nicole again for several more years until he happened to bump in to her at a consumer show. He had just gone through a difficult divorce and the beautiful young country girl and deer hunter from Illinois easily caught his eye. Even though they lived quite a distance apart, they started seeing each other whenever they could, and a long-term relationship began.

In the spring and summer of 2005, Pat once again spent many long weeks in Iowa helping edit the 13 episodes for the second season of *North American Whitetail Television*, sleeping on the floor of Ken Kemper's farmhouse in a sleeping bag. After that extremely labor-intensive, time-consuming task was finished, Pat went home to relax for a few days, feeling good about what had been accomplished for the second season's episodes. One day shortly after he finished the editing process, he was out in the woods moving some stands around when he got word that Gordon Whittington had called. Upon returning the call, Pat was told that his services were no longer needed on the TV show. The reason given for his sudden dismissal was that the show was not going in the direction the company wanted.

Pat was utterly devastated. This was the last thing he ever expected. For two years he had put his heart and soul into the production of a TV show that had received numerous accolades and top ratings, and now it had been ripped away from him. With no job and no benefits, Pat was back to square one. He had to make some major decisions. With three children to feed and another one on the way, what would he do? Fortunately, he had lots of support from friends around the country who were as shocked about his sudden dismissal as he was. "Start your own show," people told him. "You can do it."

That idea was easier said than done but Pat had little time to waste. Out of necessity more than anything else, but also out of a desire to never give up and to continue to produce excellent whitetail television, his new show, *Driven 24/7*, was born. There would be many new challenges to face and many difficult obstacles to overcome, but he would prevail. After all, he had no other choice!

THE STORY OF TOM INDREBO AND BLUFF COUNTRY OUTFITTERS

Like Pat, Tom Indrebo loved deer and deer hunting and developed a passion for bow-hunting at an early age. After filming with Pat in the late 1980s and early '90s, and after successfully producing three popular videos – *Monarch Valley*, *Legend Lane* and *Monster Alley* – Tom bought a picturesque farm in Buffalo County at an auction. Everyone thought he was crazy and that he had paid far too much for the land.

"I actually purchased this 300-acre farm in a beautiful valley at an auction in the early 1990s so that I would have a place to hunt," Tom said. "Ironically, the farm had belonged to a relative of Pat's stepmother, and Pat and his father had hunted on it for several years while Pat was growing up. Pat and his dad Keith even came to the auction. After I bought the farm, I was looking for any way I could to generate income. So I took a couple of gun hunters from Florida and it worked out very well. I enjoyed helping other hunters, and I started thinking about becoming an outfitter. I knew I'd be giving up my personal hunting life, but the outfitting business would give me the opportunity to be in the woods year-around. It would turn my passion into a business, and that thought was very appealing."

Although whitetail outfitting in Wisconsin was still in its infancy, Tom's business took off. He built a bunkhouse and made many improvements to the property, working hard to make Bluff Country Outfitters as hunter friendly as possible. Because of the quality of the deer it produced, Buffalo County soon became a destination for nonresident hunters. A number of well-known TV personalities in the hunting industry, including Jackie Bushman, hunted there with Tom in the mid-1990s. In 1996, Tom's brother-in-law Monty Nichols killed a massive non-typical scoring 206-6/8 inches – a buck everyone called "The Boss" – one of the first-ever net B&C bucks from Buffalo County.

A story about Bluff Country Outfitters appeared in *Deer and Deer Hunting*, and Tom's business received a great deal of positive publicity. That trend has continued to this day. Bluff Country Outfitters is now regarded as one of the premier whitetail hunting operations in the country, and its owner Tom Indrebo, is held in great esteem by the whitetail community at large.

CHAPTER 4

MOSES
A BUFFALO COUNTY LEGEND

During his lifetime, Moses became one of the most sought after deer in Buffalo County, Wis. Pat developed a special passion and affinity for the big whitetail, and his pursuit of the trophy buck from year to year became a true obsession.

Moses first appeared on the radar screen as a 3½-year-old in 2003. By the time he was 6, he had grown to be a local legend.

In 2003, my good friend Tom Indrebo of Bluff Country Outfitters in Buffalo County, Wis., started getting trail camera photos of a promising young buck. Hunters who manage their property for whitetails are always on the lookout for good bucks. You become aware of a certain buck through photos or actual sightings, and you tell yourself, "This buck has a lot of future potential. I'll certainly be looking for him next year to see what he does." This buck was definitely one of those deer.

At the time, the buck was 3½ years old. He had a 9-point typical frame with split brow tines, giving him a total of 11 points. He had a wide rack and grossed around 150 inches. I was hunting with Tom whenever I could so I was also well aware of this deer. Between trail cameras photos and several hunter sightings everyone knew this was a buck to keep an eye on for the future. He wasn't yet a shooter but he certainly would be in a year or so.

The following spring, I was out shed hunting with Tom and his family, and I found his sheds. One of his sheds had been found a year earlier when he was a 2½-year-old and he had since made a big jump from 2½ to 3½. Since we knew he had made it through the 2003 hunting season, everyone was very excited to see what he would do in the fall of 2004 as a 4½-year-old.

Sure enough, Tom started getting velvet photos of him in late summer and he had made another big jump, at least 25 inches. We now estimated he would score around 170.

That fall of 2004, I really started focusing on him because now he was a definite shooter. I didn't have a great deal of time to devote to hunting him because I was doing a lot of traveling that year, but I hunted him whenever I could. Tom's farm in Buffalo County is not too far from where I live in southeast Minnesota and I can be there in just over an hour.

Shane Indrebo poses with Moses' shed antlers from the buck's fourth year. Shane's dad Tom found the antlers in the spring of 2005 on a part of the farm where the buck had never been seen. This told Tom and Pat that Moses had shifted his home range.

A MUCH SOUGHT-AFTER TROPHY

Tom's hunters, as well as hunters on surrounding properties, were also starting to look for this buck. At the time, he was probably one of the biggest resident bucks we knew about on Tom's farm. Interestingly enough, the ridge where he ended up getting killed as a 6½-year-old was the same ridge where we'd found his 3½-year-old sheds. After we found his sheds, though, he seemed to relocate to another part of the farm because we stopped finding any trace of him back in that area until he was killed several years later. We figured he'd probably shifted his home range because of hunting pressure.

At 4½ he became a lot smarter and he was only seen once or twice during the entire season. This was the year he earned his famous nickname. Donnie Hansen, one of Tom's guides, saw him running across a cornfield one day. Since Donnie knew the deer was big, old and smart he called him "Moses" – as a tribute to the Moses of historical and biblical significance. The name stuck.

In the early spring of 2005, Tom found Moses' sheds on a different part of the farm from where they'd been

As time went by, Moses grew to be a living legend in Buffalo County.

*At age 4½, Moses did what many mature bucks often do. He became almost exclusively nocturnal.
He was rarely seen during daylight hours.*

found previously. Once again we knew he had made it through the season and we were very excited about the prospects of seeing what his antlers would do later that year. By now, he was one of the oldest bucks on the farm and there was much talk about hunting him in the fall. Since he was a resident deer – that is, he had lived most of his life on Tom's farm, and since Tom had accumulated so much documentation on him – he was now gaining quite a reputation with local hunters.

At 5½, nearly everyone who booked a hunt with Tom that year wanted to shoot him. I felt the same way. I thought: *Wow if I can shoot Moses with a bow it'll take my TV show to a whole new level.*

That summer, I was no longer part of *North American Whitetail Television* and was in the process of starting my own show, *Driven 24/7* on the Men's Channel. Obviously my TV career was important, but Moses held a special place in my heart. Because I had found his sheds and followed him for several years, and because I'd guided for Tom and knew his farm so well, hunting Moses became very personal. Any time you can outsmart a mature, 5½-year-old buck like Moses you are doing something extraordinary. Shooting Moses would be the ultimate challenge.

That fall, Tom and I had figured out some of Mo-

ses' travel patterns and we were trying to determine where he lived. For the past couple of years, he had relocated to the east side of the farm which, generally speaking, is very difficult to hunt because the terrain is so steep and rugged. As a buck matures, his home range usually starts to shrink. That is, he doesn't venture out and travel as far as he once did, and he'll set up shop in a small, confined area where hunting pressure is light and where he knows he's safe. When he does leave his core area, it's usually under the cover of darkness. That's exactly what Moses had done.

One of Tom's neighbors owned some land on the end of the bluff where Moses had relocated to and we felt like he was probably bedding on that property. Tom's neighbor didn't hunt much so the hunting pressure there was minimal. It doesn't take a mature buck long to find that right pocket where he doesn't get pressured. We were still getting a lot of trail camera pictures of Moses on Tom's property, but most of them were taken at night.

As you enter Tom's property and drive to the lodge, you enter from the east side, and Moses was sighted in the headlights along the road there at night by several different people. So we felt certain he was hanging out on that side of the farm.

Pat poses with the buck he shot on the spur-of-the-moment in 2005 while he was setup to hunt Moses. The instant Pat released his arrow, he deeply regretted making such a spontaneous decision.

A HARD PILL TO SWALLOW

Before the 2005 season opened, I hung several stands not far from the neighbor's property on the bluff and hunted Moses religiously once the season opened. I placed one stand on a hillside near a large apple tree that was full of apples. I also put a camera on that apple tree and soon discovered that Moses was consistently coming in and feeding on apples. After a few hunts from that stand, however, I began to suspect something. It seemed like every time I went in there to hunt Moses he never showed up, but every time I wasn't there I got photos of him feeding on apples. It was almost as though he knew when I was in there hunting him. In hindsight, I'm sure he did.

Not that I wasn't extremely careful. I never over-hunted the apple tree stand location and I never went in there unless the wind was just right. Around the first week in November, I felt like the time was getting right to see him. I was getting frequent pictures of him feeding on apples and I planned to go in there one particular afternoon when the conditions looked good

to hunt. I opted not to hunt the apple tree stand that morning because I felt like it was more of an evening location.

With that in mind, I hunted another morning stand located on the other side of the ridge. I didn't think it was as good a location as the apple tree stand, but figured being out in the woods somewhere was better than sitting in the lodge.

As I sat in my stand that morning, a nice 2½-year-old buck came by chasing a doe. I had no intention of shooting this buck, but I told my cameraman Donnie Hansen to turn on the camera because I wanted to do an encounter scene strictly for video purposes. I planned to draw back, let down, and then look at the camera and say something like, "He's a nice buck folks, but I'm gonna pass on him because I've really got my sights set on shooting Moses."

As the buck got within range, he presented a perfect shooting opportunity. Somehow, all of the pressures and frustrations of that year suddenly got the best of me. I had only taken one deer so far that sea-

Shortly after Pat arrowed a much smaller buck in lieu of waiting for a chance at Moses in the fall of 2005, he and his cameraman saw Moses standing on the side of a hill while they were leaving the woods. Pat was understandably dejected.

son, and that had been almost two months earlier in September. I was trying desperately to get my new TV show off the ground and I'd been faced with numerous obstacles.

Suddenly I thought to myself, *I'm going to shoot this deer.* I asked Donnie if he was on him with the camera, and he said, "Yes, why?"

I let the arrow fly, and Donnie couldn't believe it. "What are you doing?" he asked in amazement. "I thought we were hunting Moses."

I had never wanted to retract an arrow as badly as I did when I let that arrow go. I still have nightmares about it today. The buck was quartering away when I hit him and we spent the entire day looking for him. Finally we recovered him late that afternoon. He was a fine buck but he wasn't the buck I had come to hunt. I felt ashamed and embarrassed.

Too add insult to injury, after we loaded the buck onto Tom's Polaris four-wheeler, we had to drive past the apple tree stand location on our way back to the lodge. As we rounded a corner near that stand, we looked up and there stood Moses on the side of the hill right near the apple tree with a hot doe.

"Look! There he is!" Donnie yelled.

"No joke, Sherlock!" I said dejectedly. I was sick. (Actually I used a little stronger language.)

That really put the nail in the coffin for me. It was almost as if the deer gods were punishing me for what I'd done. Moses was standing right where I expected to see him, and if I had been hunting there that afternoon as planned, I might well have gotten a shot at him. But now my opportunity was gone and my tag was attached to another deer. I had let the pressures of TV get to me and I felt terrible. I vowed to never let that happen again. I vowed to be more patient, and let things work out.

When I got to the lodge and put that deer in the trunk of the old beater car I was driving to head home, I felt the lowest of lows. Things were not looking too prosperous. I had 13 TV episodes to produce for my new show *Driven 24/7*, and so far I had only filmed two successful hunts. Based on the *North American Whitetail Television* shows I had produced for the two previous seasons, in which we aired two hunts per show, I was 24 hunts shy of having a successful season. It was a bit overwhelming.

The next day I would be heading down to Illinois to bow-hunt in Schuyler County in my old Buick Skylark clunker with its poor brakes and leaking gas tank. I hoped my fortunes would change – and they did. As things turned out, I ended up killing my 200-inch gross typical megabuck during that unbelievable hunt. I soon went from the lowest of lows to the ultimate high. That hunt in Schuyler County turned my career and my life around!

CHASING MOSES IN 2006

As the 2006 season approached, I was still on a high from shooting the buck of a lifetime in Illinois and was determined to focus my attention on Moses. He had survived yet another season by being very adept at outsmarting Tom's hunters in 2005. He knew where he was safe and how to avoid danger. He knew how to move through Tom's property to avoid hunters. He had only been glimpsed once or twice the entire season. When he did move around during daylight hours, he was going through the thickest, steepest cover he could find.

Since I now had a huge typical buck under my belt from the previous season, the thought of shooting a big non-typical like Moses was foremost on my mind. After my regrettable mistake of the previous season, it would mean more than anything to harvest a deer like Moses. In addition, Tom Indrebo was one of my best friends in life and I felt like he honestly wanted me to shoot Moses. So I was very committed to the task.

Tom and I talked about the best places to put up a stand for Moses and we sort of put two and two together. Several years earlier when I had guided for Tom we'd hunted a deer named "Tilter" on that same bluff, and we both agreed that Moses was following some of the same patterns Tilter had followed. There seemed to be a lot of similarities between the two deer.

That fall, Tom's son Shane found Moses' shed antlers in the bottom of the valley lying very close together. At 5½, he had started growing a few non-typical points. With a total of 21 points, his rack scored well into the 180s. He was also huge in body size. At 6½, I knew he'd be one of the biggest bodied deer I'd ever hunted. I couldn't wait to see how big his rack would be in 2006.

I felt like the key to hunting Moses as a 6½-year-old would be to gain permission from Tom's neighbor

Shane Indrebo displays the massive pair of shed antlers that Moses carried as a 5½-year-old. Shane found the antlers in the spring of 2006.

to go on top of the ridge and hunt him close to his core area. After analyzing my 2005 season, I knew I couldn't hunt him on the same side hill where I had hunted him the year before. I figured Moses most likely had either seen me or smelled me each time I approached my apple tree stand. I felt certain he'd been hidden away somewhere on top of the ridge above me. From his position, he was always able to detect me. In order to outfox him, I knew I'd have to get above him and hunt very close to his bedroom.

So I called Tom's neighbor during the summer and asked him if I could hunt Moses and film the hunt for TV on his property. He said, "Yes, go ahead. I'll give you permission to set up one stand on my property."

During the several-year period between 2004 and 2006 when Moses was being heavily pursued by numerous hunters in Buffalo County, dozens of trail camera photos were taken of the elusive whitetail.

The place we decided to set my stand was only about 60 or 70 yards from Tom's property line, but I knew that was the spot I needed to be because of the difference in topography. There was an old road that came up the hill nearby that Tom had often used in the past to drop hunters off at the top of the ridge. I knew Moses was used to seeing a certain amount of traffic up on the hill road. So I asked Tom if he would drive my cameraman and I up and drop us off near my new stand, and then drive away so that Moses would think that any potential threat was gone. That high point also overlooked the apple tree stand location on the hillside below.

While scouting that high point back in the summer, I'd found a perfect tree to hang my stand on the end of the point. With a south wind, my scent would be carried out over the valley instead of back toward the ridge. From past experience, I'd learned that bluff country bucks liked bedding on the ends of the ridges where they had the wind at their backs while being able to see anything in front of them approaching from below. So with a south wind, I felt like Moses would feel completely safe because he'd have the wind at his back with good visibility below him.

I knew I couldn't hunt a north wind. With a north wind I felt certain that Moses would probably bed in another spot anyway. He wouldn't feel comfortable being there with the wind in his face because he wouldn't be able to smell anything behind him, so it wouldn't be natural for him to bed there under those conditions. I learned a long time ago that mature whitetails will always reposition themselves to a spot where they can use the wind to their advantage. That's just basic whitetail behavior. So a south wind would be perfect for my tree stand. It was a great spot to fool Moses. Hunters who are able to find these types of "opportunity" spots are guys who are going to kill a lot of deer, especially in bluff country.

I got my stand hung well in advance of the season and trimmed out a good shooting lane. I found a quick way to get in there and knew this was crucial to my success. It just so happened that there was a little dry wash that came off the ridge that I could sneak up from the road. It was a steep erosion ditch that was almost vertical, but it offered me the opportunity to climb up it by pulling my way up from sapling to sapling, right to the tree where my stand was located. I had already removed all of the debris for a quiet approach through the ditch.

The plan was for my cameraman and I to sit on the tailgate of Tom's truck and ride up the hill. When we got to the steep, sandy ditch, we would quietly slide off and sneak up to the stand while Tom drove off. Even if a deer like Moses heard the truck, he would also know it had driven away and the danger would be gone.

A BITTERSWEET EXPERIENCE, A HAUNTING MEMORY

I knew that if I was going to be successful I would have to get Moses early in the season while the foliage was still on the trees. Once the leaves were gone, I'd be silhouetted and sky-lined on the ridge and much easier to see. So my plan was to focus in on the first week of the season before he felt any hunting pressure, while he was still moving around on a normal feeding pattern and before he started getting interested in does.

There was still one big obstacle to overcome before I could get a buck tag and hunt Moses. That year, Buffalo County still had the "Earn-a-Buck" requirement and you had to shoot a doe before you could legally get a buck tag. Fortunately, I shot a doe on the first afternoon of the hunt and was very thankful. Sometimes it's not easy to shoot a doe, especially in an earn-a-buck county. So now all I had to do was wait for a good south wind and I'd be in business.

As luck would have it, the wind was right that next afternoon in mid-September. Once again I was hunting with cameraman Donnie Hansen. Donnie, who had also guided for Tom, wanted to see Moses get shot and capture it on camera as much as I wanted to shoot him. So we were essentially both hunting the deer together.

We carefully climbed the ditch and settled into our stands. To our amazement, we started looking around and saw several does bedded around us. They just sat there. They weren't the least bit alarmed. They knew something was in that tree but I think they viewed us as nothing more than big raccoons. We sat there for a while and eventually another doe came right by us. She had no idea we were there and that gave me even more confidence about my stand location.

With less than an hour of daylight left, I suddenly saw the body of a large deer out of the corner of my eye. I knew immediately it was Moses. After years of studying photos of him I knew it was him. The moment his huge rack came into view, I got buck fever. Never in my life had I ever experienced buck fever like I did that afternoon, not even when I shot my 200-incher the year before. This deer meant so much to me because I had such a long history with him, and because he was such a giant non-typical. At that moment, I would have traded every deer in my col-

During the fall of 2006, Pat suspected that Moses was bedding on the edge of some property adjacent to Tom Indrebo's farm. Pat obtained permission from the owner to hunt the deer on one corner of that property and his suspicions proved correct!

lection for Moses, with the possible exception of my 200-incher. Moses was that important to me!

Now here was walking directly toward my shooting lane 15 to 20 steps away. I knew I was going to get a shot. I knew from experience that once a buck like Moses gives you an opportunity, you'd better take it because you seldom get a second chance. Once he came into my shooting lane he was quartering away slightly, not the perfect position for a double-lung shot, but still a very lethal shot. I pulled back to full draw. Looking through my peep sight, I waited for him to take a step and put his shoulder forward before I released my arrow. Instead of putting his shoulder forward and getting perfectly broadside though, he took a side step to his left as he fed on acorns.

It was now or never. The shot looked good through my peep sight and I released my arrow. The arrow hit him behind the shoulder and he immediately bolted off. He didn't do a leg kick but I felt like it was a good hit. I could see my Lumenok arrow buried up in him as he ran off, and I felt an overwhelming sense of accomplishment. I had just now anchored the second biggest buck of my career and it was a great feeling. I knew the arrow was not a pass-through, but I felt like it had a fair amount of penetration and I was certain it was a fatal shot.

I turned to the camera in jubilation and said something like, "I just killed Moses!" I actually thought I had seen Moses go down in the woods as he was just going out of sight. I was certain I'd killed him. We celebrated and stayed in the tree for a little while until we calmed down. I think Donnie was shaking

as much as I was. We finally got down and went and found Tom and told him we had just shot Moses. Word spread through the camp like wildfire.

Just to be safe, we decided to wait until morning before going after him. That night we watched the footage back and forth and everyone agreed that it looked like a great shot. Everyone agreed that Moses had to be dead. People were high-fiving me and I certainly felt like we were going to be taking recovery photos in the morning. Things were looking good.

The next morning we were back in the woods at first light. I don't think I slept a wink. We started trailing him and initially there was a good bit of blood. Every time I went around a little twist in the trail I was looking ahead for his body and rack. He dropped off the point and went down through a valley and the blood started tapering off. I still felt like we were going to find him at any moment. Then, all of a sudden, he started going up a big, steep ridge. I immediately got a sinking feeling in the pit of my stomach. I'd had a lot of experience tracking wounded bucks like this shot by other people. In this country, when they started climbing uphill, it usually indicated a nonfatal wound.

The blood trail was getting sparse so I actually called a guy with a dog to come in and track him. We found one bed where Moses had bedded down in the next valley over but there was no more blood after that. He had stopped bleeding. We spent the next two days looking for him and we covered every inch of ground. In all, I spent the better part of the next two weeks looking for him. He simply vanished. Tom stopped getting any trail camera pictures of him and we thought he was dead for certain.

MOSES LIVES!

About a month later, one of Tom's hunters was coming down the driveway toward the lodge and there was Moses in all his glory – standing out in the open with a doe like nothing had happened. He showed no weight loss, no sign of ever being hurt and he looked perfectly healthy. Of course, when this hunter got to camp and told everyone what he'd just seen, it was like the second coming. There was a renewed hope that someone in camp might still get him. I thought maybe I could still get a crack at him.

So I continued to hunt him in late October whenever I was home. I planned to be in a tree that first week in November when the rut started kicking in and this time I vowed to hold out for Moses. There would be no shooting a smaller buck like I had done the year before.

Once again, he had changed his habits. He had moved off the ridge where I'd shot him earlier in the season and we were at a loss as to where he had gone. Tom got a few trail pictures of him near one of his ponds, so I set up a stand near that pond. There I was sitting in a tree by that pond the first week in November when I heard something coming. All of a sudden a doe ran right by the tree and there was Moses right on her trail. He ran right up to the base of the tree we were in and stopped directly underneath me. It was getting dark, and I was worried about having enough shooting light. I asked the cameraman if he had enough light and he said, "No, I'm out of light."

Moses was standing right under me, and I could've shot him but I didn't. To this day, I still ask myself why. I wanted to shoot him so badly, but I wanted to do it on camera. When you're filming a hunt for TV, you're under a lot of pressure. You get so caught up in trying to make sure everything is right for the camera that nothing else matters. In this case, I'll always regret not shooting because I wanted that deer more than anything. I should have shot anyway but I didn't. So he ran off and that was the last time I ever saw him. I guess some things are just not meant to be.

During the past decade, Buffalo County, Wis., has deservedly gained a reputation as one of the nation's top big-buck destinations.

On Nov. 15, 2006, Tom Indrebo got a broadside trail camera photo of Moses stretched over a scrape and lifting his head high up to a licking branch. Note the healed-over wound directly in the kill zone where Pat's arrow had penetrated the buck's ribcage.

View this video to see the unbelievable footage of Pat's amazing, yet devastating bow-hunt for Moses in 2006.

On Nov. 15, 2006, Tom got a broadside trail camera photo of Moses stretched over a scrape and lifting his head high up to a licking branch. The healed wound where my arrow had hit him just behind the right shoulder was clearly visible because the hair around the wound had not yet grown back. To this day, that photograph still haunts me.

Four days later during rifle season, local hunter Trevor Oleson killed Moses with a rifle on Tom's farm. Trevor's dad Geno had been good friends with Tom for many years. After Tom bought the land Geno and Trevor had been hunting on for his outfitting business, he continued to let Trevor and Geno hunt on the property because they were such good friends.

On the day he was killed, Moses had crossed Tom's big valley and gone back to the area where I'd found his 3½-year-old sheds. We had not seen him in that area for at least two years. With 20 scorable points, he ended up grossing just over 200 non-typical inches. He netted 194.

After Moses was killed, the mystery about where my arrow had gone was solved. Tom examined his body cavity and determined that my broadhead – a 100-grain fixed three-bladed Muzzy – had squarely hit one of his ribs and broken it solidly. But instead of going straight into the deer's cavity, the arrow deflected along the ribs and skidded up underneath the buck's shoulder blade and into his neck region. It appeared to be a lethal shot as he was running off. And Moses did lose quite a bit of blood. But in the end, the big deer quickly recovered from the broken rib and flesh wound. The arrow was never found but it must have worked its way free fairly quickly.

After my hunt for Moses aired on the TV show, we got great feedback from it. Everyone makes mistakes, and I felt that if I could help at least one

Four days after the classic trail camera photo of Moses poised over a scrape was taken, local hunter Trevor Oleson shot the legendary buck on Nov. 19, 2006 while hunting with a rifle on land belonging to Tom Indrebo.

Outfitter Tom Indrebo (left) and hunter Trevor Oleson proudly show off Trevor's trophy of a lifetime.

Over time, Buffalo County outfitter Tom Indrebo collected several years' worth of shed antlers belonging to Moses. On the far right is a replica of Moses' rack the year the big buck was killed.

hunter be a little more patient by watching what I'd done, it might increase their chance of success. I'll be the first to admit that I was very excited when I made that shot.

CONCLUSION

I certainly had regrets for my two missed opportunities at Moses, but I'd known Trevor for a long time and I was very happy for him. In many ways, Moses lived a charmed life, but Trevor made his shot count when it mattered most. That put an end to the Moses saga for me. In a way, I felt a huge sense of relief because he had consumed so much of my life, and hunting him had been such an emotional roller coaster. Now I could re-channel some of my hunting efforts and start hunting on a normal basis again. With that said, I'll never forget all of my close encounters with this great deer, and I feel certain that getting to know him on such a personal basis has made me a better hunter in many ways.

CHAPTER 5

DRIVEN DREAMS
HUNTING ADVENTURES IN SASKATCHEWAN
Five Amazing Years of Hunting Big Bucks

No wonder Pat's favorite place in the world to hunt whitetails is in Saskatchewan! These two bruiser bucks were taken in 2011 on Pat and Nicole's annual pilgrimage to hunt with Buck Paradise Outfitters.

SASKATCHEWAN 2008

PAT AND NICOLE'S FIRST YEAR OF HUNTING AT BUCK PARADISE

In October 2007, Nicole and I traveled to Saskatchewan to hunt with an outfitter that was recommended to me by a guide I met while brown bear hunting in Alaska earlier that year. It was Nicole's first-ever trip to Saskatchewan and she was very excited. On the second day of the hunt, she managed to arrow a massive 181⅞-inch Canadian brute, her largest buck ever by bow. Two days later, I shot a beautiful 157-inch buck with my bow while hunting on the ground.

It was a memorable hunt for both of us, and we naturally wanted to return to Saskatchewan in 2008 if possible. That summer, I talked to the outfitter we had hunted with in 2007 about a possible return trip. At the time, the TV show featuring our 2007 hunts had not yet aired, and the outfitter was reluctant to invite us back until he could see what kind of response his business would receive as a result of the TV publicity. That was certainly understandable, but Nicole and I needed to nail down our fall hunting schedule.

I had heard good things about another nearby outfitting service – Buck Paradise operated by Grant Kuypers – just across the lake from where we hunted in 2007. Some of the Mossy Oak and Primos crew had hunted at Buck Paradise and highly recommended it. So I gave Grant a call and explained to him what Nicole and I were doing with the TV show. He invited us up for a whitetail hunt in the fall of 2008, and we've been going back to Buck Paradise every year since – for black bears in the spring and whitetails in the fall. That first hunt turned out to be the beginning of a great relationship.

We were all set to return to Saskatchewan in October 2008. Since my dad had spent so much time teaching me to hunt when I was a boy, I had always wanted to show my gratitude by taking him to Canada on a whitetail hunt. Nicole and I decided that 2008 would be the year. Two good friends, Bryan Lemke and his dad Dale, also went along on the trip with us. (Bryan later became our full-time cameraman.) The plan for the first day was for my dad to hunt by himself while I filmed Nicole hunting with a muzzleloader. If and when she filled her tag, we would shift gears. Nicole would

Pat took these photos from his ground blind during the day while hunting.

Pat always has a still camera in his hunting bag in case any unusual photo ops come along.

then film me hunting with a bow.

Upon our arrival, Grant recommended that Nicole and I hunt a very remote part of the forest known as Deep Ravine, where a number of big bucks had been photographed by Grant's trail cameras. In order to get from the lodge to the area we would be hunting, we had to make a strenuous 2½- to 3-hour quad ride deep into the forest each morning well before daylight. That was fine with us, but getting there each day was a real adventure as well as a physical challenge. We traveled down rough, bumpy trails, crossing over beaver dams and going through numerous sloughs and bogs. Once we finally got back into that remote country, we definitely felt like we were in the middle of nowhere – a true wilderness setting. It was at least 12 to 15 miles from the lodge to Deep Ravine, maybe more. The trip alone was like a roller coaster ride!

This daytime photo of a big chocolate-racked 10-pointer was taken back in a remote area called Deep Ravine. It took Pat and Nicole three hours to get there by quad each morning before daylight.

We had no idea what kind of deer we might encounter. We had seen pictures of some nice bucks, but this was the kind of place where a world record could step out at any moment. The deer in this country had obviously never seen a human before and we never saw any tracks or sign of other hunters back there. Because of the time it took to get there, we were always the first

An always beaming Nicole poses with the fruits of her labor in 2008.

During his first year of hunting with Buck Paradise Outfitters in 2008, Pat's big 10-pointer made its appearance during the middle of the day.

ones out of the lodge in the predawn darkness and the last ones to return at night. It was an exhausting trip but well worth the effort.

The first day back in Deep Ravine, Nicole and I hunted out of a very well-hidden ground blind tucked into a cedar tree. I love hunting on the ground because it puts you at eye level with the deer and the video footage is always so much more dramatic. Late that morning, Nicole missed a shot at a big, mature 10-pointer. The scope on her muzzleloader had somehow been knocked off its zero, possibly during the long quad ride. After remedying the situation by adjusting the scope and shooting the gun to make sure it was again driving nails, we went back to the same spot the next day.

Unbelievably, the big buck Nicole had missed the day before made a second appearance. Big mistake on his part! This time, Nicole "Annie Oakley" Jones didn't miss with her Thompson/Center Pro Hunter. She made a perfect shot and the huge buck only went a short distance. Nicole's 2008 Saskatchewan bruiser had a main frame 5-by-5 rack with several stickers. He scored in the mid-150s. She was absolutely thrilled to shoot such a fine buck!

PAT'S TURN

Now it was time to shift gears and let Nicole run the camera while I hunted. Our guide Kyle Gardner had obtained numerous trail camera photos of another big buck about two miles away, so we decided to try for him.

The third morning of the hunt found us in our new spot hunting out of treestands. Around high noon, we were both sort of nodding off when I happened to open my eyes. Sometimes that little voice inside tells you something is about to happen, and this was one of those times. I looked out and saw a very wide 10-pointer coming toward us along the top of a ridge almost at eye level out in front of me. This was very surprising because

Watch Nicole "Annie Oakley" Jones knock down a Saskatchewan bruiser in 2008.

View the chocolate-antlered brute Pat arrowed at 15 yards in 2008.

Smiling broadly, this driven husband and wife team proudly shows off the results of a highly productive 2008 hunt to Saskatchewan.

Payback time! In 2008, Pat was thrilled to be able to take his dad Keith to Canada where he shot the buck of a lifetime with a T/C muzzleloader.

A proud father and son team smile for the camera as Pat's dad Keith shows off his 165-inch 6-by-6 mega trophy.

most of the deer we saw earlier that morning had filtered out of a thick, boggy area just below us, and that was where we expected to see any big bucks appear.

But this old boy was approaching from the top of the ridge, silently walking along the four-wheeler trail we had driven in on. I quickly nudged Nicole back to reality and she got on him with the camera as quickly as possible. In order to make the shot with my bow, I had to stand up and turn slightly to face the deer. Since we were almost at eye level and there was almost no cover between us, accomplishing that goal was very tricky. I moved as slowly as I possibly could and brought my Mathews to full draw. As soon as he turned broadside and looked away, I made a good shot at 15 yards.

A smiling Nicole waits patiently in her ground blind for Mr. Big to appear.

While filming Nicole's hunt, Pat had to chase these moose away from their ground blind.

With beautiful, chocolate-colored antlers so typical of Canada, my deer turned out to be a 5-year-old brute that scored 158 inches. In just three days of hunting, Nicole and I had taken two outstanding bucks. Once again, our whitetail hunting in Saskatchewan was over for the year. That same day, my dad killed a beautiful 6-by-6 that scored 165 inches. He was totally thrilled and we were all very happy for him. The Lemkes both filled their tags as well, and it was a successful hunt all the way around. What more could we have asked for? Now, Buck Paradise was easily our favorite new place in Saskatchewan to hunt whitetails!

BUCK PARADISE 2009

Needless to say, Nicole and I couldn't wait to return to Buck Paradise in 2009. We planned to bow-hunt, but Grant asked us to hunt with rifles instead of bows since his outfitting business caters primarily to rifle hunters. He felt like the publicity he would get from the TV show would do him more good if we were seen using rifles. We were glad to accommodate him and we left the bows at home and broke out the rifles.

We arrived during rifle season in early November, and it was a little colder than it had been the year before, and with plenty of fresh snow on the ground. Nicole went back to the same ground blind in Deep Ravine where she hunted the year before on the edge of an open meadow. As usual, she was hunting first and I was doing the filming.

On the first day of the hunt, several moose came out in front of our ground blind to feed on the hay and peas in the field. Although they were interesting

Because of the brushy habitat where large trees are scarce, Pat and Nicole have found that hunting from a pop-up ground blind in Saskatchewan is highly effective.

to watch, we had a difficult time scaring them away. We were using hay and peas to attract the deer. Baiting is legal in Saskatchewan and if hunters didn't use bait in that remote country, they'd seldom see a whitetail.

With that style of hunting, you usually see a lot of deer activity all day long since the deer are concentrated at the food source. You never get bored because you get to observe lots of different deer behavior – bucks chasing does, bucks fighting and other pre-rut activity.

Later that morning, a beautiful, big-bodied mature buck came in. He had a heavy 5-by-4 frame, and was much too nice to pass up. Nicole made a good shot on him with her 7mm magnum and we had one big buck on the ground.

Nicole poses with another big bruiser taken with favorite outfitter Grant Kuypers at Buck Paradise Outfitters in Saskatchewan.

Pat also fared well during the team's 2009 rifle hunt.

The end of a great 2009 hunt – two exceptional bucks taken with T/C rifles.

Pat and Nicole's special friend Don Pickle also fared well on the first day of the 2009 hunt.

Now it was my turn. We went to a different location in Deep Ravine the next day and hunted out of a different ground blind. Even though our 3-hour quad ride was always an adventure, it was definitely not for the weak at heart and always tested our limits. Six hours on the quad every day made for an extremely long, tiring day. Shortly after daylight that morning, I passed up a beautiful buck with a heavy 6-by-6 rack. Even though he tempted me, I asked myself, *Why shoot that deer when he'll truly be a giant next year?* So I decided to let him go.

Another mature buck had been observed in the area with trail camera photos and I decided to set my sights on him. He was a hefty, thick-necked 5-by-5 with a split G-3 on the left side. He'd probably score around 150 inches. The day before, my good friend Mike Jahnke had also killed a nice buck, and we'd stayed up a little too late celebrating. All morning long I kept

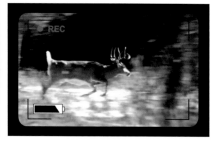

Mike Jahkne and his guide Johnny Prosak often traveled to their hunting spot by boat on Green Lake. It was a co-o-old way to travel!

to experience firsthand some of the great hunting Saskatchewan had to offer.

Our camp was adjacent to the 18-mile-long Green Lake. Since Grant Kuypers' concession included most of the lake frontage, Mike Jahnke discovered a unique way to hunt – by boat. He could travel down the lake in a boat and get out and hunt any number of good spots along the way that might hold some promise for a big buck.

Once again, Nicole and I were all set to go back into our special Deep Ravine area. The trip was always a challenge but we looked forward to it nonetheless. It was the price we had to pay to be able to hunt some of our favorite old spots. Little did we know how different, or potentially

dozing off in the blind. Around noon, I suddenly woke up and saw a big buck coming my way. I knew it was him. I waited for him to get in a good broadside position and I shot him with my custom .300 Ultra-Mag. He ran about 50 yards and piled up. Note: I'd been on a dream hunt to Alaska for Dall sheep the year before, and had a nightmare experience using an inferior production rifle in which I missed a relatively easy shot because the gun would not hold a pattern. After that, I had master rifle-maker Bobby Hart of Pennsylvania build custom rifles for Nicole and I to use in the future. Our hunt in Saskatchewan proved the value of having dependable guns.

So our much-anticipated 2009 hunt was over in only two days. For the second year in a row, we had an unforgettable hunt at Buck Paradise. Grant was very happy about the response he'd gotten from our TV show and invited us to come back for a third year.

BUCK PARADISE 2010

We couldn't wait to get back to Buck Paradise in October 2010. Team member Mike Jahnke was back for the second year in a row and we also brought along another team member, Dan Meyers, as well as our good friend Don Pickel. They had heard us talking about how much we loved Buck Paradise and wanted

Pat and Nicole were not prepared to get wet during their three-hour quad ride in 2010 when heavy snow covered all the trees and bushes. "It was the coldest day I ever spent in a stand," Pat later confessed.

These nighttime trail photos of the buck Pat nicknamed Stickers revealed a mature buck worth going after!

10/20/2010 10:36 PM

10/19/2010 9:02 PM

dangerous, the long quad ride would prove to be on the first day of our 2010 hunt.

Because the quad ride took almost three hours, it was usually just beginning to break daylight by the time we reached the Deep Ravine area. It was always a cold ride on that quad and we wore extra clothes to compensate. Despite everything we put on, we would still freeze going there in the mornings because of the wind. We always took two quads with trailers. One was loaded with hay for bait and the other held all of our hunting gear and camera equipment.

On this trip, Nicole and I made an agreement that I would hunt first. In past years she always hunted first, but she was fine with letting me hunt first this time. The good news was that our guide Kyle Gardner had been getting trail camera photos of a big buck in the same exact spot on the same ridge where I had shot a nice deer with my bow the first year we had hunted with Buck Paradise. This particular buck was a big 6-by-6 with several stickers around his bases – so we nicknamed him "Stickers." There was also a younger 6-by-6 in the area that looked a lot like Stickers, but was only slightly smaller.

Stickers had a basic 6-by-6 rack that gross scored 175 inches.
Pat shot the big buck from the same location where he arrowed his 2008 10-pointer.

This close-up photo reveals how Stickers earned his name.

Back at camp, it was time to celebrate Nicole's successful hunt for yet another North Woods monster! Standing next to Nicole on her left is Buck Paradise owner Grant Kuypers.

Check out Pat's hunt for the buck he named "Stickers" after enduring an extremely cold and wet day in the stand.

THE QUAD RIDE FROM HELL

As luck would have it, it had snowed quite a bit during the night. When we left on the quads in the predawn darkness, everything was covered with a wet snow; the branches, the bushes, the trees, everything. This had never happened to us in previous years and we certainly didn't think about the possible consequences as we left camp that morning. So the entire several-hour trip that had always been an adventure in the past now turned into a miserable test of endurance. The quad trails are very narrow, and every time we hit a low-hanging branch holding snow, the wet snow would go down our necks and work its way inside our clothing. By the time we reached the treestand we planned to hunt from, we were soaked through and through because of all the wet snow. It was certainly not a good situation to face in the Canadian wilderness when the outside temperature was in the 20s.

As I climbed up into the tree that day I remember thinking, *How will Nicole and I make it through the day being totally wet, and sitting out in the open in the wind and the elements like this?* I'm sure Nicole had the same thoughts. If we'd thought to put on our rain gear for the long ride this never would have happened. But that thought never crossed our minds. My only consolation – as I grimly faced sitting in a cold treestand for the next 8 or 10 hours – was the hope that I could shoot a deer early in the morning so we could go back to camp early. Because of the long distance involved, our guide didn't go back to camp after dropping us off. Instead, he parked the quads some distance away and spent the day in the woods waiting for us. During the day, he would put out bait in other stand locations, or check trail cameras, or just watch the deer and tell us what he had seen.

Despite being cold and completely wet all over, we settled into our treestand. The thing that really saved us that day was the ScentBlocker base layer Nicole and I each had on underneath our outer clothing. Even without the snow, the quad ride was always very cold, so we always wore a base layer to help keep us warm. Containing a high percentage of Merino wool, that base layer helps retain body heat even when wet, as was the case now.

We started seeing deer right away. The minute the quad leaves, the deer usually start coming out to the bait. They know! Sometimes they come out while the quad is still there! Of course, the big boys don't usually show themselves until very late in the afternoon. We sat there all day long in that cold tree. I don't think I've ever been more cold in my entire life. We were very surprised to see the younger Stickers during the

During her 2010 hunt, trail camera photos revealed that the big 5-by-5 Nicole decided to pursue had a sticker point near the base of its right antler.

Upon seeing a mouse run across the floor of her ground blind, Nicole let out a bloodcurdling scream. Hubby Pat was not too pleased!

"After spotting the mouse, Nicole must have kept her feet in the air for a good 10 or 15 minutes," Pat recalled in frustration.

middle of the day. We watched him awhile but had no intention of shooting him.

About an hour before dark, just when everything seemed to be really bleak, I looked up and spotted a big buck sneaking through the trees. Stickers was coming right in! Nicole got on him instantly with the camera. I feel so lucky to be with her when she's running the camera because she has a natural ability to stay calm and get the camera focused right on the animal as soon as it's spotted. This is so important when videotaping a hunt. Because of the way we were situated in the tree and the elevation of the land, I was almost at eye level with the deer as he came in, so I had to be very careful getting my bow off of the hook and getting my release clipped in so he wouldn't see me.

It was a storybook setting. He turned broadside at about 25 yards and I made an excellent shot. He ran a few yards, stopped and started looking around. I felt certain he was well hit but I wasn't about to take any chances. I nocked another arrow and put it into his boiler room. He ran into the timber a few yards and fell over.

He was an absolute stud of a buck, big and heavy with a huge neck. As mentioned, he was a clean 6-by-6 with several stickers. We gross scored him later that night back at camp at 175 inches. Considering the circumstances that day, I was pretty tickled to have pulled it off. Our teammates, Dan Meyers and Mike Jahnke, had also each shot a nice buck that day. As usual, except for being cold and wet, Saskatchewan had treated us like royalty. We were having a grand old time!

But making it through that day had been a true test of endurance. The temperature was in the mid 20s,

Despite a tiny mouse that almost ruined her hunt, Nicole managed to gather her senses long enough to make a perfect shot on this beefy, 165-inch 10-pointer. The awesome buck obviously had a body to match its huge set of antlers.

and being exposed to the constant wind all day long in that treestand unquestionably made it the coldest day I'd ever spent in a stand. Nicole felt the same way. I don't know how she did it. She's one tough lady! Late that afternoon the temperature started dropping. I think our inside clothing probably dried out a little as the day progressed but it was still cold and miserable. I'm surprised we both didn't get hypothermia! Someone upstairs was definitely watching over us that day.

A MOUSE IN THE HOUSE

Now we had one buck down and it was Nicole's turn to hunt. We planned to go back in to the same general area and hunt a spot near a big opening where Kyle had gotten a number of trail camera photos of an extremely large 10-pointer. The buck had a sticker on one side of his rack and a beautiful double white throat patch. He was often seen with another big 10-pointer that Nicole and I had seen the previous year. Kyle said, "This buck is really on a pattern and he's very regular. I think we can get him if we use a ground blind."

I asked him to go ahead and set one up, although I was a little concerned about hunting a ground blind that had just been put out. I would have much pre-

ferred to let it sit out for several days to let the deer get used to it. But we didn't have that luxury. Because of the light hunting pressure, I knew these Canadian deer often acted differently than the Midwestern deer we were used to hunting, so I thought we'd be all right.

We got settled in the ground blind early in the afternoon and pretty soon had several deer feeding out in front of us. I was happy to see they paid almost no attention to the ground blind. After we'd been sitting a while, I heard something scampering around in the leaves. I thought, *Oh no, please don't let it be a mouse.* Nicole is deathly afraid of mice. Sure enough, it was a mouse. Nicole heard it too. I could see her tense up as she said, "What was that? Was that a mouse?"

Trying to get her mind off the mouse and knowing how she would react if she saw it, I said, "No I think it was just a bird."

Moments later the mouse ran across the ground inside the blind and she saw it. She let out a blood-curdling scream that could've been heard three miles away! As you can imagine, all of the deer immediately cleared the field. She pulled both legs up onto her chair, keeping her feet off the ground. I was furious. "Get down off that chair," I whispered. "You just spooked all the deer."

Pat and Nicole proudly show the results of another successful year at Buck Paradise in Saskatchewan.

Nicole must have kept her feet in the air for a good 10 or 15 minutes. It had to be a great ab exercise, but eventually she started letting them down and finally put both feet back on the ground. She was looking everywhere for that mouse and wasn't paying the least bit of attention to what was going on outside the blind.

Gradually the deer started coming back to feed, but we saw no sign of the big 10 with the sticker we hoped to see. We sat there for a while longer and the clean 10-pointer we had seen the year before came out alone. I said sternly, "Whatever you do, don't you dare spook these deer again."

The 10-pointer had a beautiful rack that would have scored in the 150s, but after talking it over we decided to let him go. About 2:30 or 3:00 p.m. – just after everything had pretty much gotten back to normal – the mouse reappeared. I'd actually seen him a few minutes earlier and kind of kicked at him to scare him away when Nicole wasn't looking. But now he was back again and this time she saw him right away.

She completely lost it. She gave out another blood-curdling, bawling, crying shriek. Then she went into a fit. If Bigfoot himself had been there, he couldn't have competed with such a terrifying scream. She forgot all about hunting and that we were watching a big 10-pointer and screamed again. All of the deer

On the first day of his 2010 hunt, cameraman Shane Indrebo accidentally dropped the camera out of the tree he and team member Mike Jahnke were sitting in. Despite considerable damage to the camera including a total loss of audio, Shane managed to capture the action when this impressive buck appeared.

See Nicole shoot this absolute brute 10-pointer after an exciting afternoon in the blind.

These three daytime trail camera photos led Nicole to believe that she could successfully hunt this big 10-pointer. And she did!

in front of us once again cleared the area, running for their lives. Tails were waving everywhere you looked and it sounded like 100 different deer were blowing at the same time. They obviously had never before heard such a terrifying sound from a woman.

Now Nicole was up on her chair permanently. This woman had hunted bears and other dangerous game and had always exhibited nerves of steel. Now she was coming unglued – all because of a tiny mouse. She was on her chair muttering, "I'm not enjoying this at all. I want to go back now!" I was getting madder by the second. She was hysterical.

"Come to your senses and get off that chair immediately," I demanded. "I'm not gonna sit here any longer and watch you scare off all the deer because of a stupid little mouse."

The deer were gone, the mouse was gone, I was fuming mad, and just about at the end of my patience. About that time I happened to glance out the window of the blind. Walking directly toward us as if he didn't have a care in the world was the big 10 with the sticker that we'd been hoping to see all day long. He was halfway across the opening in front of us and was closing fast.

"Get off your chair now," I ordered in a serious tone. "Here comes the big one."

She thought I was making it up. But she did manage to peak out the window and see him. She timidly put her legs down, still searching the inside of the blind for the mouse. Then she grabbed her bow and

clipped on her release – all in one smooth motion. Just as the deer stopped broadside at 25 yards she came to full draw and released her arrow. It all happened in a whirlwind moment. After the shot, she started looking for the mouse again.

The deer took off. It looked like a good hit but the arrow hadn't penetrated very far. But I did notice that the buck's tail was sort of going around in a corkscrew motion as he ran off, and that's always a good sign. We waited awhile and decided to follow him up. We didn't have far to go. He only made it about 60 yards and piled up. Nicole's arrow penetrated just enough to catch both lungs. He was an absolute brute of a deer that ended up scoring 165 inches.

It was almost too good to be true. We were batting 100 percent. We'd taken two outstanding bucks in only two days of hunting – plus all of the guys on our team had also tagged out!

On the first day of the hunt, a bizarre incident occurred with our fellow team member Mike Jahnke. Mike was hunting with cameraman Shane Indrebo, son of my good friend Tom Indrebo, when the camera he was using accidentally dropped out of the tree they were in. For all practical purposes, the camera was destroyed.

As they were looking at it in disbelief, a really nice buck came walking in. Even though the viewfinder and microphone had been broken off, Shane was able to get the camera up and running. Using only the eyepiece, he filmed Mike shoot the buck with no audio,

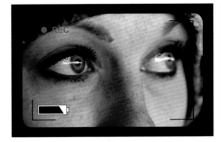  

Nicole shows off her awesome 10-pointer taken in 2011 as her guide Kyle Gardner looks on.

and then filmed the buck as it ran off. Later on they got another camera to shoot the recovery and all of the other re-creation scenes that had to be filmed. In the end, they managed to produce a great hunting segment despite what had happened. It's amazing what a little determination and ingenuity will do. That's why we like to think of ourselves as being driven!

As we were leaving camp, our outfitter Grant Kuypers said, "Great job this year! You're welcome to come back next year!" We definitely planned to return the following year for another archery hunt. In fact, Nicole had already decided on bringing a very special person with her. She said, "Next year, when we come back, I'm bringing my dad with us." Although he'd been an avid whitetail hunter all his life, Jim Jones had never been out of Illinois on a deer hunt in his life. Nicole was determined to give him this special hunt as a Christmas gift or Father's Day gift

People often ask Nicole and I what we do with all of our venison. When possible, we always take it home with us to eat. But in situations where we are traveling by air or traveling long distances from home, we often donate our meat to local food banks. In the remote areas of Canada, where poverty abounds, we usually donate our meat to those in need. They are always very grateful and utilize every part of the deer. Nothing goes to waste.

These 2011 trail camera photos were taken of the buck that Jim Jones later nicknamed "Flames" because the rack's double row of short tines resembled flames shooting upward.

as a small token of her appreciation for what he had done for her as a young girl. So as 2011 approached, she had a lot to look forward to.

BUCK PARADISE 2011

THE ADVENTURE CONTINUES
JIM JONES' DREAM HUNT WITH NICOLE

Nicole had always wanted to take her dad with us to Saskatchewan, and in 2011 she made it happen. I had taken my dad in 2008. He'd a great time and shot a beautiful buck. Now it was Jim Jones' turn. This was a dream-come-true for both father and daughter!

It was the end of October and already very cold. Everyone would be bow-hunting including Jim. Jim is a lifelong bow-hunter, and he put a bow in Nicole's hands as soon as she was old enough to draw back the legal weight in Illinois. Naturally Nicole and I wanted to hunt our familiar old spots back in Deep Ravine, but we were a little worried about Jim having to make that grueling, three-hour quad ride (especially after our experience the year before when we had gotten soaking wet from the fresh snow).

Being in his late 50s and having had some serious health problems in the past – including cancer, we didn't know if he was physically up to the challenge. But our worries were totally unfounded. Jim was all for it. He considered it a great adventure and savored every minute of the long ride. Like his daughter, Jim has a wonderfully adventurous spirit. Obviously that's where she gets it from! So we all jumped on the quads

and headed for the wilds of northern Canada.

The plan was for me to film Nicole on the first day, as usual, while Jim hunted alone in a different spot. He was all for that too. It was cold that day, about 20 degrees. Just as we got to Jim's treestand in the predawn darkness to drop him off after the long quad ride, a pack of wolves started howling fairly close by. They were probably less than 200 yards away. If you've never heard wolves howling before, I can tell you it's an eerie feeling, especially *that* close in the darkness. Our guide Kyle Gardner told Jim, "That's not a good sign if you're hunting deer. You may not

Jim Jones' Saskatchewan adventure began with seeing a pack of wolves, and it ended with this heavy-framed non-typical brute he called Flames. Nicole filmed all the action for her dad.

Jim Jones poses with his beautiful daughter after his memorable 2011 hunt – his first-ever Canadian whitetail hunt. It was just like old times for the father/daughter team and a memory they will never forget.

see anything all day. When the wolves are in the area the deer know it and usually leave."

Jim wasn't the least bit concerned, in fact, he was pretty excited. He said, "Heck I just want to sit here anyway. It's pretty cool to hear wolves. Maybe I'll get to see one."

So we said goodbye to Jim and off we went to Nicole's blind, the same ground blind we had been in the year before when the "mouse from hell" had terrorized her so badly.

Kyle was great to work with and he was always on top of things. Knowing our style of hunting from previous years, he had all of our stands set up in advance. He always allowed us to make our own decisions about where we wanted to go and which deer we wanted to go after. He'd been running trail cameras back in that area for several weeks so he had plenty of pictures of promising bucks.

Nicole had passed up a nice 10-pointer for two years in a row in this area – the same 10-pointer that we had run out of the field during her hysterical mouse

Witness Nicole's father, Jim Jones, shoot a true North Country non-typical in 2011.

panic. Now he had turned into a 5½-year-old brute of a buck and was back in his old stomping grounds. He was definitely a buck Nicole wanted to put on the wall.

The moment we stepped inside the ground blind, Nicole began to worry about seeing another mouse. I had visions of her freaking out again so I went on mouse patrol with my flashlight to make sure no mice had invaded the ground blind. I tried to shift her attention to hunting the big 10-pointer because we both knew he was a dandy.

Shortly after first light, a nice young buck came in and started feeding. We sat and watched him for a long time. About 9 a.m., he suddenly snapped his head up and looked toward the timber. I knew by his body language that something was coming. Sure enough, the big 10-pointer we were hoping to see came strutting into the field. I prayed that no mouse would suddenly appear and again ruin our hunt. As the buck came closer, Nicole had plenty of time to grab her bow, concentrate and set up the shot. She made a perfect shot and the hunt was over.

There we were on opening morning and Nicole had filled her tag. So we spent much of the day taking pictures and filming the follow-up shots. Kyle wouldn't be coming to get us until late afternoon and I was in cameraman's heaven because I knew I had the luxury of time to do everything we needed to do the right way. You don't always get that lucky. On most hunts, we never seem to have enough time for one reason or another and we're always rushed. But that day, I had all the time in the world to film outside the blind and do all sorts of special things. I shot a time lapse and photographed other deer coming in to feed. In short, I was able to shoot video of a lot of those extra major elements that we never seem to have time to get. Being able to devote the right amount of time to a production is crucial toward producing a good TV show. So it was a day well spent.

Jim didn't shoot a deer that first day but he did pass on a nice 150-class buck. Most bow-hunters would have taken a deer of that size without a second thought, but Jim spent the day taking in the sights and sounds of the Canadian wilderness, and loving every minute of it. He did, in fact, get a glimpse of the wolves, which gave him a real thrill. Now that she had her buck on the ground, Nicole planned to hunt with Jim and film him shooting a deer. Sometimes things really work out for the best!

Kyle came and got us late that afternoon as planned. We set up another ground blind a short distance away and brushed it in for Nicole and her

These night photos were taken of Pat's awesome crab-claw buck.

Catch a glimpse of Nicole arrowing a great Saskatchewan 10-pointer from a ground-blind in 2011.

A beautiful view of Green Lake; part of Grant Kuypers' Green Lake hunting concession in Saskatchewan.

Another great photo of Pat's incredible 2011 crab-claw bruiser.

Despite having to hobble around on crutches because he had just suffered a broken leg, team member Mike Jahnke managed to arrow this magnificent trophy whitetail from a ground blind in 2011. That's what being driven is all about!

dad to hunt from the next day. Kyle said that a very good buck he'd seen in previous years was coming in to that spot on a regular basis. The old warrior was a short-tined non-typical with a row of inside tines. He was a real dandy and Jim said that was the buck he wanted to go after.

Jim was excited about making another long quad ride back into Deep Ravine the next morning. He and Nicole spent a special day together in the woods. In many ways, it was just like hunting together in the old days, except they were now in the Canadian wilderness instead of Illinois. Unbelievably, the storybook setting had a storybook ending. The old non-typical came right in that afternoon as if it had been planned all along. Jim made a great shot on the buck with his bow, and Nicole got the entire drama on film. It was a great ending to a great day. Once again, the father and daughter hunting team of Jones and Jones shared an unforgettable memory together!

The same day Nicole and Jim were hunting together, I planned to hunt a good spot near the lake by way of the boat, where Mike Jahnke normally hunted. Although he was along on the trip as usual, Mike had broken his leg several weeks earlier and he couldn't do a lot of walking up and down steep terrain. It was also difficult for him to get in and out of the boat

Driven team member Mike Jahnke, cameraman Bryan Lemke, cameraman Mike Stephan and Nicole pose for a fun-filled airport photo in 2012. Do you think the team brought along enough luggage?

on crutches, so he wasn't able to hunt the spot he'd planned on.

I decided to go there and hunt out of a ground blind, and stayed there all day without seeing much. By the end of the day, I was pretty disappointed and planned to go somewhere else the next morning.

Just as I was leaving, however, I decided to check a camera that had been set out a few days earlier. I was shocked to see pictures of a giant 10-pointer in the very spot I'd been hunting! The photo was from the night before during the early morning hours. There were several other pictures of the buck from previous nights as well. Those photos changed my focus right away. I was determined to hunt that spot and that buck for the remainder of the week.

The buck was a huge main-frame 5-by-5 with long split brow tines that had crab claws on the ends. The tips of his main beams angled downward giving his rack a lot of character. "That's the buck I'm going af-

While waiting for the "big one" to show up, Pat took this photo of an outstanding 10-pointer from his ground blind.

The Busbice boys, owners of Wild Game Innovations and Evolved Habitat who sponsor Pat and Nicole's TV show, shared a memorable 2012 hunt with the Driven team in Saskatchewan. Pictured from left to right are Matt and Ryan Busbice, Nicole, "Big Bill" Busbice and Pat.

Driven TV cameraman Bryan Lemke, center, shows the gang some great video footage from the day's hunt. Looking on from left to right is Driven team member Mike Jahnke (sitting); Keith Heperer, Mike's good friend and cameraman (standing); Pat; and Dean Kuypers, co-owner of Buck Paradise.

ter," I told myself. "It's either him or nothing." I knew from the photos that he was a nocturnal deer. But I also knew that sooner or later, he might change his habits and show up during the day to feed, especially if the weather got colder. With a little luck, I might get a shot at him.

The following day, Nicole came along to film me since her dad had filled his tag. We planned to sit all day in the ground blind. During the early part of the afternoon, when I least expected to see this nocturnal buck, I saw a deer coming through the trees. I looked up and saw antlers and could see his tall brows. I was blown away. "Oh my God, it's him!"

I told Nicole to get ready with the camera. As he came in, he circled downwind of the blind through some of the thickest stuff imaginable – a typical thing for a mature buck like him to do. When he was completely downwind, he stopped and apparently got a whiff of something he didn't like. He quickly turned around and went back in the same direction from which he had come. He never looked back and he never offered me a shot. My heart sank. *That's the last time I'll ever see that buck,* I thought.

We sat there for several more hours. Right before dark, Nicole looked up and said, "Oh my gosh! It's him! Here he comes again!"

I couldn't believe it. He was extremely nervous, but eventually came in and offered me a broadside shot. I released my arrow. It appeared to be a good hit, although a little high. The last thing I wanted to

do was pressure him, so we backed out and decided to wait until the next morning to look for him. Just as we pulled up to the shore by boat the next morning, I could hear the ravens calling out in the woods. In Canada, that's always a good sign and a tip-off. Ravens love to gather close to a downed deer and raise Cain. After my shot the night before, the buck had only gone about 60 yards before going down.

Mike Jahnke also shot a great buck that day while hunting on crutches. Here we were: four bow-hunters with four big bucks down. Nicole's dad had a great buck, Mike Jahnke had a great buck and Nicole and I had both filled our tags as well. What an amazing trip in 2011!

BUCK PARADISE 2012

In 2012, Grant Kuypers turned over his old Green Lake hunting concession to another outfitter, so Nicole and I learned that we'd be hunting a brand-new area in mid-October. The camp we'd be hunting out of was located near Good Soil and Grant's nephew, Brandon Schreiber, was co-owner.

In addition to our fall deer hunting and all of the great memories at Deep Ravine, we'd also been bear hunting with Grant at his Green Lake concession for the past four years in row. Our spring bear hunting had turned into a real family affair. My daughter Olivia shot her first bear at Green Lake, and my son Carson sat in my lap and "helped" me shoot a bear with a smokepole because he was still too young to shoot

Pat and Nicole's good friend Pete "Doc Pete" Stanton arrowed this high-tined 8-pointer in 2012 while cameraman Bryan Lemke captured the hunt on film.

for something new.

We weren't sure what to expect. It was mid-October and we planned to bow-hunt. As we were driving in, we saw a lot of deer out feeding in the fields along the road. That was definitely an encouraging sign. When we arrived in camp, Brandon showed us several trail camera photos of deer he thought we might be interested in hunting. One was a big 6-by-7 that looked like a real brute. Brandon already had a ground blind set up for me to hunt this deer and he had a big 10-pointer picked out for Nicole.

The camp was full of old friends. Team member Mike Jahnke was with us as usual, as was our good friend Dr. Pete Stanton. Our special friends from Wild Game Innovations – Matt, Ryan and Bill Busbice were in camp, along with Troy and Jacob Landry, the very popular hosts of the *Swamp People* TV series. With all of these great people it was going to be a fun hunt, and hopefully a lot of great deer were going to be hanging on the meat pole by the end of the week.

On the first morning of the hunt, we had planned to let Nicole hunt first, but the wind was bad for her spot so we went to my spot instead. We sat in the ground blind all day long hoping to see the big 6-by-7 but he never showed. I did pass on a good 10-pointer. The weather was nice, the temperature was in the low 30s

one legally on his own. And of course, Nicole had taken four great bears at Green Lake for four years in a row. So that old concession had been very good to us and held a special place in our hearts because we'd hunted there at least twice a year for the past four seasons. But change is good and we were ready

This photo gives some real perspective as to the massive body size of Pat's 2012 nocturnal monster.

Team member Mike Jahnke arrowed this heavy 4-by-4 on the last day of his 2012 hunt.

and we photographed lots of deer. I actually took several very good still photos from the blind of a couple of mature bucks, so I was very pleased.

That night, while we were all sitting around the lodge making plans for the next day, Brandon showed us trail camera photos of several nice deer. One buck in particular really caught my eye. It was a night photo of a huge-bodied, thick-horned giant of a deer. I didn't say anything about it at the time, but later on I asked Brandon where the deer had been photographed. "Oh that's a deer that we photographed way up north of here but he's almost totally nocturnal and we really haven't gotten set up on him yet this season," Brandon answered. "We hunted him a few times last year but he's so nocturnal we never saw him."

"Well I hunted one last year at Green Lake that was a nocturnal deer and I ended up getting him," I told Brandon. "I sure would like to give this one a try."

"Let's just see how tomorrow goes in your ground blind and we'll see," he said.

Even though Nicole would be filming me the next

day, I told her to bring her bow just in case. So we both took our bows the next morning and back in the blind we went. When we got inside, I told Nicole to sit in the shooter's chair. "What if the big 6-by-7 comes in?" she asked.

"I'll just have to think about it," I answered.

We sat there for a while and pretty soon a couple of nice bucks were feeding out in front of us. One was a mature buck and he suddenly yanked his head up to look into the timber. We knew something was coming in. Sure enough, in walked the big 6-by-7. "Do you want to switch seats?" Nicole asked.

The buck was a big-bodied brute of a deer. He had dark, chocolate antlers with long main beams. On the left side his main beam pointed downward like a drop-tine. Both brow tines and both G-2s had stickers. He was probably 4½ years old and had lots of character. He'd probably score around 160. It wasn't easy passing him up.

"No, you go ahead and shoot him," I answered. My mind was spinning. A little voice inside was tell-

Nicole's main-frame 6-by-6 tallied up an impressive 167 inches.

ing me that I needed to be hunting the big nocturnal buck instead.

The buck came in. Nicole waited for a good shooting opportunity. As soon as he turned broadside, she released her arrow. The shot was a little far back. He ran off and disappeared. We decided to back out and give the deer plenty of time to go down. I radioed our guide and told him we were going to pull the ground blind so that we could use it to set up on the big nocturnal buck. When the guide picked us up, we pulled the blind and went back to camp. The guide and I then drove back to the spot where the nocturnal deer had been photographed. It was a little like going into Deep Ravine. The area is very remote and it took us an hour to get back in there from camp. We set up the blind, brushed it in well, and then it began to snow. I thought, *Oh, no, this snow isn't going to help us find Nicole's deer!*

We backed out of there as fast as we could and drove like crazy to get back to where Nicole had shot the big 6-by-7. By the time we returned, about 1½ inches of snow already covered the ground. Not a good situation for blood trailing a deer. We started looking around and couldn't find a single track or

drop of blood. We searched randomly throughout the woods without finding a trace of the deer. Naturally, we were really bummed out. Back at camp that night, we talked it over and decided on a game plan for the next day.

Our good friend Pete Stanton had shot a nice 8-pointer that cameraman Bryan Lemke had filmed, so I planned to take Bryan with me to film the next day while Nicole looked for her deer with a search party of volunteers. Early the next morning, Bryan and I drove to the ground blind and sat in it all day long. We passed on a beautiful 10-pointer but never saw the nocturnal buck. When we returned to camp after dark, we learned that Nicole and her search party had spent most of the day looking for her buck without finding a trace.

So now we were bummed out even more. But, I learned a long time ago that when things are not going to your liking, they have a way of turning around when you least expect it – *if* you just hang in there. The next day Bryan and I went back to the ground blind and hunted the entire day without seeing our buck. When we got back to camp that night, we were surprised to learn that several people were very sick,

Pat and Brandon Schreiber (left), co-owner of Buck Paradise, admire Pat's last-day brute. The Saskatchewan heavyweight had an estimated live weight of 360 pounds! The huge white-tail had a main-frame 5-by-5 rack with several stickers on each side and bases measuring 6½ inches in circumference.

including Nicole. We weren't sure if a flu virus was going around or if the cause was from some type of food poisoning, but it seemed as if almost everyone in camp had come down with a severe case of Montezuma's revenge. Bryan and I were the only ones in camp who felt halfway decent. I was up all night with Nicole. It was bad enough that she had not been able to find her deer, now she was throwing up every five minutes and feeling absolutely miserable.

I started thinking about the 10-pointer I had passed two days earlier. Had I made the right decision? We were rapidly running out of time and things didn't seem to be going our way. We were down to our last day of hunting and in two days we were planning to drive to Alberta for a mule deer hunt.

It snowed all that night. When Bryan and I reached our blind the next morning, everything was beautifully white. Shortly after daybreak, a doe came out and started acting very odd. *Could there be a big buck*

close by? I wondered. Sure enough, we continued watching her and saw movement in the trees. A nice buck suddenly appeared. At first I couldn't tell how big he was. Then he stepped out into the open and I gasped. It was the big one!

In order to get a solid foundation and come to full draw, I had to slide off the bag chair I was sitting in and rest on my knees. Fortunately, I knew this might be a problem and had practiced doing it several times earlier. As I slowly got into position to shoot, Bryan got the camera on the buck. The moment he turned broadside at 20 yards, my arrow was on its way. The buck only went 10 yards and fell over! He was a giant of a deer, the biggest-bodied deer I'd ever shot. He easily had a live weight of 350 pounds! Although his main beams were fairly short, he had a dark, heavy, main-frame 5-by-5 rack with several stickers on each side. His huge bases measured 6½ inches in circumference. He was at least 5½, maybe even 6½ years old. Because of the severity of the winters, I think bucks in Canada take a little longer to reach their maximum body size and antler growth, but this buck had clearly attained his maximum size. He was massive!

We instantly got on the radio to our outfitter and asked him to talk to Nicole about coming out and hunting the big 10-pointer I had passed up. We knew she was sick, but the big 10-pointer we had seen was well worth going after if she could manage it. Always a trooper, that's what she did. The outfitter brought Nicole out and picked up me and the deer, Brian stayed to film Nicole. She was still feeling pretty ill but was willing to give it a try.

My plan was to go back to camp with my nocturnal monster and photograph him there while Nicole hunted. Then, if time allowed, I planned to quickly go to her old spot and hang a stand where she'd lost her deer. We hadn't given up on finding him but our chances of doing it didn't look too good. The next morning we would only have a couple of hours to hunt before we had to leave for Alberta. So I spent the next several hours taking pictures. Then, with just a little bit of daylight left, I grabbed two Big Game treestands, and the guide and I went out to the spot where Nicole had shot her deer. The moment we turned off the ATV, we heard ravens in the distance.

As so often happens in situations with lost deer, the birds were calling out in the opposite direction from where everyone thought Nicole's deer had gone. The ravens were behind us in the woods about 200 yards away, but the search for Nicole's deer had been concentrated out in front of us. I instantly knew those ravens were on her deer. We walked back in there and

Another successful year hunting with Grant Kuypers and Buck Paradise Outfitters in Saskatchewan! Pat's 2012 buck was a gargantuan whitetail, weighing around 370 pounds on the hoof. Nicole's awesome 6-by-6 was also a dream buck!

sure enough there he was. He had gone back into some thick, almost impenetrable cover and died. He was so well hidden that I couldn't find him until I was only a few feet away. Nicole, at one point, had actually walked within 50 yards without seeing him.

Because of the cold, the meat was still good so we field dressed him and cleaned him up for some photos. Then we covered him with a ground blind so that the coyotes wouldn't be able to get him. Nicole didn't know that we had found her deer, and I prayed that she hadn't shot another one that evening. Fortunately she hadn't. She was surprised, relieved and very happy to learn that we found her buck.

Talk about turning things around! Everything had looked so bleak the day before. Now, on the last day of the hunt, I managed to shoot the elusive nocturnal buck – and we had found Nicole's awesome 6-by-7. Plus, Mike Jahnke ended up shooting a great buck that same afternoon. It was definitely time to celebrate. We came back the next morning and shot some great vid-

eo and photos of Nicole's deer in the snow. Then we loaded up the truck and headed off to Alberta to start the process all over again.

Over the years, Canada really has been very good to us.

As a cameraman and TV producer, filming a hunt is almost like being a homebuilder. You start from scratch and put a tremendous amount of effort into all of the various aspects of telling a good story and filming a show. In the end you put all of the finishing touches on it and polish it up as much as possible. You lay down a doormat at the front door of your beautiful new house and at last the job is finished. But here's the clincher: The moment you finish one house, there is no time to admire your creation because now you have to grab that hammer and start the process all over again. When filming a TV show, however, you only have four or five days to get the job done. It's exhausting work, but it's never a job; it's a way of life. I guess that's why we call our show *Driven TV*!

In order to shoot a big buck, you have to hunt in areas where big bucks live. That's why Nicole and I like to hunt Canada so much – because of the great hunting opportunities. Over the years we've taken a lot of special people with us to Buck Paradise, and we've always had a great outcome. No one has ever been disappointed. This speaks volumes for our outfitter. Another reason we've enjoyed hunting with Grant Kuypers so much is because he understands what it takes to film a TV show. Grant is a real professional, and he always goes the extra mile to see that we have what we need.

If you want to hunt truly giant bucks, give Canada a try. Certainly you'll always find a few bad outfitters in the mix, but if you do your homework properly you'll avoid having problems. Nicole and I have never had an issue getting through customs. In many ways, it's much easier than dealing with the TSA at airports in the states. You must have a valid passport and all firearms have to be registered. You pay a small fee for this, but it's well worth the money and any extra effort you may go through because you could end up shooting the buck of a lifetime!

CHAPTER 6

LIKE FATHER, LIKE DAUGHTER

THE DAY NICOLE AND HER DAD SHOT THEIR BIGGEST BUCKS EVER

Through an incredible twist of fate, Nicole and her dad Jim Jones were hunting in different parts of Illinois on opening day of the firearms season in November 2011, when they each downed their best bucks ever.

Wherever they travel to hunt mature whitetails, Pat and Nicole seem to have a knack for making things happen, often under adverse conditions.

ILLINOIS, NOVEMBER 2011

It goes without saying that while Pat loves Saskatchewan, Illinois is Nicole's hands-down favorite place to hunt whitetails in North America. Her roots are firmly entrenched in southern Illinois where she grew up hunting with her dad and two brothers, not to mention the fact that the Prairie State is one of the premier big-buck states in the country. Prime time in Illinois usually runs from around Nov. 1-20. The rut usually kicks in around the first of the month, and by the 15th the big boys are chasing does fast and furiously.

Pat and Nicole typically try to bow-hunt the week before the first gun season begins. Then they switch over to muzzleloaders (you can use either shotguns or muzzleloaders during firearm season) and hunt the three-day gun season. That first gun season always

falls on Friday, Saturday and Sunday around the 18th to the 20th of the month.

In November 2011, Pat and Nicole were hunting with Tom Gaylord of Spoon River Outfitters in Fulton County, Ill. Fulton County is the home of some of the biggest bucks in Illinois – including the 37-point Jerry Bryant buck taken with a crossbow on Nov. 15, 2001. Unbelievably, Bryant was turkey hunting from a ground blind when he shot his mammoth buck. At 304⅜ non-typical inches, the Bryant buck is a world record with a crossbow – and an Illinois state record non-typical.

The plan was for Pat to bow-hunt the week preceding gun season while Nicole ran the camera. Then on Friday, the first day of gun season, Nicole would switch over to her trusty Thompson/Center muzzleloader and

During the week preceding the first firearms season in Illinois in November 2011, Pat arrowed this white-antlered 9-pointer. While hunting, Pat had actually seen the huge whitetail that Nicole later shot with her muzzleloader, but the buck never came close enough for a bow shot.

Pat would do the filming. They were both hoping to shoot mature bucks, but they never dreamed that Nicole would end up with the biggest buck of her life. What an unbelievable hunt this would turn out to be.

A BUCK NAMED "ROUNDER"

"We had never hunted with Tom before although we always bumped into him at the Illinois Deer Classic, and he had invited us to hunt with him several times in the past," Pat said. "I knew Tom's property was located in a fantastic area. Terry Drury owned some ground nearby and legendary baseball player Jim Thome, who grew up in Peoria, also had prime land in the area. The day we arrived, Tom showed us trail camera photos of some of his mature bucks. One in particular that stood out had been nicknamed 'Rounder.' He was a huge non-typical that had been photographed over and over again. Any time I see that many photos of the same buck I know he has to be a

resident deer living on the property. Why is that so significant? Because I've learned through experience that you have a much better chance of shooting a deer like that, and sooner or later, a resident deer is going to slip up and make a mistake.

"Tom said he had a good stand set up in the area where he was getting most of the photos of Rounder so Nicole and I went in there to hunt him. I planned to bow-hunt Monday through Thursday. Nicole would start hunting on Friday when gun season opened.

As luck would have it, we had an encounter with Rounder right off the bat on Monday morning. He was following a doe. The doe went into a brush pile about 60 or 70 yards from the tree we were in and simply locked down in there. She would not come out and he would not leave her side. I tried everything. I grunted and snort wheezed. That got his attention, but he was not about to leave that doe. We watched them for several hours and finally the doe got up and went off in

Nicole proudly shows off her largest buck ever, a massive non-typical nicknamed Rounder by outfitter Tom Gaylord of Spoon River Outfitters. Nicole was hunting with her T/C muzzleloader in Fulton County, Ill., in 2011. With 14 total points, Rounder gross scored in the mid-190s.

the opposite direction.

"We hunted that same general area the rest of the week but I never saw Rounder again. On the third day of the hunt I did end up shooting a large-framed 9-pointer that grossed in the high 130s. He had a beautiful rack with very white antlers. He certainly was not a giant like Rounder, but was a very good buck and I was happy to get him with my bow.

"Now it was Nicole's turn to go after Rounder. On Friday morning we decided to go back to the same area where I'd shot my deer near the top of a ridge. But it was extremely windy that day. As we were walking in that morning, we decided instead to sit at the bottom of the ridge where I'd had the Monday-morning encounter with Rounder because the wind would be easier to deal with. Bucks love to move around near the tops of ridges, but on windy days they'll often drop down the ridge for a distance, or even go all the way to the bottom of the ridge so that they can better use the wind to

their advantage.

"We planned to sit the entire day. Because of the timing of the rut, we thought we might see some buck movement during the middle of the day. About an hour after daylight, we saw a couple of does. An hour or so went by and Nicole happened to spot a big deer up on the top of the ridge. After studying him with our Nikons we realized it was Rounder. He was looking down toward the does and started coming downhill toward them.

Nicole got her muzzleloader up and he came right to us – well within bow range. At 25 yards Nicole stopped him with a bleat and squeezed the trigger. Because of the smoke cloud, she couldn't see his reaction to the shot, but since I was sitting above her with the camera, I could see that she'd hit him perfectly. He ran like a streak up the hill a short distance and stopped. He stood looking around for several seconds and then just tipped over.

"Did I get him?" Nicole asked.

"He's down!" I answered excitedly.

We both knew the caliber of this deer. He was a monster, and without a doubt, was probably Nicole's biggest deer ever.

When I told her the buck was down, she fell apart. She couldn't believe it and knew she had done something really special. I think she even looked at me and said, "I love you!" I don't know where that came from, but I said, "I love you too honey!"

She was very emotional and it was really genuine. We celebrated in the stand and later went and recovered the buck. He had a massive 6-by-5 frame with a total of 14 scorable points. He had a sticker on his right brow and several more on his right G-2. He also had extra-long brow tines and grossed in the low 190s. We figured he was probably 4½ years old.

But the story gets even more interesting…

From the time she could barely walk, Nicole was determined to be with her dad in the woods as soon as the Illinois shotgun season came along.

ALWAYS ON MY MIND

"No matter where I am sitting in a treestand, I always think about my dad and the special times we had when I was a little girl," Nicole reflects. "I might be thousands of miles away in Canada, or hunting in the Midwest somewhere, but I always think about my dad and we're always together in spirit. Always!

"Sometimes I'll send him a text or call him on his cell phone when Pat and I are in a treestand together. On this particular hunt in Illinois, it was very ironic because here I was in a treestand in the northern part of the state, and Dad was hunting on his place in Jackson County in the southern part of the state. Since it was opening day of shotgun season, I could almost picture him out there with his beloved H&R 12-gauge single shot with a bull barrel. As soon as it was light enough to see, I sent him a couple of text messages. I think I asked him things like, 'How are you this morning?' 'Seeing anything?' 'What's the weather like?' 'Not seeing much here but hearing some distant gun shots.'

"I didn't get an answer right away. I later found out Dad was hunting on the ground in a low area and his phone reception was bad. It was very windy where

Pat and I were hunting and we weren't seeing much movement. Around 9:30, I suddenly got a reply from Dad saying, 'I just killed the Kicker buck.' I knew he was ecstatic. He'd been hunting this old buck for several years and had found one of his sheds the year before. He never expected to kill him. We were both very excited for him.

"Another hour or so passed. I looked up on the ridge and suddenly saw a big buck. I got my binoculars on him and realized it was Rounder, the very buck we had hoped to see. We'd been watching some does out in front of us near the bottom of the ridge as Pat mentioned earlier, and Rounder immediately locked in on them. He started walking down the hill. I immediately got my muzzleloader on him and followed through the scope. He kept getting closer and closer. When he got within 25 yards, Pat said, 'I'm on him with the camera. Go ahead and shoot any time you're ready.' Whenever we're filming together, we always have to make sure the camera is on the deer before the shot is made. As soon as Pat gave me the okay, I squeezed the trigger.

"After the shot, a huge cloud of smoke made it impossible for me to see anything. 'Did I hit him?' I asked

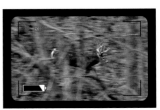

Jim Jones gives a thumbs-up for his daughter's first-ever video hunt. Nicole was videotaping a hunt in Kentucky with her father when she arrowed this nice 10-pointer. Little could she imagine what the future would have in store for her!

Pat. I was so excited that I had to sit down to regain control because I knew he was a giant. Pat said he was down. As soon as I was able, I called Dad on my cell phone to tell him the news. 'I just shot a huge buck,' I told him with a shaky voice. I fell apart. I was crying.

"'Why are you crying?' he asked.

"'Because I just shot the biggest buck of my life,' I answered excitedly.

"'Well that makes two of us,' Dad eagerly replied. 'Kicker is definitely the biggest buck I've ever shot too!'

"The events of that incredible morning took a little while to sink in. When everything did sink in, it was unbelievable. Within the span of a few hours, my dad and I had each shot the biggest bucks of our lives while hunting in our home state several hundred miles apart. Plus we had been in communication with each other while we were doing it. Knowing my dad had shot his biggest buck ever was very special, but having been in communication with him that morn-

ing made it even more remarkable. It was almost as if we'd been hunting together just like we used to in the old days.

"There's a humorous sidebar to the story. Since Pat had seen Rounder four days earlier on Monday while he'd been bow-hunting, he now jokingly accused me of doing something to sabotage his hunt that day. 'I know what you did,' he said. 'While you were behind me running the camera, you were waving your arms and trying to scare Rounder away so that you could come back and shoot him with your muzzleloader. I'll get back at you for this!'

"In truth, Pat was thrilled that I'd taken such an amazing buck. We spent the rest of the day photographing Rounder from every conceivable angle. The next day, my mom and dad drove up from southern Illinois to the lodge where we were staying in Fulton County. Dad brought his trophy with him so that we could take pictures of both bucks together. Pat took some great photos. Plus, Dad shot another good buck later that season with his bow. He was also blessed with the birth of his first grandchild. 2011 would be a hard year for him to top!"

BATTLING CANCER

"When I was two years old in 1986, my dad was diagnosed with Stage III Hodgkin's Lymphoma," Nicole remembered. "Some of his doctors doubted if he would still be around in six months time. He was on a rigid protocol of chemotherapy for almost a year. In addition to being miserably sick from the chemo, he lost a lot of weight. During deer season, his friends actually took him out, put him in his treestand and tied him in so he wouldn't fall out. The odds were against him but somehow he made a full recovery.

"In later years, he had several malignant melanomas that were also treated with chemotherapy. Then, in 2009, he was diagnosed with prostate cancer and had to have surgery. Somehow, his strong will, his strong faith and his passion for deer hunting helped get him through those tough times.

"In October 2011, I realized a lifelong dream when Pat and I took my dad to Saskatchewan where he shot a beautiful non-typical brute of a buck with his bow. It was the first time in his life he had ever traveled out of Illinois to go whitetail hunting, and it turned out to be one of the greatest adventures of his life. (See Chapter 5, Driven Dreams).

My mom also had a bout with thyroid cancer when

Deer hunting has long been a family tradition for the Jones family. After many years of hunting in southern Illinois and passing on the love of hunting to Nicole and his two sons, Jim poses with his best buck ever taken in 2011, a high-racked buck he fondly called "Kicker." Nicole's mom Susan was always a big part of deer camp as well – cooking meals, passing out snacks and supporting her deer hunting family any way she could.

Nicole holds up a set of sheds belonging to Rounder that were found by outfitter Tom Gaylord. The sheds were probably two years old.

I was in junior high school. She had to have her thyroid removed. Now both of my parents are doing great. They look forward to spending lots of time with their adopted grandkids in the future!"

A SPECIAL BOND

"It's been so neat for me to be able to witness the special bond that Nicole and her dad have forged over the years," Pat says. "Both of them had worked very hard at becoming good whitetail hunters and now, by some miracle, they had each taken their biggest bucks ever on the same day. They might have been hundreds of miles apart geographically that day, but in spirit, Nicole was sitting right there with her dad like she had when she was 8 years old.

"Nicole is just like her dad in so many ways. I feel extremely fortunate to be married to her and to be a part of her life. Jim Jones really did an amazing job raising his daughter!"

Whenever she and Pat are hunting anywhere in North America, Nicole always tries to stay in touch with her dad and keep him abreast of what is going on. Although they might be thousands of miles apart, they are always together in spirit.

CHAPTER 7

THREE LUCKY VELVET BUCKS IN NINE DAYS

It's difficult to fathom the amount of work that goes into a setup like this. Pat and Nicole spend hundreds of hours in treestands each year in all types of weather, knowing that their determination and dedication will ultimately lead to success.

Pat and Nicole really love archery hunting and the added challenge it provides. It takes year-round practice with quality equipment to stay sharp, especially when hunting in open country where long-distance shots are common.

Although I'd always wanted to hunt trophy whitetails in velvet, I'd never had the opportunity. I knew there were only a few places in North America with early enough archery seasons to make it happen; primarily North Dakota and Alberta. In 2009, things sort of fell in place and Nicole and I planned on making it a two-part trip. First we would travel to northwestern North Dakota and hunt on private land in early September, and then we would head north across the border to east-central Alberta and hunt with Neil Johnson of North Star Outfitters.

In early September we headed for the badlands of North Dakota with cameramen Shane Indrebo and Bucky Beeman. We would be hunting on a private 3,500-acre ranch belonging to Jeff Moengen and his dad. Jeff had been managing the prop-

The Badlands of northwest North Dakota contain some rugged terrain, but the deer tend to congregate near the river bottoms where most of the food sources are located.

Whenever they arrive at a new hunting destination, Pat and Nicole always take time to make sure their Mathews bows are shooting accurately. Exact distances are always determined with Nikon rangefinders.

Pat was able to outfox this high-racked velvet 8-pointer in North Dakota by setting up a ground blind inside a corral, near the spot where he'd watched a bachelor group of bucks come out of the timber to feed late in the afternoon. The strategy worked like a charm!

erty for big bucks for a number of years, and with 5½ miles of river-bottom frontage on the Little Missouri River, he had turned the land into a whitetail paradise. It was exciting to think we'd be hunting in the same general area of the badlands, and the same system of river bottoms where Teddy Roosevelt had hunted whitetails in the early 1880s and later made so famous in his classic writings.

Much to our liking, this would be a do-it-yourself hunt. Upon our arrival we hung some stands for Nicole just inside the woods overlooking a large alfalfa field adjacent to the Little Missouri. Typical of the end of summer and early fall, bachelor groups of bucks were coming out to feed in the alfalfa late in the afternoon.

Nicole set up near several trails where Jeff previously had seen some mature bucks coming out of the woods. Because we were hunting a food source, most

Watch Pat's hunt for a beautiful North Dakota velvet-antlered whitetail.

of our energy was focused on hunting in the afternoons. Morning hunts were tough because trying to get into our stands before daylight without spooking the deer that were still in the alfalfa at daybreak was almost impossible. However, I did set up a pop-up ground blind and hunted it the first morning.

We hunted the first two afternoons without having much luck. We were seeing a lot of deer but they were all well out of range. Nicole had a close encounter with a wide 8-pointer that had just shed its velvet. But the deer walked right under her stand without offering a shot. She slowly turned around as the deer walked away on the other side of the tree. But she had a difficult time anchoring her shot in such an awkward position. The buck turned broadside and she shot right over his back. She was not a happy camper but those things happen to everyone, especially when you hunt as much as we do.

Most of the trees along the edge of the alfalfa field were not very tall, making them difficult to hunt from. I hunted mostly out of a ground blind.

Two special North Dakota whitetails! Nicole's buck had recently rubbed off its velvet but she was thrilled to fill her tag nonetheless.

After five days of hard hunting, an elated Nicole shows off her last-minute buck taken on the final morning of the hunt.

Nicole and Shane were able to find a suitable tree for a double stand set. Anytime you're sitting in a tree with a cameraman, the deer are twice as likely to see something they don't like. It's hard enough for one person to get away with it. But with two people you double the odds of getting picked off. You leave twice as much scent and there is twice as much for a deer to see, especially with a big production camera. In order to pull it off, being well concealed is a must.

For the first four afternoons of our hunt, I watched several bucks across the field work their way around an old corral in order to get to a more lush part of the alfalfa. Whenever you're hunting a large early-season food source like alfalfa or soybeans, there will always be a section of the field the deer seem to favor. Whatever the reason, you'll see that the deer always gravitate toward this area every afternoon because the food source is probably just a little sweeter. Scouting and simply observing the deer helps you figure out where these spots are located.

Such was the case in the portion of the alfalfa where the old corral was located. A small bachelor group made a beeline for that area every day. The way it jutted out into the field made it a natural pinch-point because the deer had to walk around it. Even though I was watching from a considerable distance away through binoculars, the deer appeared to be passing within bow range of the corral. So I got a crazy idea. There were no trees around there for a treestand setup, but what if I put a pop-up ground blind in one corner of the old corral? The more I thought about it the more it made sense. The fencing in the corral would help camouflage the ground blind, and the deer might just pass by within bow range and offer me a shot. It was now day four of our hunt and I only had one afternoon left to make something happen. I decided to go for broke.

I waited until the deer had cleared the field the next day and gone back to their bedding areas in the timber. Later that morning, Bucky and I went over to the corral and set up a Primos Double Bull ground blind. It

This photo shows the open, rolling river country in Alberta that Pat and Nicole love to hunt. Most of the larger agricultural fields are found near the river systems.

Check out the video of Pat getting his Alberta open-country velvet buck.

was a "cool" 90 degrees that day. Despite the heat, we knew the deer still had to eat. Plus, I was happy to see that the wide boards of the corral fencing really did help camouflage the blind. Would the deer notice it and give it a wide berth? Only time would tell.

In most hunting situations, it takes a few days for the deer to get accustomed to a ground blind that has just been set up. So I always like to let a ground blind sit for at least several days, if not weeks, before hunting from it. But in this situation, I was down to the wire. I didn't have the luxury of time. This was the fifth and final day of the hunt. We were planning on leaving the next day for Alberta. It was now or never.

Bucky and I settled inside the ground blind by early afternoon. We knew nothing would happen until prime time so we waited in the heat. About a half hour before dark, we looked and saw the same three velvet whitetails I'd been watching for the last four days. They walked past the corral as they had always done, hardly giving the ground blind a glance. All three of the bucks were beautiful velvet 8-pointers, but one was heavy with very tall tines. I vocally grunted him to a stop at 25 yards and made a perfect shot.

He only went a short distance. When we reached his side, I could see that his velvet was in perfect condition. At this time of year, the velvet is sometimes torn and starting to shred, but in this case it was perfect. This great buck was everything I had hoped for and more. I finally had the velvet buck I had always dreamed about!

A heavy rain had just fallen on the third afternoon of Pat's Alberta whitetail hunt when this outstanding 10-pointer entered the field.

Because Alberta contains so much vast country, Pat and Nicole usually hunt close to the river bottoms where most of the prime food sources are located.

Now it was the end of our hunt. I had a buck down and Nicole still had an unfilled tag. She had hunted hard for five days and had several close encounters – all to no avail. Our plan was to get up early and head to Alberta, but I really wanted some good daylight photos of my buck before we left. So I suggested to Nicole that she should plan to hunt for several hours the next morning while Bucky and I were taking pictures.

"I can't," she said. "I've already taken down all my stands because I thought we were leaving."

So late that night, we went traipsing back out to the alfalfa field wearing our pajamas in the rain to put up a new double stand set for Nicole and Shane. The weather was supposed to be bad in the morning and things didn't look good. Nicole got up early and went hunting. I slept in – since we were planning to take pictures, we had to wait for the best morning light and there was no reason to get up early! Shortly after daylight, I was still in bed when the door suddenly burst open. It was a beaming Nicole. "I got him!" she yelled excitedly.

Only moments after shooting light had arrived that morning, a big-bodied 130-class 8-pointer walked right by Nicole's stand and offered her a shot. Nicole, who always seems to come through in a pinch, made a perfect double-lung shot on this "last minute" buck. The buck had already rubbed off his velvet, but he was a prime trophy nonetheless and Nicole couldn't have been happier.

Not only had our adventure to North Dakota been successful, it was also very memorable. After several days of hunting, we had finally figured out what the deer were doing and adjusted our strategy accordingly. Even though time had been working against us, we had made something happen at the very last moment and were both very happy. Things don't always work out the way we hope they will, but in this case they had, and we left for Alberta with smiles on our faces and high hopes for our next hunt.

ALBERTA, EARLY SEPTEMBER, 2009

We drove all night long from North Dakota to east-central Alberta and arrived dead tired early the next morning. We would be hunting with Neil Johnson of Northstar Outfitters in Marwayne, Alberta, near the Saskatchewan border. We had hunted black bears with Neil the previous spring and knew he ran a great operation. He had invited us to come up and try some early-season bow-hunting for velvet whitetails. If we got lucky and filled a tag early, the plan was to also bow-hunt for a big muley in velvet.

After a few hours sleep, we went out and set up some treestands for the first afternoon hunt. Once again, I would be hunting over a prime early-season food source – alfalfa. This would be very similar to the type of hunting we had done in North Dakota, only the field we were now hunting was much smaller. The first two afternoons of hunting and watching the deer feed in the alfalfa were uneventful. However, I once again noticed that they seemed to gravitate toward a certain part of the field where the alfalfa must have been a bit more rich and sweet tasting.

Even though I was hunting the same food source, Alberta was quite different than North Dakota. In North Dakota we had been hunting in the rugged badlands, but the topography in Alberta was much flatter. Because the topography is so different, the deer also act differently, especially mature bucks. The good

Hunting velvet whitetails is exciting because the bucks are still fairly predictable early in the season. Once the velvet is off, however, their patterns change drastically.

news is there are plenty of big bucks to hunt and hunting pressure is extremely light. But because of large numbers of predators – mainly coyotes and wolves – the deer don't move much during the middle of the day. When they do move they are extremely cautious. Seldom do the larger bucks come out until just before dark. That trait seems to be ingrained in most of the Canadian deer I've hunted over the years. So the best way to hunt them is to set up early in the afternoon and wait until prime time just before dark.

Everything came together on the third afternoon. I was hunting from a tree overlooking a small, secluded alfalfa field when a sudden rain shower came through about midafternoon. It wasn't much fun sitting out in the rain, but once it stopped we knew we were going to see deer movement right away. After a heavy snow or an intense rainstorm, you can usually count on seeing deer. When the snow or rain stops, the deer usually start feeding right away. This situa-

Velvet muleys are generally found in more open country away from the river systems, but like whitetails, their feeding patterns are very predictable before their antlers are rubbed clean.

tion was no different.

Shortly after the rain stopped, a beautiful, heavy-framed 145-class 10-pointer, still in full velvet, came walking into the field directly across from us with several does and smaller bucks. He walked straight over to our side of the field and started feeding. He eventually worked his way right out in front of my treestand and offered me a good broadside shot at 25 yards. My Muzzy broadhead hit him perfectly, and he didn't run far. I now had my first Canadian whitetail in velvet. I was pumped!

As is often the case with early-season food sources, trying to hunt the alfalfa in the mornings was risky. The deer were bedding around the edges of the fields, and trying to get into a morning setup was all but impossible without spooking a lot of deer. So Nicole and I did the next best thing. We went coyote hunting. Early the next morning, I called in a big coyote and Nicole made a great shot on it with her Thompson/Center .22/250. Nicole had seen several nice whitetails over the past three days of hunting but nothing

had come in close enough for a bow shot. At least now I had a good buck on the ground and that motivated her to fill her tag as well.

That afternoon, I hunted a different alfalfa field for muleys. My setup was off the mark, but it didn't take long to figure out what the deer were doing. We could see a bachelor group of mule deer bucks bedded during the heat of the day in some high grass and brush near a small lake just to one side of the alfalfa field. Late in the afternoon, when it was time to get up and start feeding, they worked their way down a fence line and jumped the fence into the field.

Armed with this knowledge, on the second afternoon my cameraman Shane Indrebo and I decided to sneak in and try to find a spot where we could set up on the ground near the location where we'd seen the deer enter the field the day before. We found just the right spot. The brush was fairly high and provided good cover for us to hide in.

If you can't find a suitable tree for a treestand setup, going into an area on the fly and making a natural

Catch the up-close footage of Pat arrowing his monster Alberta mule deer buck – in full velvet!

Everything came together for Pat and cameraman Shane Indrebo when they decided to set up on the ground in some 3-foot-high grass near the spot where the deer were jumping the fence to enter the alfalfa field.

ground blind can really pay off. In this case, we simply hunkered down on the ground in the brush and small saplings that grew along the fence line next to the alfalfa. I made sure I could shoot off the ground in a kneeling position by coming to full draw several times, and then I leaned back against a small tree and waited to see what would happen. Shane and I felt confident that we might get some up-close-and-personal action later that afternoon, and we weren't disappointed.

About an hour before dark, a mature mule deer buck we'd seen the day before jumped the fence and started feeding 20 yards away. Although he was a 4 year old, he only had a 2-by-2 rack, but with fairly long tines. I hoped to see the much larger buck he had been with the day before. By now, one of my legs had gone numb from sitting on it and I could hardly make it move. I slowly worked my way into shooting position and waited to see what would come next. The next buck in line was a 2-year-old 4-by-4 in velvet. Then all at once, Mr. Big stepped into view! He was a giant, mature, high-horned, main-framed 4-by-4 with several stickers and short brow tines. He was still in full velvet and was perfectly beautiful. He was feeding right on the edge of the field only 10 paces away! We had hoped to get close – but in this case we were too close!

Suddenly he looked over and saw something he didn't like – probably the camera lens. He got very nervous. As I came to full draw, he jumped back away from the field edge and paused for a split second. He

*What more could Pat ask for? In nine days of hunting, he arrowed
two exceptional velvet whitetails and this bruiser of a mule deer.*

was standing broadside at about 20 yards and that was all I needed. Before he could take another step, the arrow was on its way. Once again, my Muzzy broadhead did its job. He ran all the way across the field with the other two bucks and went down just inside the woods. Shane captured some outstanding up-close footage of the entire drama.

Before we started on this two-part odyssey to North Dakota and Alberta, I had never taken a trophy whitetail in velvet with my bow. Now, in the course of only nine days, I had taken two beautiful whitetails and one giant muley. The hunting gods were really looking out for me. I couldn't believe my good fortune. Nicole ended the Alberta hunt without filling her tag, but she had been successful in North Dakota. She was very happy for me. That's the great thing about having a hunting partner like Nicole. She's always so supportive and she never gives up, even when things are not going her way. Maybe next time the hunting gods will favor her!

CHAPTER 8

PAT AND NICOLE
DRIVEN TO ACHIEVE EXCELLENCE

When Pat decided to start his own show in the summer of 2005, he had an outpouring of support from many of his deer hunting friends and sponsors. Two years later he bumped into Nicole at an outdoor show by chance, and they started doing some hunting and filming. Today they have one of the most popular shows on outdoor television.

Despite the fact that Pat is a perfectionist who can often be very demanding as a TV producer, he and Nicole work together extremely well. "She is as good in front of the camera as she is behind it," Pat says. "She has so much God-given talent!"

After his dismissal from *North American Whitetail Television* in August 2005, Pat knew he had to make some quick decisions. He had long dreamed about having his own TV show. Now, because of events beyond his control, moving in that direction seemed to be the logical thing to do. Although he'd gained plenty of experience, starting a TV show from scratch was a huge undertaking. Hunting season was only a few weeks away and Pat was scheduled to go on several hunts that had been lined up months earlier. What should he do? He only had a matter of days to decide.

Pat called several key sponsors he had worked with in the past and with whom he felt like he'd developed good enough relationships to feel them out about sponsoring a new show. Among those were Mathews, Nikon, ScentBlocker, Muzzy and Thompson/Center. In the outdoor industry, major sponsorships are not easy to obtain. The competition is fierce. Hundreds of TV shows compete for precious sponsor dollars.

To Pat's surprise, all of these sponsors said they would support his new show. That spoke volumes for the respect these companies had for him and his abil-

ity. Pat then went to his bank and applied for a $7,000 loan with which to buy a good used camera. The lending officer looked at him and said, "Let me get this straight, Mr. Reeve. You don't have a job, you have no money coming in and you want to borrow $7,000 dollars?"

"That's right," Pat said.

"Okay," the officer said. "Sign here."

Pat got his money and another huge hurdle had been overcome. He immediately went out and bought a used Sony DSR300.

"I had so many good people who got behind me and assured me I could make it doing my own show," Pat said. "That meant so much to me. I knew I couldn't do the entire show by myself so I decided to put together a pro staff team. I called some of my good friends who had been former cameramen or guys I'd hunted with in the past. These guys were all great hunters in their own right and I knew they would enhance the show. Steve Snow, Mitch Hagen, Dennis Williams, Chad Nolte and Mark Wimpy made up the original pro staff. Paul Brazil and Donnie Hansen also helped out a great deal. When I first called them they basi-

During Pat's first year of filming for his new show in 2005, his five skilled and hardworking team members posed with him for a classic photo. Pictured from left to right are: Mitch Hagen, Mark Wimpy, Chad Nolte, Pat, Steve Snow and Dennis Williams.

cally said, 'Hey, we're here to help in any way we can. We'll film for you or do whatever you need us to.'

"Next I needed a name for my new show. Instead of some catchy name, I wanted it to be something that best described and defined me as a person, a hunter and a TV producer. So I decided to call the show *Driven 24/7*. In this sense, the term *driven* meant that I was always working to improve what I'd done in the past. I was *driven* to be a better cameraman, *driven* to be a better hunter, and *driven* to match wits with big whitetails. In short, I wanted to define myself as a driven person who lived and breathed what I did. That seemed to fit my personality perfectly so that became the name of the show.

"Even though a number of good sponsors agreed to sponsor the show, those sponsors' dollars would not start coming in for almost a year. So I was eating crackers and running on a lean budget for many months. I went from the end of August 2005 to the

first of July 2006 without a paycheck. As mentioned in Chapter 1, I had a brand-new diesel Ford truck sitting in my garage, but it had been painted with the logos of my former employer and I was not about to be seen driving it. I couldn't afford to have the truck repainted, and I really couldn't afford to put fuel in it, so I went out and bought an old $400 Oldsmobile Cutlass Supreme that would have to serve as my main travel and hunting vehicle in 2005.

"I was ready to hit the road. The gas tank of my old clunker leaked, and I could only put in $10 worth of gas at a time. In addition, the car had almost no brakes because I tore them out in a cornfield. But that old Red Rocket got me to Kansas, Wisconsin, Illinois, and back home again and that's all that mattered. The guys I was working with all came to love that old clunker. It represented something, it stood for determination and the spirit of never giving up.

"I knew I couldn't afford to put my show on Outdoor Channel because of the cost involved, but I was able to get on the Men's Channel, an up-and-coming cable channel that was airing a number of good hunting shows. The plan was to produce 13 original episodes that would air three times per week starting in the third quarter of 2006. As things turned out, we had a fabulous hunting season in 2005. My pro staffers shot some great deer, and after shooting my record 200-inch buck in Illinois, I got so much positive feedback when the show started airing that I knew we were going to make it.

"We had another great filming year in 2006 and the show was on its way. All of the sponsors were happy. At last, the future looked bright. As mentioned in Chapter 3, I first met Nicole back in 2003 when I was producing *North American Whitetail Television*. A friend in Illinois who thought very highly of Nicole's hunting ability had introduced us at a trade show and I immediately decided to use her in our opening montage during the second year of airing the show. That opening montage later won a Golden Moose Award on Outdoor Channel.

"Several years went by and I was hard at work planning what would be my third year of filming and producing *Driven 24/7* when I bumped into Nicole at a different trade show in 2007. I had just gone through a divorce but was fortunate to have four wonderful children with whom I was very close. Nicole and I hit it off right away. We had so many things in common.

"We got reacquainted and pretty soon were dating. I knew she'd grown up deer hunting with her father in Illinois. She had killed a lot of deer and turkeys with a shotgun and she loved to bow-hunt. We shared the same passion for deer hunting, and the thought of sharing that passion with someone like Nicole and spending time with her was very appealing. It filled a lot of voids in my life and took things to a new level.

"Having graduated from Southern Illinois University, Nicole was teaching third grade. She was a great teacher. She loved kids and they loved her. But she decided to move up to Minnesota late in the summer of 2007 so that we could start hunting and filming together that fall. It was tough for her to give up teaching but she was very excited about her new future.

"She joined right in and helped me run the business in many ways. I needed help in the office – with the web site, with handling orders and with other various aspects of running a TV show. She complimented the business and the show in every way. She was a natural in front of the camera, and she brought a special look to the show that I certainly couldn't compete

During Pat's second year of filming for North American Whitetail TV, Nicole made a cameo appearance in the opening montage.

Nicole, as the flag girl, prepares to start the race in Pat's opening montage for North American Whitetail TV, which later won a prestigious Golden Moose Award.

with. Her outgoing personality and friendliness always seemed to shine through because she genuinely liked people."

FILMING WITH NICOLE

"Nicole had not had much experience with running a camera but she picked it up amazingly fast. She's a quick learner and doesn't have to be told twice. She understood how important it was to film every phase of the hunt from start to finish. All the pieces of the puzzle have to fit together to make a good story line. The videographer's challenge is to make all of the elements flow both visually and through sound. Lots of people fail in TV production because they don't get all of the elements necessary for a good story line. I would explain certain things to her while we were hunting – 'this is why I pan the camera' –and other things like that.

"I think the reason Nicole is so good is because she has an eye for detail and she doesn't get rattled. When you get rattled you don't pay attention to detail. A good cameraman has to remain calm from the start and capture all the action and the shot. Then he has to get the hunter's reaction. After the action and reaction, he has to recreate the hunt. In order to do this successfully, a good cameraman must have the presence of mind to remember the details and the chain of events.

"Within just a month or two of filming with Nicole, I didn't have to worry about her making mistakes in the tree with the camera. Whenever I did critique her or show her how to do things a little differently, she understood what I was talking about. Frequently we would go back and watch the footage and critique it for camera work and style. She had excellent vision and always kept things tack sharp. That's so important in our line of work. We use production cameras and we shoot everything on manual, so keeping everything in sharp focus is critical. Yet, I've seen a number of cameramen who never quite master that important aspect of videography.

As a dedicated videographer and TV producer, Pat always strives to capture the action in each part of the story he is telling by using camera angles that are unique and unexpected. He sees things that other cameramen seldom see.

Whenever they are in a stand together, Pat and Nicole use every advantage they can think of to end the day successfully. Over the years, calling has been a very productive means of getting big bucks within bow range.

"When you hunt almost every day of the season, you spend a lot of time in a stand or blind waiting," Nicole says. "But even during our downtime in the middle of the day, we are always ready to jump into action on a moment's notice."

On any given hunt, Pat will often film Nicole for a couple of days, and then Nicole will get behind the camera and film Pat. This partnership has worked out well during the past seven years.

TRADEMARK DISPUTE

"During our first year of filming together in 2007, Nicole and I got home from a trip one day and were in the process of washing our clothes and packing to leave on another hunt when the doorbell rang. It was the mailman. He handed me a certified letter from a person in the hunting industry who claimed that he had trademarked the term '24/7.' This person threatened to sue us if we didn't change our name. As you might imagine, I went into a panic mode. Everything we owned had our *Driven 24/7* logo on it – our clothing, the truck we drove, all of the CDs and DVDs we sold, T-shirts, our web site – everything. Just when things seemed to be going my way, here was yet another curveball being thrown at me.

"I contacted my attorney right away. After checking into the situation, he determined that the person had in fact trademarked a name with '24/7' in it. Although we could have fought it in court, because '24/7' is a widely used term, we decided it wasn't worth the time, energy and money it would take to do so. Nicole and I weighed all the options and decided to change the name of our show to *Driven with Pat and Nicole*.

"The next few months were grueling for us. We had to change our web site. We could no longer sell our DVDs. We had to replace all of our clothing and get the truck repainted. We lost a lot of revenue during that time, but we learned a valuable lesson in business. If you have a logo or company name that you want to use, get it trademarked! That experience took a lot of our attention and in many ways took the focus off what we were doing. But we got through the crisis. We refocused and kept pushing and finished the year on a very strong note. If there was any consolation to the incredible headaches the trademark dispute had caused us, we went to Canada several weeks after it happened and Nicole shot her 181-inch monster!

"During that first year of hunting and filming together, an amusing incident occurred while we were on an antelope hunt out West. Having grown up in Illinois, Nicole had never had much experience shooting a rifle. She had always used a shotgun for deer, and most of her shots had been less than 100 yards. Now she was trying to shoot antelope at distances out to 350 yards and she missed her first three shots at three nice antelope bucks. It was almost comical watching her try to shoot an antelope with a rifle at those distances, although she certainly didn't think it was very funny at the time.

"Prior to the hunt, we had never given this a second thought. Nicole is a natural at shooting a shotgun or muzzleloader, but now these long-range shots were really playing mind games with her. On the fourth buck of the afternoon, we snuck up to the top of a little hill where she took two shots and missed again. She handed me the gun in disgust and said, 'This is it! I'm done with antelope hunting!' She was not happy.

"Amazingly, the antelope buck was still standing there. Since I also had a tag, I raised her gun, took aim

Pat and Nicole pose with one of two Golden Moose Awards won in 2013; one for best show opener and one for best big-game hunt. To the left of Nicole is cameraman Bryan Lemke, and to the right of Pat is editor Adam Helwig.

and squeezed the trigger. It was a very lucky shot on my part and the buck dropped in his tracks. My antelope turned out to be a B&C-class animal and I gave Nicole a hard time about her four misses. She went home and started practicing with a rifle. It didn't take her long to become very proficient shooting at long distances.

"After surviving the trademark crisis of 2007, Nicole and I were thrown yet another curve when the Men's Channel went belly up in 2008. For us, it was one more obstacle to overcome, one more mountain to climb. But we got through that crisis as well and we ended up moving our show over to Outdoor Channel. Maybe that was a good thing after all. In the years since, we've had 18 Golden Moose Award nominations and we've won six Golden Moose Awards. Winning awards may not be the most important thing in the world, but it is a way in which your peers judge you. The TV business is a very ego-driven business and we're very proud of what we've accomplished.

NICOLE AS A MOM

"Since Nicole has always gravitated toward kids, she hit it off with my four kids right away. Now she's a surrogate mom to them. She takes care of them like they were her own; feeding them, bathing them and getting them dressed. She loves them and they love her. Once I realized that things were good with Nicole and the kids, I knew she would be a lifelong partner. I knew there might be some criticism when we got together, but I was interested in being happy and building a future with someone special. In that respect, things have worked out far beyond anything I could have imagined.

"With Nicole, what you see is what you get. There is nothing phony or made-up about her. She always thinks about other people first. She likes to please people. If she has a weakness, it's that she goes out of her way to help people out and please them. But that's a good thing. It's a special characteristic that a lot of people don't have. Nicole is also very natural. She has very little ego. She's just Nicole, the girl from

Illinois who grew up hunting with her dad and loving every minute of it. And make no mistake about it, the girl can hunt. She has amazed me time and again. She has also learned how to run a camera very efficiently.

"Nicole has had a lifetime passion for bow-hunting. She loves it. She has a lot of natural ability for both hunting and filming. She knows what to do and when to shoot. No one has to tell her. On her very first hunt in Saskatchewan, she shot a monster 181-inch whitetail on the second day as mentioned in Chapter 2. She tried to trick me and tell me it was a small buck. We were both very proud of the fact that her great buck later made the cover of *Big Buck* magazine in Canada. Since then, she's taken several more

very large whitetails. In 2011, she shot a buck with a muzzleloader in Illinois that grossed in the mid-190s.

"Although whitetails will always be our passion, we've hunted lots of other North American big game together; elk, mule deer, antelope, caribou, moose, black bears and turkeys. Nicole even shot a 12-foot alligator in Louisiana. Nicole loves life! She has a real spirit of adventure and she's always willing to step out of her comfort zone to try something new.

"We've also done a lot of international hunting together. She successfully stalked and shot a male lion on the ground in Africa with a bow. That was a dream of hers, something that was on her bucket list. Later we went to New Zealand where we both hunted red

Although Pat and Nicole have a rigorous schedule that takes them away from home on hunting trips and personal appearances for many days of the year, the moment they return home they can't wait to spend time with the family. Usually that involves doing something outdoors. This family portrait, taken a couple of years ago, includes (left to right) Cole, Carson, Isabel and Olivia. As of the spring of 2013, Isabel was 7, Carson was 9, Cole was 12 and Olivia was 16.

Living the dream! One ingredient that has greatly contributed to Pat and Nicole's amazing success is their passion for what they do. Hunting for a living involves an incredible amount of stamina, drive and determination. When you are living your dream, it becomes a way of life instead of a job!

Don't miss Nicole's heart-stopping stalk for a massive African lion!

View the footage of Nicole arrowing a dangerous Australian water buffalo at only six paces!

stag and tahr. We've hunted high in the mountains on top of the world, and there is nothing to compare to that. It was absolutely breathtaking. Standing on top of the world like that you quickly realize your presence on earth is pretty small and insignificant.

"After the hunt, Nicole wanted to go skydiving. We had one day left on our New Zealand trip, so off we went to the skydiving place. We took our two hunting guides with us as part of their tips. We all suited up, got in the plane and climbed to 12,000 feet. I was supposed to be the first one out and I don't mind saying the 'pucker factor' set in. I've always been afraid of heights anyway, and now I was having second thoughts. But there was no turning back. Out I went strapped to my instructor. We did a free-fall for a minute or two and then the chutes opened. It was incredible, floating down over New Zealand. When I hit the ground I said, 'My gosh, that woman has really gotten me into a lot of stuff!'

"We went to Australia where Nicole shot a dangerous water buffalo with her bow at six paces. It was a very tense situation but she never missed a beat. I was filming her at the time and we were both standing in a crocodile-infested river. She always stays cool under pressure. In that particular situation,

Nicole shot this hefty male lion in South Africa in 2011 after a heart-thumping on-the-ground stalk. "She always stays cool under pressure," Pat says proudly. "She's amazing!"

Nicole shot this very dangerous water buffalo from six paces in New Zealand in 2010 after a long and difficult stalk. She shot the massive beast from the water's edge as it walked along the riverbank five feet above her while she stood in a crocodile-infested river. Pat stood in the water behind her and captured the entire hunt on film.

our outfitter had inadvertently left his rifle sitting on the riverbank 15 feet away, so we essentially had no backup when she made the shot. The show featuring that high-energy hunt aired in 2011, and in 2012 we won a Golden Moose Award from Outdoor Channel for Best Big Game Footage. Nicole's lion hunt aired in 2012, and it too won a Golden Moose Award for Best Big Game Footage in 2013. As mentioned, we've won a total of six Golden Moose Awards since 2004.

"We've actually hunted Australia and Africa twice now. If we hadn't been together, hunting as a couple, I seriously doubt if I would have made most of those international hunts by myself. But being able to do it with Nicole made all the difference in the world. For us those trips were lifetime adventures, and sharing adventures in Africa or Australia with your soul mate is special. We did it because we wanted to share the adventure together.

"As a school teacher, Nicole had the ability to influence 20 or 25 young minds every day, and she was a great role model. Now, because of her exposure in the TV industry, she touches and affects thousands of lives, young and old. It's common to see large numbers of daughters and wives with their dads and husbands at deer shows, and they all hunt together as families. You never saw that 10 or 15 years ago. Women like Tiffany Lakosky, Kandi Kisky, Vicki Cianciarulo, Nicole and many others have changed a lot of attitudes in recent years. Not too long ago, a 77-year-old woman came up to Nicole and said, 'I watched you hunt on TV and decided to do it myself. I've been married for over 50 years, and my husband always went alone. Now I won't let him leave the house without taking me. I love it!'

"Several years ago at one of the many deer classics we do every year, we met and became friends with a young man named Drake who had dwarfism. He made and sold his own jewelry and he really touched our hearts. He was a special young man. We also became friends with a beautiful young girl named Emily who we saw every year at a different show. She had a serious lung condition. Sadly, Drake and Emily both passed away in early 2013.

Things like that really bring everything into focus for us. Nicole and I are so fortunate to do what we do. It's not about the bucks we have hanging on the wall. It's about the places we've seen and the friends we meet. That's what keeps us Driven!"

Pat and Nicole believe that life should always be an adventure, and that dreams can come true if you work hard and believe. Their philosophy is, "Be the best you can be." They try to live by that creed every single day.

CHAPTER 9

HUNTING TIPS AND CALLING CARDS

Plant it and they will come! Food is obviously one the biggest calling cards you can offer deer. Pat and Nicole work hard at having plenty of good year-round food available on the properties they hunt, especially around home. Here they are preparing to disperse some Evolved Harvest clover seed.

Hunting over water sources has proven to be very productive for Pat and Nicole. Over the years Pat and his good friend Tom Indrebo of Buffalo County, Wis., have mastered the art of building small, isolated waterholes on or near ridgetops. Deer have to drink and bucks often visit these waterholes during the middle of the day.

MANUFACTURING "CALLING CARDS" TO ENHANCE YOUR STAND LOCATION

Every time Nicole and I set up a stand in a tree or on the ground we always look for ways to make that location the best it can be. We try to enhance each stand location by making sure there are one or more "calling cards" available to the deer. What is a calling card? A calling card is some type of physical object or contrivance that will entice a deer to come close to your stand and offer you a shot. Since we bow-hunt so much, we have to get close. A calling card can be natural or manmade, visual or airborne – such as scent. Sometimes a single calling card is all you need. Other times it might be smart to have several.

We always try to think about the different aspects of each situation and then try to offer calling cards that fit those specific circumstances. Many hunters don't think about doing extra things to enhance their stand locations. They simply find a good spot along a trail in the woods or maybe just inside the woods on the edge of a food plot, and they put up their stands and hope a big buck will come by. But think about it – if you can do something to entice a buck to come within 20 or 30 yards of your treestand or ground blind, why not do it?

Say you are sitting on the edge of a bean field in the early season and the deer are feeding out in front of you 100 yards away. How can you entice that big buck you are watching to walk over to your stand location and offer you a 25-yard shot? Yes, you can try to call him in by grunting or rattling, and that might work. But what if it doesn't? Calling is not always 100 percent successful. One excellent way to entice a feeding buck to come your way and offer you a close shot is by having a small, man-made waterhole nearby. Sooner or later those feeding deer are going to get thirsty and come over for a drink. In this case, the waterhole may be just the calling card you need to close the deal.

There are many examples of calling cards: waterholes, rubs, scrapes, licking branches, small interior food plots, minerals, bait where legal, apple trees and other fruit bearing trees, and decoys. Nicole and I use most of these throughout the season and we've had enough success to know they work.

WATERHOLES

Even though water sources are fairly abundant in most of the places where Nicole and I hunt – there are plenty of creeks and rivers in the Midwest where

People ask me when my favorite time to hunt is. Every day is my favorite time. I love the early season. You've waited all year long and you haven't hunted deer in many months. It's really an exciting time. It's hot sometimes and not as comfortable, but I love being out there. I love the rut because of the weather. It's much colder and the sights and sounds are more exciting. I love to hunt the post-rut in the late season. The weather is worse, the temperatures are much colder and you have to key in on food sources. You know what they say: the worse the weather, the better the hunting. The day deer season closes I feel like I've been cheated. I never get enough. I don't ever want it to end.

we live – deer are a lot like humans. They'll take the path of least resistance and go to the most convenient and safe spot to get a drink. On properties where we do a lot of hunting for mature bucks, we frequently build waterholes in the timber and close to bedding areas where bucks feel comfortable coming in and getting a drink during daylight hours. We also like to build small, isolated waterholes in flattened areas on ridgetops.

Most hunters think you have to build a pond or waterhole in low areas where you have natural drainage. Not true. Most of the waterholes we build are small, scooped-out depressions about the size of a trampoline where the rainwater and runoff can gather. These holes are shaped roughly like a cereal bowl. The edge of the bank pools and collects water and rainfall. You really don't want a lot of runoff anyway because in times of heavy rain, runoff can easily blow out your pond and ruin it.

Using a small dozer, I like to build our ponds in the flatter areas where there is no runoff. That's one reason we like ridgetops so much. Normally a small waterhole will collect enough rainfall during the summer months to pretty much fill up and stay full during hunting season. Some evaporation always takes place, but as the waterline recedes, the deer follow the taper of the bank down to the water's edge.

You can build a waterhole one day and have deer using it the next if you have a fresh rain. I've seen that happen many times. Deer love to play around waterholes and splash around in the water, much like children. Time after time, I've seen mature bucks use old, stagnant waterholes where the putrid-looking water has been sitting for months. Often you'll find a clear running creek only a stone's throw away. I don't know why deer prefer stagnant water to clean water – but they definitely do.

Someone once told me that there is some sort of mineral or bacteria in that nasty, stagnant water that deer crave. I don't know if that's true or not, but it could have something to do with water temperature. I think deer prefer to drink tepid water at warmer temperatures. Fast running creek water is much cooler than water that has been sitting in a small man-made pool.

Some humans are the same way about drinking cold water. Nicole is definitely one of those people. She doesn't like to drink ice water. Instead she prefers to drink water at room temperature. I've known other people with this preference as well. I think deer are very much like people in this respect.

Over the years, Nicole and I have killed a lot of nice bucks in a number of different states hunting over waterholes, both in the early season and during the rut. Deer can go without food for an indefinite period of time but they can't go without water, especially during the rut when bucks are out running themselves ragged. Bucks have to have water on a regular basis or they'll get dehydrated. Smart bucks also know that does get thirsty too. Does tend to frequent water holes as much as bucks do – particularly those secluded little ponds located close to bedding areas.

Bucks also like to cool down in water on warm days. I've seen a number of bucks walk out into small waterholes and just stand there. With their thick win-

Pat and Nicole have taken a number of big bucks in several different states hunting over waterholes. Manufactured waterholes come in all sizes and shapes. This one is fairly large, but much smaller depressions that gather rainwater and runoff also attract deer. In fact, deer love to congregate around large waterholes.

When a buck is being chased by predators, or when a buck chasing a doe gets overheated, it will often seek out a body of water in which to cool off and rehydrate. Wounded deer often seek out water as well.

Through observations over the years Pat has learned that mature bucks often prefer small stagnant pools over fresh running streams nearby. A well-located stand near an isolated waterhole close to a known bedding area can be dynamite.

ter coats, they tend to overheat very quickly on unseasonably warm days. That cold water helps them cool off and rehydrate. Elk and other big-game animals are the same way. Elk love to wallow in wet mud. That caked mud certainly helps keep the insects at bay, but the cold water also helps cool them off.

A number of companies now make waterproof liners for small ponds for landscaping purposes. If you live in an area where the soil is too rocky or too sandy to build a viable waterhole, liners work extremely well. You can also buy molded plastic pools in different shapes, sort of like children's swimming pools. One drawback to these pre-shaped pools is that deer don't like having to step down into them. So using a waterproof liner or tarp where the angle is gradual is much preferred. If you do use a liner, make sure you cover it well with soil. Also, if you have an existing waterhole of this type that starts leaking, a mineral called Bentonite can be put in the water and used to seal any holes. Bentonite is a natural clay-like mineral that can be bought in bags and is harmless to water and wildlife.

As a rule of thumb, I'd say that on an average 100-acre farm, you should have at least two waterholes, if not three. My good friend Tom Indrebo of Bluff Country Outfitters in Buffalo County, Wis., is a master at building small, isolated waterholes. He'll sometimes have two on the same ridge. He's discovered from his trail camera photos that certain deer have definite preferences for going to the same waterhole day after day. There may be another small pond just over the ridge 150 yards away where other deer prefer to

go for a drink. Deer really are creatures of habit. If they weren't, we might never see a mature buck in the woods!

Nicole and I always try to set up multiple stands over each waterhole we hunt so that we can take advantage of various wind conditions. Having several good options is extremely important. Waterholes are great calling cards for deer, but they also create an oasis for many other species of wildlife; birds, small game, even frogs and lizards. Probably 90 percent of the bow-hunting that takes place in Africa today is done over waterholes. If you haven't already done it, build a few waterholes on your property and make them part of your overall management program.

Pat and Nicole seldom hunt from stand locations that do not have either natural or manufactured licking branches nearby. Since every buck in the area will almost always stop to sniff and scent-check a licking branch, Pat says you have nothing to lose and everything to gain by making sure you place one within 30 yards of your stand.

LICKING BRANCHES AND SCRAPES – NATURAL OR MANUFACTURED

Deer have a fascination with licking branches. I think it's safe to say that if a buck is walking through the woods, he'll stop to scent-check and investigate practically any licking branch he comes across that has been used by other deer. So whenever I set up a new treestand in a promising location, I don't trim any overhanging branches that might become potential licking branches. Instead, I always leave them right where they are. I want them to become licking branches and potential scrape sites.

If there isn't a licking branch close by, I'll manufacture one. One way to do this is find a good branch that is too high for a deer to reach. I'll cut it off and wire it to a tree a few yards from the tree I'm sitting in. You don't want it to be too close. Fifteen to 20 yards is a good, safe distance. I'll hang the limb about 4 feet off the ground so that it'll attract the next deer that comes along. I always go a step further by clearing out the leaves and other litter on the ground below and making a mock scrape. I'll often sweeten the scrape with a little deer scent. It's very important to make sure the limb over the scrape is green and moist. If it's brittle and dried out, it'll easily break off. When that happens, it kills the scrape. Sometimes I'll break a small limb off the licking branch, mangle it slightly and then place it in the scrape. That's just one more visual sign for a deer to see. Now I've turned this spot into a calling card. These types of setups work extremely well along old logging roads and field edges.

Why wouldn't you have a licking branch or mock scrape near your stand? Anything you can do to increase your chances of bringing a buck over to your location can only help your odds. At worst, a buck might not pay any attention to it, but it definitely won't alarm him. Licking branches and scrapes are perfectly natural to the deer. They're a big part of a buck's communication system. So bucks certainly won't shy away from them. I've been amazed at the number of times I've had bucks start using fake scrapes and continue using them throughout the season.

Here is another great trick that has worked for us on many occasions. Often, when Nicole and I are hunting out of a tree on the edge of an open field or food plot, I'll cut a little tree 5 or 6 feet long or a large limb with plenty of branches on it, and bury it in the ground several yards out in the field in front of our stand. I'll make sure one of the branches is hanging down so that it looks like a licking branch. This becomes a calling card just like a trapper setting out a trap for a coyote. Since we often put up our stands weeks before we intend to use them, the deer have plenty of time to adapt to the new licking branch and use it every time they pass by.

Most feeding deer will come over to investigate. In fact, we've had a number bucks feeding out in front of us get curious and come right over to check out the new licking branch. Those same deer might not have ever gotten that close to us if we hadn't enticed them to do so. Even if the deer totally ignore your calling card, you haven't lost anything. And if a big buck does that I know who manage their property for big bucks will establish several mineral licks per hundred acres. These mineral licks are just part of the overall nutritional program. Once you establish one or more mineral licks on your property, deer will visit these sites on a year-around basis.

We usually put out our mineral supplements as soon as the snow starts melting in early spring. We've had a lot of luck using Black Magic Rack Rock, a natural mineral supplement made by Evolved Habitat. It comes in blocks that look just like a rock. It contains calcium, phosphorous, magnesium, sodium, as well as some other trace minerals. We've also used other granular mineral products, but the deer seem to especially love the rock and it has worked extremely well for us.

Mineral licks are excellent locations for trail cameras because the licks attract so many deer on a regular basis. It's hard to say how much some of these minerals and vitamin supplements actually help antler growth, but they certainly can't do any harm to the local deer population. Some of the sweeter tasting deer attractants on the market today don't have

Once you establish one or more mineral licks in key locations on your property, deer will come by and visit them on a year-round basis. Mineral licks are great sites for trail cameras and also great sites to hunt over.

come over to check it out, it'll distract his attention while you are preparing for the shot. It might also stop him long enough to get a good, broadside shot. I always use rubber gloves to minimize my human scent when setting up licking branches or making mock scrapes. Remember – whitetails are naturally curious. Calling cards like licking branches and scrapes are 100 percent natural to them.

MINERALS AND MINERAL LICKS

Just like licking branches and mock scrapes, Minerals and mineral licks are great calling cards. Today there are numerous mineral supplements on the market that attract deer. Most hunters and landowners

Whenever possible during the off-season, Pat and Nicole spend a lot of quality time fine-tuning their hunting areas so that when the season opens the deer will have multiple calling cards to draw them in and keep them on the property.

Large, well-located internal food plots will help keep deer on your property, and offer them a safe place to feed in the open without having the worry of being harassed by road hunters.

much, if any nutritional value, but they do draw deer into specific locations. In some states where baiting is not legal, certain commercial deer attractants could be construed as bait, so check your local laws carefully before you use these products.

SMALL INTERNAL FOOD PLOTS

The small, internal food plots that we sometimes plant back in the timber are designed more for hunting purposes than for nutritional purposes. Internal plots are great calling cards because deer feel very safe coming into these isolated openings in the woods. They're usually located very close to bedding areas and are surrounded by good cover.

Our average hunting plots are small; anywhere from ¼ acre to 1½ acres in size. Nutritional plots are always much larger. The object of a nutritional plot is to have food available to your deer throughout the winter and into early spring. If a buck is in poor condition going into antler growing season, it'll take him a long time to catch up. He may never catch up. But if he's had plenty of good food to carry him through the winter, he'll be in much better condition to start grow-

ing some large antlers.

Internal plots can be difficult to hunt for several reasons. Once you start penetrating the timber, you run the risk of giving away your presence to the deer, especially mature bucks. Getting in and out without being detected is crucial. The biggest mistake most hunters make is tipping off the bucks they are hunting. The number one key to success in hunting big bucks is to keep this from happening. A quiet approach to your stand is vital. Also, the wind must be in your favor at all times.

My good friend and pro staff member Mark Wimpy has an 80-acre tract in Illinois. He has one small interior food plot on that property where he consistently kills big bucks every year. He hunts only that food plot and he never goes into the timber. He waits until the timing is just right, and he lets the deer come to him in that food plot. If you try to go to the deer in the timber, they're going to win the game 90 percent of the time. Sure, you might get lucky once in a while, but the damage you can do by going into the timber is hard to measure. Mark is living proof that you don't necessarily have to have a huge tract of land in order

Whether it's building a pond or clearing a spot for a new food plot, there's something special about being in a tractor or bulldozer and working the land. It gets in your blood!

to consistently kill big bucks. You just have to have the right calling card!

Sometimes we use the brush and other debris from clearing a small internal plot to funnel the deer into specific areas. We'll push the trees and brush into a pile and arrange it in such a way that it creates a barrier the deer have to walk around. By doing this, you can actually funnel the deer to the spot where you want them to enter your food plot. Stringing barbed wire through the woods also works well as a means of funneling deer into certain spots. I'll usually put up three strands of wire at least 5 feet tall. Then I'll run parallel strands five to eight feet away. With two separate fences that close together, the deer are very reluctant to jump either fence because they don't want to cross two barriers. So instead they walk the fence line until they reach the opening you have purposely made for them. Either one of these barriers can be very effective.

We try to offer a variety of different calling cards in our internal plots by planting several different food choices including corn, beans, clover and wheat. Several years ago I built a 1½-acre internal food plot on my 35 acres in southeast Minnesota. On one edge of the plot I also built a small pond. We use this internal plot mostly as a place for my kids to hunt. Over the past few years, they've taken some good bucks there. Just inside the woods on the edge of the opening I have a permanent, elevated ground blind used primarily for gun hunting. A short distance away I have a treestand used primarily for bow-hunting. Both stands are very good for a north wind. It's too risky to hunt a south wind because that will blow right back into the bedding area in the timber.

Last year I initially planted three different food sources in that small plot – corn out in the open, several varieties of clover, and alfalfa in the shaded areas close to the trees and pond. In the fall, I re-tilled several spots where the corn was not growing well and over-seeded those areas with rape and turnips. They grow very well together. In the past, I've sometimes combined corn and beans together. I plant the corn first then I go back and broadcast beans. They also grow well together. But I don't plant corn every year, I usually rotate corn and beans each year so that the soil doesn't get depleted.

In addition, I planted two rows of white cedars around the exterior of my small food plot on the side closest to the bedding area. When these trees are full grown, they'll serve two purposes. They'll provide thick cover for a staging area as the deer approach from their bedding area. Deer feel a lot more comfortable if they can stage in an area that has good protective cover before they step out into the open to feed. Then during the coldest days of winter, those cedars will someday provide good thermal cover for the deer to bed in.

Because of their thick foliage, the snow doesn't tend to accumulate as much under cedars as it does under other types of trees, but when it does work its way to the ground it tends to melt faster because the temperature is usually a little warmer under those trees. Plus, the cedars will eventually offer protection for my food plot by sheltering it from the wind, and they'll serve as a good winter food source for the deer.

Planting food plots correctly requires some amount of hard work. You can't just throw out a seed and expect it to grow and produce an ear of corn. You've got to work at being a good farmer. Three important things I always monitor in my soil are the pH level, the phosphorous content and the potassium level. Generally you want your pH to run about 6.5. If it's lower

If you have one or more small, internal food plots and a fairly high deer population, it may be necessary to fence the deer out while your food sources are growing so that there will be plenty of food available later in the season when it's time to do some serious hunting. Deer can easily wipe out a small corn or bean field before it has a chance to mature.

than 6, you'll need to add some lime to help neutralize the soil. When needed, I usually put out between 2 to 4 tons of lime per acre. You have to condition your soil and make sure the pH is right. You also have to make sure you have the right amount of nitrogen in the soil. Especially when planting small internal food plots, you must make sure the woods are opened up enough to allow the right amount of sunlight in.

PROTECTING YOUR FOOD SOURCE

Protecting a small food source while it is growing can be a huge challenge. I learned very quickly that planting corn in a small, 1½-acre internal plot in an area where the deer population is fairly high is a recipe for disaster. That is, unless you take steps to keep the deer out while the young plants are growing. For instance, several years ago I planted a little over an acre in corn. But I knew that corn would never get out of the ground unless I protected it. So I fenced off the entire plot with an electric fence.

I put out five strands of wire. The first strand was

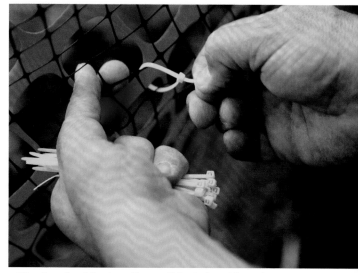

The thought of fencing off a small food plot with mesh netting at the top and plastic snow fencing at the bottom can be daunting from a work standpoint, but Pat says it's much less labor intensive than you might think.

only four or five inches off the ground. This was done primarily to keep the raccoons out. We have a huge problem with raccoons in the Midwest and they're tough on cornfields. I used a 10-mile electric solar panel and it worked very well. It'll span all of 10 miles and it gives off quite a jolt. The wire consisted of a yellow braided-rope outer section with a strand of wire inside. The rope is very easy to work with and roll up once you are ready to take down the fence. I used 8-foot metal fence posts, pounded them into the ground, and hung the five strands of wire/rope at equal distances from the top to bottom of the posts.

Our good friends Darren and Sherri Martin own a farm in Illinois with a high deer density. Darren has a 2-acre food plot in one of his river bottoms where the soil is very rich. Plenty of moisture is available in that bottom and things grow extremely well there. However, the deer literally mow everything down before the young plants can mature. In 2012, Darren planted beans. They were doing well and he was very excited. But as soon as the young sprouts got about 4 inches tall, the deer started wiping them out.

He called me and asked what he should do. I told him to fence off the 2 acres and replant. At first he didn't think he'd have time to take on such a big job. But he went out and bought some snow fencing (a flexible molded plastic). Using metal posts, he put up a 4-foot-high snow fence. Above that, he added another section of 4-foot-high mesh fencing. That did the trick. He had a great food plot and the fence kept the deer out.

Darren took down his fence when archery season opened around Oct. 1. The beans were almost chest high and his brother killed a beautiful buck hunting over that food plot. Darren was able to put up the entire fence by himself in about two days time. It was a lot easier than he thought it would be. Since all of the fencing is reusable, Darren definitely plans to put up more fencing in future seasons on several of his food plots.

I had only one instance on my food plot where a deer became tangled in the wire and pulled a couple of strands loose. But I patched that very quickly. That year I grew a great stand of corn and took the fence down about the first week in October because my daughter Olivia was planning to hunt over the food plot. As I had hoped, the deer used that internal plot for the entire hunting season and Olivia ended up shooting a nice buck on it.

In summary, our small internal plot contained clover and alfalfa for early in the season, corn for mid-season and several different grains for the late season. Between the food source and the waterhole, we had manufactured two good calling cards that made our stand location a lot more successful for hunting the deer in that area. I did everything possible within my power to enhance that stand location and make it into a good situation for hunting, and it really paid off. I think you see a lot of that happening around the country today with hunters managing their own proper-

Pat and Nicole's good friends Darren and Sherri Martin inspect a fine crop of soybeans on their Illinois farm that grew well and prospered because of the fence Darren had put up earlier.

ties for big bucks. Those hunters are taking mediocre spots and making them the best they can be with a little extra work.

APPLE TREES AND OTHER FRUIT TREES

Speaking of food sources, Nicole and I focus on apple trees a lot during early season in the Midwest. In Chapter 4, I mentioned that I set up a treestand near an apple tree in Buffalo County, Wis., that Moses, a big buck I was hunting, was visiting on a regular basis. I got numerous trail camera photos of Moses eating apples under that tree. Deer love apples, especially big bucks. They seem to crave them. I don't know whether it's the sugar content or the sweet taste, but I've seen big bucks key in on apples many times in many different areas.

Deer love the smell of apples and they're naturally attracted to that smell. We've used apple attractant in Canada where the deer have never even seen an apple and they love it. Wildgame Innovations makes several different apple attractants made from ground apple

Evolved Harvest makes a great blend of brassicas that I use in my food plot called ShotPlot. I plant it in late summer around my corn. It grows very fast and offers a good source of protein for the deer. The deer don't usually start feeding on these plants until the weather gets really cold. By then, these brassicas are the only greens around. I also use Evolved Harvest's Great Lakes Blend and ProGraze. Great Lakes Blend is intended for cooler climates and includes some brassicas and clovers. I like to plant several varieties of clovers along with my brassicas because clover is a perennial and it'll come back the next year. If someone told me I could only plant two food sources in my food plot and nothing else, I'd choose brassicas and clover over everything else.

extracts. Apple Crush and Rut'n Apples are two of their popular attractants. We've used both and they've worked well for us in Saskatchewan and the Midwest.

Bucks also love pears and fruit from other trees as well. Pears and other fruits don't do as well in Wisconsin and Minnesota, probably due to the colder climate, but they seem to do extremely well a little farther south in states like Illinois, Kansas and Iowa where Nicole and I hunt every year. In fact, Nicole's dad has pear trees on his property in southern Illinois. We don't have persimmons in Minne-

Watch Pat's exciting 2012 muzzleloader hunt for an Illinois dandy!

sota either, but I know they're as effective as apples in other parts of the country where they grow well, particularly in the South.

I've planted several varieties of apple trees near my food plot on our 35 acres. One of these days I hope to have a nice little orchard for the deer when our trees start producing fruit. If you plant fruit trees you'll probably have to cage them off for several years while they are young, because the deer will browse the tender limbs and bark and kill the trees. I also have a problem with mice. When snow is on the ground, mice will often come in and girdle the young trees. So I wrap the trunks each winter to keep the mice at bay. Keeping fruit trees alive while they are young is not always easy, but it's well worth the effort. Once the trees are established, you've produced a great calling card for bucks. Fruit trees in general provide a lot of nutrition for wildlife and there are many different varieties to choose from.

ACORNS AS CALLING CARDS

Acorns are probably the most abundant natural calling card in the autumn forest. During good mast years, deer often bed near their feeding spots right in the timber. Then, all they have to do is stand up and start eating acorns only a few feet away. After eating awhile, they'll bed down again without having traveled but a few yards. When hunting over acorns, white oak acorns are definitely the food of choice. There are also a number of commercial products on the market that we use from time to time to simulate real acorns. We've had great success with Acorn Rage Deer Attractant made by Wildgame Innovations. We've put this attractant out in remote areas in Canada where the deer have never seen an acorn and they love it.

That period of time from late September through the first week or two of October is often called the "October lull." This is a time when hunters typically stop seeing much activity. I think this so-called lull is caused by a few factors – mainly warmer weather and food availability. In years of good acorn production, the deer spend a lot of time in the timber gorging themselves on acorns. Bucks generally lie around in preparation for the pre-rut and rut. If the acorn crop is good, they don't have much incentive for leaving the timber, so that's why hunters are not seeing them in food plots.

Oak trees that are producing acorns are great places to hunt, but getting into stand locations in the timber is always tricky. For one thing, on quiet days when the leaves are crunchy, a smart buck will hear

Nothing is more rewarding than working hard at enhancing your property with one or more irresistible calling cards that enable you to fill your tag with a dream buck like this.

It's especially important to have some type of late-season food source on your property that will attract deer and keep them in the area. If you don't, they'll seek out food elsewhere.

you coming a long way off. Nicole and I always strive to fool the deer's senses any way we can. If a buck hears you approach your stand location, he's not going to get up later and come your way. In all likelihood he's been bedded there all day listening to various sounds, listening for danger. So getting to your stand as quietly as possible is crucial. So many times I've watched bucks listen to a neighbor start a truck or four-wheeler. Believe me, they pay attention to those sounds and listen intently. They stay focused on that noise until the potential threat is over. Trust me, they know when a twig snaps in their woods.

We make sure we get to our stands at least an hour before daylight. Hunting the afternoon can be tricky because the leaves are dry and crunchy. What's more, the risk of bumping deer is much greater in the afternoon because the deer are already bedded in the woods and they're going to hear any unusual sounds. Rainy days or windy days are good times to hunt acorns because the rain and the wind help cover up any noise you might make.

Nicole and I strive to make every approach and exit as quietly as possible. We often rake out the leaves ahead of time and make a path to our stand. We try to clear away all debris so that we never crack a twig, even if it's a short distance of only five yards. Given a choice, we'll have someone drive us to our stand location on an ATV or electric cart and drop us off. Generally it takes us 15 minutes to set up the camera and get into position in a double-stand filming setup. So I'll ask the person who's dropping us off to leave the engine running during that time. I know the deer are listening, and if I make any noise setting up, the sound of the motor will hopefully muffle any sound I make. Once we are set up, we wave to the driver of the vehicle and he'll make his exit.

Having someone drop you off is a very effective

way to approach a stand. There is no scent left on the ground from walking in. If we don't have access to any kind of vehicle, Nicole and I have used the ploy of having a third person walk to the stand with us, stay until we're set up and then walk back out. This has worked like a charm many times. Once again, we do whatever it takes to fool a deer's senses. Where possible, we prefer to use electric vehicles instead of gas vehicles. We have a Polaris EV that we truly love. It's got plenty of room, plenty of power and it's extremely quiet. Plus, there are no irritating exhaust fumes to deal with.

Years ago when I was guiding for Tom Indrebo in Buffalo County, we used four-wheelers quite often to take hunters to and from their stands. Some of the hills in the bluff country are quite steep, and it was always nice to have a vehicle that could take you to the top of a hill. We always found the ATVs to be a very efficient means of delivering hunters to their stands without alarming the deer. We used them so much the deer became accustomed to them. Whenever they heard a four-wheeler coming or going, they never seemed to associate the noise with any kind of danger.

One week we had a hunter in camp named Dave. Although I offered to take him up a very steep hill to his stand one morning on the four-wheeler, he insisted on walking because he was paranoid about spooking the deer with a four-wheeler. He made such a big fuss over this issue that we jokingly nicknamed him "four-wheeler Dave." On the second day, however, he was more than willing to let me take him to his stand on the four-wheeler because of the exhausting uphill walk. That day, he literally had deer all around his stand before my four-wheeler had even made it all the way back down the hill. He ended up shooting a very nice buck a short while later. That certainly changed his perspective on being dropped off at his stand by a vehicle. In some places, a four-wheeler might very well alarm the deer. But at a place like Tom's where they are used so much, the deer pay very little attention to them.

BAIT SITES

Nicole and I love to hunt whitetails in Canada. We often hunt over bait sites because that's the only way to draw deer out of the hundreds of square miles of thick forest. Our outfitter in Saskatchewan usually puts out hay and cowpeas for the deer. In Canada, the winters are brutally cold and the deer respond extremely well to bait because there is little else to eat. So bait sites become excellent calling cards.

Much like waterholes in the Midwest, we've noticed that certain deer seem to have a preference for going to specific bait sites on a regular basis, even if another is located within 150 yards. If you're hunting a certain buck, the chances are good that you'll see him at the same bait site over and over again. You'll always have some deer that like to make the rounds and go to all of the different bait sites and waterholes, but most mature bucks will get in the habit of visiting the same site on a regular basis.

Baiting with corn is legal in a number of states like Kansas, Ohio, Texas and Wisconsin. Hunting the brush country of South Texas is much like hunting in Canada. Corn is put out along senderos to attract the deer and pull them out of the thick brush. Otherwise, you might never see a gnarly South Texas buck. Of course, food plots are also very popular in Texas, but in areas where rainfall is minimal, keeping the plants alive is sometimes next to impossible. In Kansas, where Nicole and I hunt almost every year, we prefer to hunt over natural food sources like soybeans in the early season and corn during the late season.

Baiting has become a very controversial topic. Some people think that if you put out bait, giant bucks will simply walk right in and start eating. It doesn't happen that way. Bucks are always elusive animals and never easy to hunt. Even when a buck does approach a bait pile in Canada, he'll sneak in from the downwind side and often stand in the shadows of the timber until moments before dark. Or he may not come out until well after dark. So it's never a sure thing that you're going to shoot a big buck if you hunt over bait.

I believe it should be up to the individual hunter and not the state to decide whether or not to use bait. It should never be mandated by the state. What's the difference in putting corn on the ground or cutting standing corn for the deer? And when it comes to kids or any first-time hunter, hunting over bait often provides

10/26/2010 5:08 PM   Cuddeback

Bait piles are one of the few and vital calling cards that work well in the wilds of Canada. Pat and Nicole like to hunt from pop-up ground blinds in situations where bait piles are used.

the kind of positive experience that wins them over to hunting for life. A prolonged hunt where no deer are seen after hours of sitting in a stand could have the opposite affect.

In states where it's legal to do so, I like to put corn out in early season as a means of taking inventory of the local bucks with trail cameras. For some reason, bucks seem to crave corn early in the season. We've found that putting corn out in strategic spots where deer tend to congregate is a great way of getting photos of many of the local bucks and evaluating their antler growth. Most of the pictures are taken at night but that doesn't matter. You can still get a good idea of how big your bucks are and which ones you want to target for the upcoming season.

Another offshoot of baiting that people seldom think about is that it benefits numerous other species of wildlife. You may be putting corn out specifically for the deer, but turkeys, birds, squirrels, raccoons and many other animals will soon find it and help themselves. A bait pile may just help some of these animals make it through a tough winter.

USING DECOYS AS DRAWING CARDS

Nicole and I have had great success using decoys in a variety of locations at various times of the year. We've had very good luck in the early season hunting food sources in large fields or food plots. In these situations, it's sometimes difficult to pinpoint exactly where the deer will be coming out of the woods to feed. They may use one particular trail one day, and a totally different trail several hundred yards away the next. With the aid of a decoy, even if a buck comes out

200 yards from your stand, that decoy will help draw him over to your position.

We prefer to use a small-bodied decoy with a medium-sized rack. Anything larger might intimidate the buck you are trying to lure in. Primos makes one that we use on a regular basis. As soon as a buck comes out and starts feeding within sight of the decoy, I'll do some soft calling to help convince him that the decoy is real. Most bucks don't ordinarily come charging right in. Instead, they'll often start feeding slowly toward the decoy. They like to give the impression of being totally disinterested. But don't be fooled. They know right where that decoy is!

Then, as a buck gets closer, something happens. He'll finally get to the point where he simply can't stand it any longer. He has to come in and check out this "other buck." I've noticed this behavior many times. It's almost as if the decoy plays a mind game with an incoming buck. At this point, you've got him because he's definitely going to come in and check out the competition.

I always make sure my decoy is as free of human scent as possible. I used to put out deer scents around the decoy as an attractant, but I don't any more. I've found that scents sometimes alarm incoming bucks. Actually I've learned that the absence of any deer scent seems to draw on a buck's curiosity more anyways. When a buck comes in, he'll always circle around to the rear of the decoy with the intention of trying to smell the other buck's tarsal glands. In real life, of course, a live buck will never let another buck do that. He'll always turn around and face the incoming buck. But since the decoy doesn't turn around, the incoming buck will always go around to its rear and try to smell its tarsals.

For that reason the positioning of your decoy is critical. I always set up my decoy so that it's slightly quartering away from my position. That way, I'll get a shot opportunity when the buck comes in and circles to the rear of the decoy. If the decoy has movable ears, I'll put the ears back and cock the tail out slightly. I don't want the decoy to appear alert. Instead, I want it to appear to be posturing.

In the past, I've made the mistake of setting my decoy out about 20 yards from my stand. That was way too close. Whenever a buck came in and started to circle, he would often walk right under my tree and catch my scent. It's far better to set the decoy farther out so that when the buck comes in and circles to the rear of the decoy, you'll be offered a 20 or 25 yard shot. At that point, the live buck should be far enough out so that he will not catch your scent.

Pat and Nicole love using decoys. Under the right circumstances, they've had great success using them. There is nothing as exciting as watching a mature buck shuffle in with his hair bristled out and begin to posture as he approaches the decoy.

We seldom use decoys in small interior food plots because of the tight space. But we often use them in larger food plots for the reasons mentioned above. Generally speaking, we don't use decoys as much in situations where a lot of other calling cards are available, except for food of course. In most cases, we use them in situations where we hope to draw a deer into a specific area in order to get a shot opportunity.

For instance, if you're hunting over a waterhole out in the middle of an alfalfa field and it's the only water source within half a mile, you know that sooner or later those deer are going to come in for a drink because they're thirsty. So why put out a decoy because the deer already have a good drawing card. Decoys are one of the few calling cards we use that do sometimes alarm bucks, so we like to use them in situations where we believe they'll help get a big buck within bow range.

CHAPTER 10

A PASSION FOR SHEDS

Shed hunting across North America has grown to be an incredibly popular pastime in recent years. Pat has been addicted to shed hunting since his teenage years, and he has a vast collection of several thousand antlers. Here he and Nicole show off some large mule deer sheds from a recent trip to Saskatchewan.

For Pat and Nicole, shed hunting season is always a family affair. Here Pat poses with his son Cole during a typical shed hunting outing.

Shed hunting has been a lifetime passion of mine. Some people play golf and some people like to fish. I shed hunt. It's my hobby and has been for many years. I found my first shed when I was around 6 years old. I actually went out with a friend to look for sheds. We were in a public area in southeast Minnesota not far from home. I'd heard people talking about looking for sheds – my dad and others – and I'd seen one or two that other people had found. So we decided to go out and look for ourselves.

I had no idea what I was doing – where to look or anything like that – but I just happened to stumble upon a very small antler that day. It was the left side from a yearling buck and it contained three points. It was all of about 7 inches long and I was thrilled. I found it in the most unlikely spot. The tiny antler was actually on a sandbar in a crystal-clear trout stream a few inches under the water. I don't know how I ever saw it and certainly never expected to find it there. But I vividly remember that experience – seeing that shed lying in that sparkling water is permanently etched in my mind – and I've been hooked ever since.

I took that little antler home and it eventually became a coat hanger in my room when I was growing up. I drilled a hole in the base and nailed it to a board and hung hats and other things on it. Later on a friend asked me if he could have it. Impulsively I said, "Sure," without really thinking about it. I let him have it, not realizing how important it was to me. But

A young Pat Reeve shows off a very respectable set of sheds he found in Wisconsin while glassing a field from his truck.

I ended up getting it back about 15 years later because it meant so much to me. It now rests proudly in our china cabinet in the living room. Little did I know it back then, but that tiny shed antler was the beginning of a life-long passion and career. Today I probably own around 2,000 shed antlers and I've given away hundreds more that I've found.

Finding a deer's shed is special because it connects you to that animal. In essence, it creates another chapter in an ongoing story, especially if the shed is from a buck you know about. It gives a certain mystique and added quality to the idea of hunting a mature whitetail buck. If you are lucky enough to have one or more shed antlers from a big buck you have successfully hunted, it adds so much more to the story and the experience.

After finding that first antler, my shed-hunting career didn't begin in earnest until years later when I was 15 or 16. As I got older, I became more interested in trophy whitetails and started thinking more about shed antler hunting. A few people were talking about shed hunting at the time but it was still years away from becoming the huge sport it is today. I started going out with a buddy, had some mixed luck and found a few horns here and there. At that time there were a few die-hards in Minnesota and Wisconsin that you heard stories about, but most hunters didn't think much about actually finding and collecting shed antlers.

As soon as I started doing more hunting and getting more interested in learning about whitetails, it was sort of a natural progression to want to find the sheds from some of the bucks I knew about. Before long it became a passion. I began to focus a lot of energy on finding horns; spending lots of time outside walking and looking. Today, in southeast Minnesota where I live, if you don't find a buck's sheds right after he drops them, you're probably not going to own them because someone else is going to pick them up. Today you almost have to catch an antler in midair as it falls off the deer's head! That's how competitive shed hunting has become!

WHAT MAKES A BUCK SHED?

Our peak shed hunting season in the upper Midwest is from about Feb. 15 to March 15, although the exact time a buck drops his antlers can vary for a variety of reasons. Stress is a major cause of early shedding. Stress from bad weather, a wound, a particularly hard rutting season or even food availability can cause a deer to shed his antlers earlier than normal. Some bucks might be genetically programmed to shed around the first of the year, while others may carry their antlers well beyond the normal shedding period.

At the time his photo appeared on the cover of the winter 1996 issue of North American Shed Hunter, Pat was an active measurer for the organization.

I've found fresh sheds as early as mid-December and I've seen big bucks that still had both antlers in late March. Specific dates also vary across the country. But if you talk to farmers, landowners or other shed hunters in your area, you can easily find out when you need to be in the woods looking for fresh sheds.

Trail cameras can also tell you when a buck has shed. Several years ago, my good friend Tom Indrebo got some great trail camera photos of a well-known buck we were hunting in Buffalo County, Wis., named Moses. (See Chapter 4 for the full story of Moses). Moses was still carrying his antlers in those photos. The next day, Tom got photos of a bare-headed Moses; he had shed his antlers during the night. Not only did Tom know that Moses had shed, but he also knew approximately where to look for the antlers – and he immediately went out and found them.

Despite the competition and large number of people out there looking for sheds, sometimes you get lucky. The snow might cover one up after it's dropped or you stumble across it later on after the snow melts. You might even be in the right place at the right time and find one that has just been dropped. The key is to find them early, especially if you're looking in the timber or on the edge of the timber – before the squir-

Judging from the blood on the pedicle, this trophy shed antler has not been on the ground long.

Pat says finding both sheds from larger bucks is sometimes easier because they are often located close together. Big bucks don't like the imbalance of having only one antler. When one falls off, a buck will often knock the other off intentionally in close proximity to the first.

rels start working on them.

Bucks shed their antlers because of a decrease in testosterone in their body chemistry caused by photoperiodism, or an increase in the amount of daylight each day. As the days get longer in February and March, the pedicels dry up and the antlers fall off. Amazingly, a number of bucks have been photographed by trail cameras shedding their antlers on the same exact date each year for several years in a row. Whether this is just a coincidence, or whether some type of genetic clock is triggering this, is not known. What is known is that most normal and healthy bucks do shed their antlers about the same time each year, give or take a few days. But each buck is different.

Nicole and I concentrate most of our efforts to find shed antlers during the 30-day period mentioned above when snow is still on the ground. Some people wait until the snow is gone before they start looking. I love looking in the snow and I've found that fresh antlers contrast with the white snow just enough to stand out really well. When the woods are free of snow, you're competing with natural ground cover – sticks, branches and leaves that help camouflage the antlers. To me, it's much more difficult to see them under those circumstances.

If the snow has already melted and I'm hunting for the sheds from a specific buck, I generally try to wait for a damp, rainy day where the woods are wet and dark. Wet antlers have a visible sheen to them and they seem to pop against the forest floor. To me, they're easier to see under those conditions. Time is always of the essence. Not only are you competing with other shed hunters, but you're also competing with squirrels and other small rodents that seem to find the antlers as soon as the snow melts. Squirrels can chew up an antler and ruin it very quickly. I always get a big kick out of hunters who show me sheds that have just about been destroyed by squirrels and they'll think that a mouse did it. It would take an awfully big mouse to devour a large antler! But squirrels are usually the culprits and they can destroy a big antler in a matter of days. Sometimes an antler can lay in the open for years without being bothered by squirrels, but if it's in woods or close to the tree line, the squirrels will usually find it.

I have thousands of sheds in my collection. Not all are from whitetails; I have shed antlers from mule deer, elk, fallow deer, red stag and moose. To me, each antler is a piece of art and has a special memory attached to it. I like having sheds around and looking at them. I like picking them up and holding them. Some people make crafts out of them, knife handles, candle holders, etc., but I put my big sheds on the shelf to be admired like pieces of fine porcelain. Most of the sheds we find go in a large pile, but if we find a really big shed it deserves to sit on the shelf to be admired.

Pat (right) and several hunters in camp show off some nice North Dakota sheds found by their outfitter. Pat was filming a show in North Dakota during his North American Whitetail TV days. Pictured second from left is Pat's iconic cameraman, Gene Bidlespacher.

We call these sheds "shelfers." Whenever you find a shelfer, you've really found something special!

Obviously my favorite places to look for sheds are in areas where I'm hunting certain bucks because I like to find the antlers from those bucks. You get a real sense of satisfaction when you pick up an antler from a mature buck because you know he's made it through the season and that he'll probably be bigger next year. That antler represents one chapter in a buck's life, but the story is ongoing and not yet finished. That in itself is very exciting. And if you do get lucky and shoot him in the future, it makes the entire hunting adventure that much more memorable.

CHECK OUT THOSE FOOD SOURCES

Nicole and I do a lot of shed hunting around our home in southeast Minnesota and over in Wisconsin in certain areas that we hunt. It isn't the best shed hunting by far because we don't have an overabundance of big bucks in our area. I always tell people to look for sheds in areas where the deer winter. All too often, hunters search in and around their hunting property while the buck whose antlers they are seeking may be wintering several miles away due to the availability of late-winter food sources. Bucks shed their antlers near the food sources where they spend most of their time in late winter.

So I like to look for sheds in and around those food sources. I don't spend as much time looking in the timber as I do out in the open in and around the food

source. I first try to determine where that food source is, and then usually do a little scouting to try and figure out how many bucks are there and if they are big enough to go after. If they're big enough to pursue, I'll then start looking for their sheds. It's nice to know what you're up against before you waste a lot of time. If no one has harassed those bucks or pushed them out of the area, their sheds should be close by. Throughout the winter, bucks don't move great distances and expend energy traveling unless they are forced to, especially if there is any appreciable amount of snow on the ground. Instead, they bed very close to where they are feeding.

If I find one shed antler by itself, I'll start walking the trails from the food source back to the bedding area to try and find its match. I've picked up a lot of sheds in staging areas right next to the food source. Sometimes you'll find a little grassy spot on the edge of a feeding area where bucks come out of the deep woods and sort of mill around before going out in the open to feed. They might do a little light sparring or they might even rub their antlers against trees and knock them off intentionally. When bucks are back in their bedding area, they're not nearly as active. They're in their beds for most of the day. So it stands to reason that these small staging areas between bedding and feeding locations are great places to find one or both shed antlers.

Don't forget to search areas near fence crossings, creek crossings, steep ravines or steep ridges. Anytime a buck might have to jump a fence or scramble

Pat and Nicole smile for the camera amidst a small portion of their vast shed antler collection.

Pat displays the results of one day's shed hunting in Buffalo County, Wis., on property belonging to his good friend Tom Indrebo. "Sometimes it's easier to find fresh sheds in the snow because the dark antlers contrast so well against the white background," Pat says.

up a hill he is apt to jar one of his antlers loose. Sometimes a sudden jump up or down a steep hill will cause an antler to pop off. Deer love to soak up the warm rays of the sun on a cold winter's day and they'll often be found sunbathing on south-facing ridges, so check those southern slopes near feeding areas as well.

When it comes to bucks with big antlers, it's often easier to find the matching side of a shed you've just found because big bucks don't like the imbalance or lopsided feeling they get after they drop the first antler. So they'll often intentionally knock off the other antler within a short distance of where they dropped the first antler. Sometimes a big buck will carry a single antler for days or even weeks, but in most cases he'll do whatever he can to cast off the other side fairly quickly.

Sometimes you'll find both sheds very close together. The biggest set of sheds I own are from my 200-inch typical buck from Illinois taken in 2005 (see Chapter 1). They score very close to what the original antlers score. After I killed the deer, I learned that a young man named Lucas Barbie was out on his first shed hunting adventure and found the set off my 200-incher on the edge of a picked cornfield – only about 200 yards from where I shot the buck. They were lying almost on top of each other. In all likelihood, my buck probably cast off one side and then shook his head vigorously and the other side popped right off in the same spot.

Some of the largest sets of sheds I've ever picked up are no longer in my collection because I've given them to the hunters who ended up killing the buck

Pat poses with the largest set of sheds he ever found, a matched set from a Minnesota buck named "Captain Hook." The big deer was later killed by Pat's good friend and landowner John Redmond, and Pat gladly gave the sheds to John. "If someone kills a big buck and you have the sheds, I think it's only proper etiquette to give the sheds to that person," Pat says.

that once wore those antlers. I think it's always proper etiquette to do that because sheds mean so much to the hunter who harvested that particular buck. The largest set of sheds I ever found were picked up in southeast Minnesota several years ago on a lease belonging to my good friend John Redmond. Nicole and I hunt with John quite a bit. The sheds were from a great buck he had named Captain Hook, and he ended up killing the buck later that same year a short distance from where I found the sheds. Captain Hook was a gorgeous buck and the sheds were only about 20 yards apart. Of course John wanted the sheds and I was happy to give them to him. He had them mounted right alongside the original buck.

MAKING MEMORIES IN CANADA

I've literally traveled all over the North America looking for sheds. Years ago, I used to travel to Canada on a regular basis to look for antlers with a group of close friends. Those trips we made for several years in a row are among some of my most cherished memories. Our group included Tom Indrebo, Jimmy Hanson, Den-

Pat and friends during one of their annual shed hunting vacation trips to Saskatchewan in the late 1990s. Pictured left to right are: Tom Indrebo, Pat, Dennis Williams and Jim Hanson. "Back in those days, it was phenomenal," Pat said. "We would find upwards of 300 sheds."

Here's another awesome photo of the shed hunting team "super stars" in Saskatchewan. (Left to right) Dennis Williams, Jim Hanson, Pat Reeve and Tom Indrebo.

Nothing is more exciting than walking trail systems and finding a trophy shed like this!

nis Williams and myself. We would drive up to southern Saskatchewan in the dead of winter, get a motel room and search from farm lot to farm lot. In those days, southern Saskatchewan held a huge population of whitetails and they would winter-over in the farm country. The winters were so brutal that the deer would spend their entire winters eating off of haystacks and hanging around grain bins. There was little to no other food for them to eat out in the bush. So if you were going to find any antlers, that's where they'd be.

Ironically, Americans weren't allowed to hunt deer in southern Saskatchewan at that time, but we could legally hunt for their shed antlers. It was never a problem getting permission. Our good friend Garry Donald, owner and publisher of *Big Buck* magazine, helped us find a good spot and put us in touch with several landowners. The landowners welcomed us because shed antlers do incredible damage to tractor tires. The repair bill for a tractor tire can be quite significant.

Sometimes we'd pull up to a farmer's house to ask permission to shed hunt and we'd see deer trails crisscrossing the road, and half a dozen antlers out in the snow before we even got out of the truck. It was a shed hunter's dream. All of the antlers we found were from whitetails, and many of them were big and chocolate colored. We'd often find between 200 and 300 antlers every year – and we picked up some great sheds.

For the first couple of years, we'd pull up to a farmer's house to ask permission and they'd look at us like we were crazy and say, "Shed hunting? What's that?" They thought we were talking about the shed out behind the house. Then, after they understood, they'd often say, "Wait here just a minute." Off they'd go out to the barn or behind the house and they'd come back with an armload of horns. Sometimes when we came back to the truck after shed hunting all day, a big pile of antlers would be sitting beside the truck. They wanted to get rid of them and they wanted us to have them. We made great friends with some of those people and it was always a fun adventure.

Eventually we even started staying with the landowners that we had become friends with – Paul, Dennis and Norma Lamontagne – and they treated us like family. We'd spend a week with them and enjoy ourselves tremendously. We did that for a number of years until the laws changed. As soon as the Chronic Wasting Disease and Mad Cow Disease scares came along, laws were passed making it illegal to import skulls into the U.S., and only a certain number of shed antlers could be brought into the country. To make matters worse, the whitetail population in southern Saskatchewan took a major hit around 2001 due to several severe winters in a row. Where we had once seen as many as 1,000 deer wintering on a big farm lot, after the die-off we were lucky to see 100. The deer were nearly wiped out.

During that same time period, professional antler buyers started pouring into southern Saskatchewan and buying antlers from landowners to sell to the Asian markets to be ground up. So farm families and kids started picking them up and keeping them to sell to these buyers. Obviously we weren't finding nearly as many sheds, so we eventually stopped going altogether.

In May 2012, Nicole and I went to Saskatchewan for a few days and did some shed hunting with our good friends Cody and Kelsey Robins near Saskatoon. This time, we were looking for big mule deer sheds instead of whitetail sheds. Cody lives near world-renowned shed collector Bentley Cobin. Bentley is an absolute fanatic about sheds, and we got a chance to spend some time with him as well. In all, I think our group picked up around 60 sheds in three days of hunting. Nicole found a huge shed off a 190-class muley and Kelsey found a 3-by-3 shed that was definitely world class. It had an 18-inch G-2! We had a great time.

We went back in March 2013. This time, however, we only found about 15 antlers because quite a bit of

Pat shows off a massive, multi-tined non-typical shed found by a local landowner during one of his annual trips to Saskatchewan in the 1990s. The single antler scored around 108 inches.

Nicole poses with a large mule deer shed found in southern Saskatchewan.

See some shed hunting fun with friends Bentley Cobin and Cody and Kelsey Robbins in Saskatchewan in 2012.

Shed hunting is a highly anticipated event each year for Pat, his family and friends. Here Pat poses with daughter Olivia (right), good friend Dennis Williams (left) and Dennis' son Daniel.

Pat, Olivia, Chad Nolte and son Caden, Dennis Williams and son Daniel all pose for the camera during one of the group's annual trips to the Minnesota woods during shed hunting season.

fresh snow covered the ground. Interestingly enough, after the snow melted, Cody went back to the same spot where we found those sheds and he found many of their matches that had been buried in the deep snow.

FAMILY FUN

To me, shed hunting is not just about finding large quantities of antlers. It's a great cure for cabin fever because it gets you back outside into the fresh air after being locked inside all winter long. It's a great form of exercise. It's a great family activity. It's a great time to start doing some preliminary scouting by looking at last year's buck sign – old rubs, scrapes and trail systems. You might even discover a good treestand location. And as already mentioned, if you find a big shed antler you know the buck that once carried it has made it through the winter. Come fall, he'll most likely be in that same area. I can't tell you how many times I've found a big shed in the timber somewhere during the spring, and later killed the buck that dropped it within 100 yards of the spot where the antler was found.

Many people don't bother to look for sheds on public land because they feel that other people have

It's a family affair. Pat's four children – Carson, Cole, Olivia and Isabel love to get out in the woods and search for sheds.

The Reeve family displays some of the best sheds in the family collection. Pictured from left to right are Olivia, Pat, Carson, Nicole and Isabel (Son Cole is not pictured).

Shed hunting is a wonderful hobby. If you've never tried it, head out to the woods each spring. It'll be an adventure!

already gotten there first and picked over those areas. This is true to a certain extent but not always. It's usually the early bird who gets the worm on public land, so get there early and go back often during prime shedding time. Also, make a point of looking in secluded, out-of-the-way places where other people might not be willing to go. We happen to live very close to some great public land in Minnesota where a lot of big sheds have been found. If you plan to shed hunt in parks, public areas or nature preserves, make sure you get permission to do so legally.

One of the most unique sets of sheds I've ever acquired was given to me by a farmer in southern Saskatchewan. The deer actually shed its entire skull cap with both antlers attached. The skull cap measured about 10 inches wide, and had no hair on it. You can imagine what that deer's forehead must have looked like after he dropped his antlers! I've found lots of other sheds that had fairly large chunks of the buck's skull attached – but it never seems to affect the buck's health or antler growth the following year.

It's fairly easy to age sheds from bucks that are 1½, 2½, 3½ and 4½ years old by looking at the face of the pedicel. But after 4½, it becomes a lot more difficult. Of course, a large pedicel on an antler with very heavy mass usually indicates an older buck. Burr points and stickers also indicate a deer that has some age on him. You can often tell that a big rub has been made by an older mature buck by the way the bark is gouged out. A buck that has several burr points, stickers or split brows will often gouge the tree and you'll find a big pile of bark on the ground below the rub. A very smooth rub usually indicates a buck that has normal antlers with no abnormal points.

Shed hunting is a wonderful hobby. It's also a great way to get your wife and children out into the woods with you. Teaching a youngster the ropes of shed hunting is a lot like taking them hunting or fishing for the first time. If you do take your kids out for the first time, take them to a place where they have a good chance of finding a shed or two. If you see a shed on the ground, let them pick it up and praise them for finding it. Make sure they have a positive experience and they'll be hooked for life.

Shed hunting with dogs has also gotten very popular in recent years. A good shed dog can help a hunter or landowner cover a lot of ground, saving precious time and energy. There are a number of successful breeders and trainers across the nation. Nicole and I have really enjoyed watching our kids train their dog to shed hunt. They've gotten very good at it. So good, in fact, that we're now at the point where when we arrive at a shed hunting location, they take off and we don't see them again until it's time to go. They usually return to the truck bone tired with an exhausted dog and a pile of fresh sheds!

Shed hunting helps you get reconnected with nature. If you haven't gotten out there and tried it lately, grab your wife and children this winter and head to the woods.

CHAPTER 11

SEVEN STANDOUT BUCKS THAT PAT WON'T SOON FORGET

Pat shot this great Buffalo County, Wis., 10-pointer with his T/C muzzleloader in 2000 while hunting with outfitter Ted Marcum. Pat was filming for the Prime Time Bucks *video series, and at the time it was one of the largest bucks ever taken on video.*

BUFFALO COUNTY MONSTER – 2000

As a pro staffer and videographer working for Hunter's Specialties in 2000, I had filmed numerous hunts with other people in front of the camera hunting a variety of big-game species, but I was still new to being in front of the camera myself. The year before, I had shot my first whitetail ever on video while bow-hunting in Buffalo County with Ted Marum of Buffalo County Outfitters. Now I was back again, but this time I planned to hunt with my Thompson/Center muzzleloader.

I was set up in a treestand on top of a ridge. It was opening day of gun season in Wisconsin, and I'd learned that when the shooting starts, the big bucks seem to hang tight on the ridges. I'd been sitting all day and it was just starting to get dark. I'd seen a couple of nice bucks but was determined to hold out for one of the bruiser bucks that I knew lived in the area. Conditions were perfect, cold and clear. I knew I only had a few more minutes of good shooting light when I saw a big buck approaching through the timber. He was definitely a buck worth pursuing.

As soon as he got to a small opening about 75 yards away, I voice-grunted to stop him. He paused and I made a good shot. He didn't go far and when I got to his side I couldn't believe it. He was much larger than the bow buck I had shot with this same outfitter the previous year. He had an outstanding 10-point rack and grossed 162 inches and some change. He was 5½ years old, and I was very proud of the fact that I had taken this old boy on video.

That hunt really got my creative juices flowing. It jump-started my obsession with trying to shoot an even better buck for Hunter's Specialties and trying to produce an even better TV show the following year.

MUZZLELOADER MAGIC IN ILLINOIS – 2003

It was the first week of December 2003. Stan Potts and I were hunting with Rob Scott of Buckhorn Outfitters in Greene County, Ill., during the second gun season. I had hunted this same farm two weeks earlier during the first gun season without seeing a lot of big buck activity. It was our first season of filming for *North American Whitetail Television* and Blake Porter was my cameraman. I was hunting along the edge of a picked corn field and was in sort of a transitional zone because the deer were crossing the field at different times of the day going back and forth from feeding to

Pat was filming for North American Whitetail TV *in Greene County, Ill., when this mammoth buck appeared. The buck had 17 points and gross-scored 182.*

bedding areas.

I was using a Thompson/Center .50-caliber muzzleloader. It was a good spot for hunting with a muzzleloader because I could reach out and get a little more distance than I could with a bow. We were hunting on the ground – tucked back into the edge of the timber in sort of a natural ground blind, on top of a little high spot where we had very good visibility. It was a foggy, drizzly day – great conditions for mature bucks to be moving around in – but not the best for hunting with a muzzleloader.

Just after first light, I looked out and saw a big-bodied buck ghosting out of the fog and crossing the field. Blake quickly got the camera on him and I waited for him to get closer. You only get one shot with a muzzleloader and you have to make it count. I followed him through the scope. When everything looked just right for the shot, I made a mouth grunt to stop him and took a deep breath. The second he stopped, I squeezed off the shot. As the smoke was clearing, I could see him running across the field and I knew he wasn't going far.

When I walked up to him I was totally blown away.

Cameraman Blake Porter captured all the action of Pat's Illinois bruiser. The deer was crossing a field at first light when Pat connected with his Thompson/Center muzzleloader.

He was tremendous – much larger than I had originally thought. He was a heavy, main-framed 5-by-6 with tall, thick tines that were very bladed. He had a split G-2 on the left and several stickers around his bases. In all, he had 17 points. Had it not been for one broken brow tine on left side, he would have scored over 190 inches. As it was, the rack grossed about 182. As of that time, this was the biggest buck I had ever killed.

I couldn't believe my good fortune. What a great buck for our first season of filming. I'll never forget Stan's reaction. He had been hunting just a short distance away, and when he pulled up and saw my buck, he almost fell out of the truck!

PAT'S FIRST CANADIAN GIANT – 2003

While guiding hunters for Tom Indrebo at Bluff Country Outfitters in Buffalo County, Wis., during the late 1990s, Tom invited Jackie Bushman to come up and film a hunt for his Buckmasters TV show. I had the good fortune to meet Jackie's well-known cameraman and TV producer, Gene Bidlespacher. Gene's reputation had preceded him as being one of the top whitetail cameramen in the country, and I was thrilled to meet him.

Prior to going with Buckmasters, Gene had helped produce the classic video *Bowhunting October Whitetails* with Gene and Barry Wensel in the 1980s. That video is still considered one of the best ever made on hunting whitetails. Gene was my idol. Since I was a budding cameraman wanting to learn everything I could, I considered him to be the best in the business and was in complete awe of him.

A few years later, Gene left Buckmasters and moved to Montana (after 18 years producing the Buckmasters TV show). On his way from Alabama to his new home in Montana, he went out of his way to stop by and visit me in Minnesota. I was just getting involved with *North American Whitetail Television* in 2003, and he told me, "If you need a cameraman, or any help with anything else, just let me know." He knew I was interested in hunting Canada, and he even offered to help line up a couple of good places to hunt where he had filmed while working with Buckmasters. I told him anything he could do would be greatly appreciated.

Gene had filmed several times on a large private farm in southern Alberta owned by Simon and Marge Schonifer. The Schonifers were not outfitters. As landowners however, they were able to get a few transferable landowner tags each season. For a fee, they

On Pat's 2003 trip to Alberta with cameraman Gene Bidlespacher, Pat wasn't quite prepared for what lay ahead. As they drove over the top of a long ridge, Pat looked down and saw hundreds of tiny specks in the alfalfa fields below. Thinking the specks were cattle, Pat asked, "Where are all the deer?" "Those are the deer!" Gene answered.

allowed several nonresident hunters to hunt on their property each year. Gene had told me about how great the whitetail hunting was on their farm. So I finally asked him, "Can you set something up?" He called the owners on my behalf and pretty soon we were on our way. This would be the first time we'd ever hunted together and I was thrilled. Gene was both a friend and mentor to me, and I was very excited about the prospects of working with him.

Even though I was working for *North American Whitetail Television*, I had to pay for the hunt out of my own pocket. It was well worth the expense because I felt like it was a good investment in my future. I drove to Montana, picked Gene up and we headed north to southern Alberta. When we got to the general area where I knew we'd be hunting, the terrain was very open and rolling without much cover. I was quite concerned. I asked him, "Where are deer? Where are the trees?"

"You just wait," he answered with sort of a mischievous grin.

When we arrived at the farm, I wasn't prepared for what I was about to see. We drove over the top of a long ridge and stopped to look down into a wide valley below where the Schonifer farm was located. For as far as the eye could see, massive alfalfa fields now covered in snow spanned the bottoms. I could

barely make out what appeared to be hundreds of tiny dots in those fields that looked like cattle. I knew they couldn't be cattle but I wasn't sure what they were.

"When do the deer start coming out?" I asked Gene.

"Those *are* the deer," he answered.

"Every one of those dots?" I asked incredulously.

"Yes!" Gene assured me. "This is going to be an unforgettable hunt."

At that moment I knew Gene was right. And this was in the middle of the day. As we drove down into the valley and passed close to some of the fields we saw mature bucks bedded out in the alfalfa. I thought I had died and gone to heaven. It wasn't going to be a matter of *getting* a buck. It was more a matter of how big he would be. I was beside myself with excitement.

Opening day was still two days away. Simon drove us around and we did some glassing that afternoon. Just before dark, we watched a number of nice bucks come out of the willows to feed. We couldn't have asked for better weather. It was very cold with a lot of snow on the ground. In fact, Gene told me that's why so many deer were out feeding during the middle of the day. The cold temperatures brought them out. From a distance I saw one particular deer, a beautiful 6-by-6, and I set my sights on him right away. This was the buck I wanted to shoot.

The next morning we sat around drinking cof-

Pat set his sights on a beautiful 6-by-6 that they saw leaving one of the fields. Low and behold, he shot the 170-inch monster on the first day of the hunt!

fee while we watched that same 6-by-6 go back into his bedding area across the road from the Schonifer house. Opening day of rifle season was the next day, Nov. 1. Since we now knew which trail this buck was using, we decided to sneak up that creek bottom during the middle of the day and put up a couple of Big Game treestands for Gene and I to hunt from the next morning. With a little luck, we might just get a crack at the big 6-by-6. I was never more anxious or excited about an opening day in my life. I couldn't wait.

The next morning we got up extra early and headed to our stands. Because we knew a lot of deer would still be out in the fields, we slipped out of Simon's back door as quietly as possible and he drove us around to the creek bottom where we had set our stands. He dropped us off and drove away. As it started getting daylight, the parade began. We watched deer after deer as they came off the field and headed back into the thick cover to bed down for the day. We saw a number of good bucks including one wide, heavy, 150-class 8-pointer that I had a difficult time passing up.

The big 4-by-4 was very tempting, but I was determined to try to hold out for the big 6-by-6. I didn't have long to wait. A short while later, there he was, coming our way with a group of does. It was as if

our hunt had been planned out in advance. I stopped him with a mouth grunt and made a perfect double-lung shot with my Thompson/Center .300 Winchester Magnum Encore at about 150 yards. He didn't go far.

I had never shot a deer that big. He had a huge body and a set of antlers to go with it. When we walked up to him I couldn't believe that I had actually taken a buck of this magnitude. He was a wide, heavy, symmetrical 6-by-6 with long tines and almost no deductions. He had everything you could ask for in a trophy buck from Alberta and ended up scoring just over 170 inches. We took some outstanding photos that day in the snow and it was one of the best days I've ever spent in the field. We did all of our re-creating with the video camera and then we shot dozens of still photos as well. Gene was a pleasure to work with.

This hunt was a dream-come-true for me. To be in Alberta hunting with a legendary cameraman like Gene Bidlespacher, and now to have taken such a magnificent whitetail – my biggest buck ever as of that time – was far more than I deserved. It didn't get any better than this. What a great hunt and what a great friend Gene was to me!

Now I was in a quandary. We had driven all the way to Alberta and finished our hunt in one day. We still had several days allocated for Canada before we had to return to the states. I looked at Gene and asked, "What now?"

Gene to the rescue! "I know a really good place in Saskatchewan if you want to drive over there," Gene said with his typical grin.

"Let's go!" I said.

So we ended up making our Canadian odyssey a two-part trip. We drove across the border into eastern Saskatchewan and hunted with outfitter Arnold Holmes, a very good friend of Gene's. This hunt was way up in the northern wilderness and much different from what I had just experienced in Alberta. On the second day of that hunt, I shot a magnificent chocolate-horned 4-by-4 with a sticker that grossed over 150 inches. In three days of hunting, I had taken two fantastic bucks with my idol and mentor Gene Bidlespacher. And just as it had been in Alberta, it was very cold in Saskatchewan with a lot of snow on the ground. To me, those two hunts really epitomized what hunting in Canada was all about. I fell in love with hunting north of the border and knew I'd be back. I was hooked on Canada for the rest of my life!

ANOTHER SUGAR CREEK DANDY – 2006

Since Illinois is Nicole's all-time favorite big-buck state to hunt, we make a point of hunting both the archery and firearms seasons there every year. Normally we try to bow-hunt the week before the first gun season begins. Then we continue hunting with a muzzleloader as soon as that three-day gun season opens. The first gun season usually comes in around the 18th to the 20th of November. Depending on the weather, the timing is usually excellent, and the rut is still going strong.

Hunting both seasons requires getting an archery tag as well as a gun tag. In Illinois, you can put in for a statewide archery tag valid for any county in the state, but the gun tag is county specific; you have to put in for the county you plan to hunt – in this case, Schuyler County. During gun season you can use either a shotgun or muzzleloader. Nicole and I prefer to use our Thompson/Center muzzleloaders. We've found them to be extremely accurate and always dependable.

2006 would mark my second year hunting with Sugar Creek Outfitters. The year before, I shot my biggest buck ever with a bow – a 200-inch typical 5-by-5 megabuck that turned out to be the largest typical whitetail ever harvested on video. It was also one of the largest typical whitetails taken in North America by bow in 2005. That amazing hunt changed my life and helped get my new TV show, *Driven TV* on the Men's Channel, off the ground.

I had not yet teamed up with Nicole in 2006. That was still a year away. For the second year in a row, the owners of Sugar Creek, Don Barry and Don Barry Jr.,

After tagging out on the first day in Alberta, Pat and Gene drove over to northern Saskatchewan where Pat shot this outstanding heavy-framed 4-by-4. The buck grossed over 150 inches.

Pat shot this beautiful white-horned 10-pointer while hunting at Sugar Creek Outfitters in 2006 with his trusty T/C muzzleloader.

Pat was thrilled to be invited back to Sugar Creek Outfitters one year after he shot his massive 200-inch monster with a bow (see Chapter 1). This muzzleloader buck scored a whopping 169 inches.

had very graciously extended me an invitation to hunt and film both archery and gun seasons.

It was mid-November and I was hunting a large timber tract about 1,000 acres in size. Hunting in a thick creek bottom – I often gravitate toward creek bottoms or the bottoms of ridges and have had a lot of success hunting low areas – I rattled in several good bucks during bow season but was never able to get one in close enough for a shot.

Just before gun season opened, I moved my stand uphill about 70 yards. After having watched the deer during the previous week, I realized the bucks were moving closer to the top of the ridge. I knew my bow-hunting setup had been just off the mark, so I changed my strategy accordingly. Sometimes you have to take action and make adjustments to your setup when you realize the deer are doing something other than what you expected. In this case, I had been able to see what the deer were doing, and I took advantage of that knowledge and changed my stand location. It can be risky moving your stand in the middle of a hunt, but sometimes it's well worth the risk. In this case, it really paid off.

On Friday, the first day of gun season, I passed on a couple of small bucks with my muzzleloader. My cameraman was my good friend Donnie Hansen. The next day we planned to sit out all day long because the rut was still in full swing. Around noon, I heard something approaching my stand. It was a doe, and she was not wasting any time moving through the woods. Her body language told me she was being followed. As soon as I got my muzzleloader up and ready, a beautiful 10-pointer appeared about 50 yards away following in the doe's footsteps – almost within bow range. I made a mouth grunt to stop him and as soon as he stopped, I squeezed the trigger. He ran about 50 yards and tipped over.

What a trophy. An absolutely awesome buck! He was a clean 5-by-5 with tall tines and a heavy rack that scored 160 inches. We figured he was 4½ years old. Everything about him made him special. His forehead was very black and gave him a dark look with much character. I was really thrilled and the fact that I'd been able to hunt the area a few days prior to gun season gave me the opportunity to see what the deer were doing, and I changed my stand location based on what I'd learned. That made all the difference! Once again, the great state of Illinois had given me a special prize – an outstanding buck. Little did I then know that within another year it would also give me the biggest prize of all – my future soul mate and lifelong hunting partner, Nicole Jones!

FIFTEEN-MINUTE HUNT FOR A WISCONSIN MEGABUCK – 2007

In November 2007, my good friend Ron Skoronski invited me on a rifle hunt on his well-managed property near Spring Green, Wis., just east of Madison. When Ron called he said, "Conditions are perfect. You need to get down here right away. They're doing it right now!"

So I packed up the truck with my cameraman Mike Law and headed over to Wisconsin. When we arrived, only a few hours of daylight remained, but Ron said, "Hurry. You need to get out there right away. You can't afford to wait till tomorrow."

So Mike and I quickly changed into our hunting clothes and grabbed the camera equipment. We walked down a short hill from Ron's house and climbed into a permanent ground blind on the edge of the hill that overlooked a half-picked, half-standing cornfield. Ron was right. It was very cold and conditions were perfect to shoot a deer. Lots of fresh snow covered the ground and the deer were definitely feeding in the corn. As we approached the blind and got inside, we ran quite a few deer out of the field, but were confident they would come back within a short time.

Ron told me I could shoot any buck I wanted except for one. "Don't shoot a big buck that has a split G-2 on one side," he had said. "He's a young buck and I want to give him a couple more years to see what he does."

Mike and I had no sooner gotten the camera set up in the blind when I saw a huge buck coming toward us. I said, "Holy smoke, that buck is a monster!" The last thing I expected was to have a big, mature buck come in that fast after we had just emptied the entire field.

The buck had a long kickstand-type droptine coming off the back of his left side. I could also see a couple of other non-typical points and I knew this buck was definitely an old mature deer. Although Ron had described the other deer as being younger, I was in a dilemma because I wasn't 100 percent sure if this was the buck Ron had asked me not to shoot. I grabbed my cell phone in a complete panic as the buck was approaching and nervously tried to call Ron on his phone. Within seconds the big buck was right out in front of us. Ron finally answered and I quickly described the deer as being a big, mature non-typical with a droptine and several kickers and stickers. "He's just a giant!" I said.

"That doesn't sound like the young deer with the split G-2," Ron said calmly. "So go ahead and shoot him if you want to."

Pat and his cameraman had no sooner gotten into their ground blind while hunting on property belonging to Pat's good friend Ron Skoronski near Madison, Wis., when this incredible non-typical appeared out of nowhere. The giant buck grossed over 185 inches.

It didn't take me long to hang up. By now the buck had stepped into the food plot and was so close that I was nervous about trying to ease the barrel of my rifle out the window of the blind. As I did so, he must have heard or seen something because he snapped his head over in my direction and stared at the blind. It just so happened that I was filming a TV segment for *Winchester Whitetail Revolution* and I was hunting with a Winchester automatic rifle. I carefully aimed at the buck's shoulder and squeezed the trigger. There was an audible "click." The bullet had misfired. I quickly ejected the bullet and got another round in the chamber. By now the buck was fully alert and starting to walk away. But it was too late. This time when I squeezed the trigger the gun fired. He didn't go far.

When we reached the buck's side I couldn't believe how big he was. He had a massive non-typical rack that grossed over 185 inches, and that didn't include several tines that had been broken off. He was old and gnarly and his huge rack had lots of character. He had a big 17-point frame including the long kickstand flyer off his left G-2. He was at least 6½ years old, maybe older. Ron had seen him several times in the past and had numerous trail camera photos of him.

Later on after Ron came down, saw the buck, and realized which deer this was, he said, "You never quite

Pat's rifle hunt for this Wisconsin bruiser lasted all of about 15 minutes! It just goes to show – you never know when that buck of a lifetime is going to step out!

explained to me on the phone that he was *this* big! We've been after this old boy forever. He's been at the top of my hit list." But Ron was genuinely happy for me and it was a great hunt.

Being the big-buck fanatic that he is, it was very generous of Ron to invite me down to hunt on his farm. What a beautiful piece of property, and what a great experience!

LATE-SEASON BOW-HUNT FOR A BUCK NAMED "PINCHER" – 2009

I've hunted for many years with my good friend John Redmond, owner of Fair Chase Outfitters in southern Minnesota. In 2007, while hunting on John's farm, I saw a nice 3½-year-old buck that had long brow tines that were sort of "pinched" in at the top. John had a number of trail camera photos of this deer and we named him Pincher. At the time he was a 9-pointer. Even though he didn't have a lot of mass, we both agreed that this buck had good potential for becoming a great buck some day.

In 2008, Pincher played the disappearing act so typical of bucks his age. No one saw him during the

entire season and no photos were taken of him by any of John's trail cameras. Could he have been run off the property by another, more aggressive buck? It's entirely possible. It happens all the time with mature bucks.

Later that same year, John invited me to come down to his property and try to shoot a particular management buck during gun season. John doesn't normally allow any gun hunting on his property, but this was a special situation. The buck in question was a gnarly 8-pointer that was probably 5½ years old. The deer was very aggressive, and John suspected that he had been running some of his other big bucks off the property. In fact, Pincher might well have been one of those bucks. John had nicknamed the deer the "Swamp Buck." He wanted the Swamp Buck to be taken out of the herd for obvious reasons. People who manage their property for mature whitetails often have trouble with aggressive bucks like this, and it's always a good policy to cull them from the herd if possible.

I wanted to help out any way I could but never really thought I had much of a chance at shooting the Swamp Buck. On the day of the hunt, I decided to let my 4-year-old son Carson come with us. Donnie Han-

Pat had been following the buck nicknamed "Pincher," so named because of the way his long brow tines pinched inward, for several years on property in southern Minnesota owned by his good friend John Redmond of Fair Chase Outfitters.

sen was my cameraman and we were hunting over a corn field out of a homemade hay-bale blind. We were actually set up in the same little valley where I would have an encounter with Pincher the following year.

This was Carson's first deer hunt and he was pretty excited. In an effort to keep him quiet and happy, I had brought along a big bag of candy and snacks. What a mistake! After filling up on all of this junk food for several hours, Carson was bouncing off the walls of that ground blind. He was definitely on a sugar high and he couldn't stay still or quiet. He was squirming around in the blind and making all sorts of noise. I seriously doubted if we'd be able to shoot anything that day. Late that afternoon several does came out and started feeding on corn. Then all at once, I saw a buck in the trees up on the hill. As he made his way down to the field, I realized it was the Swamp Buck.

Despite all the noise and movements Carson was making, the buck eventually came out into the corn field and I was able to place a good shot into his vitals. Carson was beside himself. Because this was his first deer hunting experience, the Swamp Buck was now his deer. Seeing that kind of excitement in my son made it a very special and memorable hunt. Because of all the chaos inside the blind, I never expected to shoot a deer that afternoon, least of all the Swamp Buck. But everything turned out just fine, John was very excited to learn that we had gotten the rogue deer, and Carson insisted that we get it mounted so that we could hang his deer in his room! It's still there to this day. Now, everyone who comes to our house gets dragged into

In 2008, outfitter John Redmond invited Pat down to his property to hunt an aggressive management buck nicknamed the "Swamp Buck." Pat decided to take his youngest son Carson along on the hunt. It was Carson's first deer hunt ever and he was ecstatic!

Watch Carson's first hunt with his dad as Pat matches wits with the elusive "Swamp Buck."

To Carson's great joy, Pat successfully brought down the elusive "Swamp Buck" during the hunt. Being his first-ever deer hunt with his dad, Carson immediately laid claim to the deer as if he had killed it himself.

his room to see the legendary Swamp Buck.

The next year, 2009, I was bow-hunting at John's during the early season in October when I saw a magnificent buck that would gross at least 170 inches. It was Pincher! He was back! By now he had grown a tenth point and was definitely a shooter.

That year, John was hunting a huge, 180-inch buck he'd nicknamed "Captain Hook" that he ended up shooting. I had found both of the deer's sheds from the year before. Since John had filled his tag with Captain Hook, I decided to put all of my efforts in trying to match wits with Pincher. It was late season before I really got a handle on him. The colder it got and the more snow that piled up on the ground, the more regular he became. He was coming into a cut corn field on a routine basis.

I decided to set up a Primos Double Bull ground blind in the cut corn and completely covered it with corn stalks. The snow was so deep it was hard to keep the truck from getting stuck just driving back into the spot where I wanted to hunt. I was determined to shoot Pincher with a bow. On one particularly cold

Carson proudly shows off his dad's buck that he commandeered. Today the mounted trophy proudly hangs in Carson's bedroom.

day, we were in the ground blind and Nicole was filming me. After we'd been sitting there awhile we saw a deer coming our way. From my position all I could see was the deer's legs. But I could clearly make out some

In 2009, while hunting from a ground blind in southern Minnesota as Nicole operated the camera, the buck named Pincher, now sporting his largest rack ever, made an up-close-and-personal appearance. Pat made a perfect 20-yard bow shot.

dark tarsal glands, and I knew it was a buck.

Nicole got the cameras rolling, and finally the entire deer came into view. It was Pincher! Just about the time I saw him he looked over and eyed the ground blind suspiciously. He suddenly slammed on the brakes and stopped – fully alert. Another two seconds or so and he would have been gone. But it was too late. I had my 20-yard pin on him and the arrow was on its way.

My Muzzy broadhead did its job and he didn't go far. I was very happy and excited. I had hunted all year for a deer of his caliber and now I finally had one at the end of the season. To do it with a bow made it even more special. Nicole was just as excited as I was, and it was a great hunt and a special day to be in the woods with Nicole.

Pincher was a basic 5-by-5 but he had long, bladed brow tines that gave his rack special character. Even though he was 5½ years old, he never did put on the body size or heavy mass in his rack that you would expect to see in most mature bucks. Some bucks just never do. But he was still an outstanding animal. He would have scored around 170 inches, but his right G-4 had been broken off and was missing several inches. Pincher was definitely a buck I would never forget!

THE BEST OF THE BEST IN BUFFALO COUNTY – 2010

Over the years, the Hurlbert family has been very gracious to allow Nicole and I to hunt whitetails on their one-of-a-kind farm in Buffalo County many times. Whenever they extend an invitation for us to hunt on their property we always get excited. We have a great relationship with the owners Ron and Kent, and they seem to like what we do on TV. I've known Ron for over 20 years. The family had been managing their 5,000 contiguous acres for big bucks for at least that long. Each year they allow us to hunt some of their big management bucks, or bucks that are very old and going downhill. To say that this land contains an above-average number of mature bucks running around on it would be an understatement. Nicole and I consider this land to be one of the best pieces of property in the entire state of Wisconsin – if not the entire Midwest for big whitetails.

In 2010 Nicole had been having a frustrating year. We'd been hunting hard together all season long, with Nicole doing most of the hunting while I did the filming, and she had not taken a single deer with her bow. She had come close to shooting some really great

Late-season hunts can be so productive at this time of year when the temperatures are cold and the snow is deep. As the saying goes, "the more miserable the weather, the better the hunting!" And it's very true. It's a great time to shoot that big boy you've been after all season long. With a little work, you can usually figure out where he's bedding because it'll never be far from a good food source. Then, all you have to do is wait for a cold, nasty day and set up over that food source. Usually it's just a matter of time before he'll show up.

Most late-season hunting is done in the afternoon. It's very difficult to find a good early-morning setup over a food source because the deer usually stop feeding at first light, or shortly thereafter, and bed down in the adjoining woods – sometimes right next to the field. They never go far, so trying to get into a good food source before daylight is risky because the chances are good that you'll blow most of the deer out of the area.

It's far better to sneak into your stand location early in the afternoon, let things settle down and wait for the deer to start filtering back into the field late in the afternoon. On particularly cold days, they'll often start feeding early in the afternoon. Usually the big boys are the last ones to make an appearance, oftentimes only moments before good shooting light is gone for the day. So dress warmly, be patient and get ready for some exciting late-afternoon action!

bucks so many times but something always seemed to happen at the last minute.

Since we travel out of state so much during the season, we love to spend a few days hunting close to home and recharging our batteries whenever we get a chance. The Wisconsin border is so close that we re-gard Wisconsin and Minnesota as home states. We'll often take off to a nearby location like the Hurlbert farm for an afternoon hunt since it's only a 30- or 40-minute drive from our house.

By the late season in 2010, I still had an unfilled Wisconsin tag. Always thinking of others, Nicole unselfishly encouraged me to try and fill that tag on one of the monster bucks we knew about on the Hurlbert farm. Usually by this time of year, we have several big Hurlbert brutes pinpointed from trail camera photos and sightings made earlier in the year. These deer are placed on our ongoing bucks-we'd-like-to-shoot hit list.

There was one old bruiser I'd seen several times during the course of the season, but he never would come in close enough to offer me a shot with my bow. He was an ancient main-framed 5-by-5 with very tall brow tines. He had a thick, heavy body and lots of battle scars. By late season, the deer were getting more predictable and coming into food sources, so I decided to hunt the spot where I had seen him several times. Nicole was behind the camera. Our treestands were set up on the edge of a field, but by this time of year there was very little cover around us. I had been picked off by does on several earlier hunts. But I decided to give it one more shot because this old warrior was well worth going after.

He came into the field late in the afternoon just before dark. The moment I saw him, I knew it was going to be nip and tuck because I was afraid he would see me in the tree. He slowly worked his way into position out in front of me and offered me a nice broadside shot. I made a good double-lung shot with my Mathews and he didn't go far.

I was elated because I'd had such a long history with this deer. Kent had trail camera photos of him from previous years and he was just a bruiser of a buck. Within a day or two of that hunt, Nicole shot another brute in Minnesota. So by the end of the season that year we had two big bucks down and we couldn't have been happier. There was lots of snow on the ground that season and the temperatures were cold; ideal conditions for taking a mature buck. As a rule of thumb, if the outside temperature is below 20 degrees and lots of snow is covering the ground, the truly big bucks will be hanging close to any available food sources. If the property you are hunting has any standing corn or beans left at this time of year, you're sure to see some good action from the big boys. Hunt the food and they will come!

I ended the 2010 season with another memorable hunt on the Hurlbert farm. That property is definitely a piece of whitetail heaven!

Pat was able to get an arrow in this old warrior late in the season. He'd seen the buck several times earlier while hunting on prime property in Buffalo County, Wis., belonging to the Hurlbert family.

CHAPTER 12

FIVE STANDOUT BUCKS THAT NICOLE WON'T SOON FORGET

"There's nothing like the rush you get after you've made a great shot on a great buck and you're on the trail to recover him," Nicole says. "That's when the adrenalin starts to take over!"

NICOLE'S FIRST VELVET BUCK EVER – 2007

It was early September 2007 when Pat and I loaded up the Chevy truck and headed west to North Dakota. I was pretty excited. This was my very first whitetail hunt for *Driven TV* and my very first hunt for velvet whitetails. A landowner Pat knew had invited us to come out and hunt on his river-bottom property in the northeast part of the state. It was open, flat country, with lots of small woodlots and wooded draws. This was potato farm country. We would be hunting early season food sources, mainly soybeans. We had actually driven out to the property several weeks before the hunt to do some scouting and set up some treestands. However, it was still sort of a shot in the dark. We had never hunted this land before, but from everything Pat had been able to find out the area looked very promising.

Do-it-yourself hunts like this are both fun and challenging. In most cases, you have to do some quick scouting when you get there. Then, depending on what the deer are doing, try to set up your stands to your best advantage. We stayed with one of Pat's good friends, John Hanson. John has killed some incredible velvet bucks in the early season with his bow, and it seemed like he shot a monster in North Dakota every year. He was a big part of the reason we decided to make this hunt.

We had previously set up our treestands on the edge of a bean field. On the first afternoon out we saw quite a few bucks, two of which were really nice. I'll never forget that afternoon because it was one of the first times I had ever been in a treestand with Pat. At this point, we had been dating for several months but had not yet hunted and filmed together.

It was so quiet that evening you could have heard a pin drop. We were watching a beautiful 150-class buck feeding out in the field about 70 or 80 yards away, hoping that he would eventually feed over in our direction. We were actually sitting in two separate trees. Pat was facing the field in one tree, and I was just in front of him facing toward the woods. All of a sudden Pat passed some gas and it was quite loud. He couldn't help it; it was just one of those things that happen.

At first I was shocked, then we both started laughing. I had never heard him do that before and I almost fell out of my tree laughing. It was so funny. We ended up putting that on the TV show and people loved it. Everyone got a big kick out of it. But the joke ended up being on me because even to this day, many people

Nicole's first hunt ever for Driven TV *in 2007 proved to be memorable in more ways than one. Although she got very sick during her North Dakota hunt, she managed to put an arrow in this awesome velvet 4-by-4.*

who viewed the show thought it was me, not Pat, who had let one rip!

It took us two afternoons of hunting to really pinpoint the deer and figure out what they were doing. They had actually changed their feeding habits since we had hung our stands several weeks earlier. After the first frost, the beans where we were hunting had yellowed somewhat and the deer were feeding on other side of field where the plants were much more green. So we relocated our stands accordingly. On the third afternoon, everything was perfect. The deer came out right where we expected to see them and started feeding slowly along the field edge in our direction.

A beautiful 4-year-old 4-by-4 in velvet with a split brow tine worked his way into range, and I made a good shot on him. However, my arrow hit him a little far back, so we decided to back out for the evening and give him plenty of time to go down. We returned early the next morning at first light and found him piled up just inside the woods near the edge of the field. He hadn't gone 60 yards. I was absolutely thrilled.

While Pat and I were filming the recovery another

funny thing happened. As I walked up to the deer for the first time, Pat was behind me running the camera. There was a large hole in the ground covered with debris just in front of me that I didn't see and I stepped right in it. Suddenly I went down for the count and disappeared out of the view of the camera. I was up to my waist in that hole! We both got a big laugh out of that one.

This was my first velvet buck ever and a special hunt with Pat that I would never forget. While we were in North Dakota, a not-so-memorable event also occurred. I got extremely sick for several days. Since we were hunting out in the middle of nowhere and the closest little town was probably 30 to 40 miles away, poor Pat had to drive to a drugstore in that town several times to get me some medication. Since this was our first hunt together, I'm sure he was thinking, "What have I gotten myself into?"

Despite being sick, the entire North Dakota experience was an unforgettable adventure. To this day, my beautiful 4-by-4 whitetail is the only velvet buck I've ever taken and his rack is gorgeous in every way. The day I killed him, the velvet was perfect and not yet starting to split off. We saw a few bucks that were already starting to rub their velvet off, so I really lucked out. We've been back to North Dakota several times during the early season since, and I've taken other bucks, but none were still in velvet.

OPENING DAY BOW-HUNT IN MINNESOTA – 2007

After my unforgettable hunt for a velvet buck in North Dakota in early September, Pat and I immediately headed to southeast Minnesota to hunt opening day of archery season with Pat's good friend John Redmond of Fair Chase Outfitters. (Archery season usually opens around the middle of September in Minnesota.) This would be my first time hunting in Minnesota and second time filming for *Driven TV*. I was still on a high from my successful hunt in North Dakota, so once again I was very excited.

Since it was early season, we planned to hunt over a waterhole. Although I'd heard Pat talking about how common this was in Minnesota and Wisconsin while the weather was still relatively warm, this strategy would definitely be another first for me.

When we arrived in camp we met two other bow-hunters, Dale and Bryan Lemke, a father and son team from Pennsylvania that Pat had known from his days of guiding with Tom Indrebo. We hit it off with them extremely well and have all become very good friends, and have gone on several more hunts together over the next few years. Then, after graduating from college in 2011, Bryan relocated to our hometown of Plainview, Minn., and went to work for *Driven TV* as our full-time cameraman.

On opening day, Pat and I got on our Polaris four-wheeler early in the afternoon and rode it to the base of a very high ridge where we planned to hunt. We went through the gate and about 3/4 of the way up the steep ridge before we parked the four-wheeler. We soon discovered that the landowners of the adjacent property where we had gone through the gate operated a buffalo farm. It was strange to see big, shaggy buffalo roaming around in areas where we expected to see deer. We later had a neat opportunity to visit the buffalo farm and meet the owners. We soon learned that one of the animals in their herd had been a famous movie star, a big male named Cody was used in several scenes of Kevin Costner's blockbuster 1990 movie *Dances with Wolves*. We got to pet him and see some of the other buffalo as well.

After parking the four-wheeler, we hiked the rest of the way up the really steep hill. Being mid-September, it was hotter than hot. John had carved out a several-acre food plot in the middle of the woods on top of the ridge, and had also built a small waterhole right smack-dab in the middle of the food plot. Our treestand overlooked that waterhole. The weather had been extremely hot and dry for the past few weeks, and John told us the deer were coming to the waterhole literally all day long.

Pat got up in the tree first so that he could set up the camera equipment. The moment he got to his stand, he looked around for a second and then looked down at me and said, "You're killing a buck tonight!" Then he gave me a double thumbs-up sign.

I thought, *That's nice to know but what would make him say that?* I really had no idea why he was suddenly so excited.

After I had climbed up to my stand I understood. The waterhole was surrounded by deer tracks – hundreds of deer tracks. It was unbelievable. The entire area around the waterhole was pounded down with deer sign. We knew we were going to see plenty of deer so we got set up as quickly as possible. We sat for a couple of hours and saw several does and fawns and a couple of small bucks.

Then all of sudden, we looked over and saw a mountain of antlers headed our way. A large buck was walking up the wooded ridge toward the food plot. At first, all I could see was a massive rack swinging from side to side just above the horizon of the ridgeline. Finally the head and body of a big, mature buck popped over the horizon and there was no question that this

Within several days of returning to Minnesota from her successful North Dakota hunt, Nicole was hunting with Fair Chase Outfitters in the southern part of the state when she arrowed this gnarly old warrior.

Dale Lemke also shot an incredible trophy the same day Nicole shot her buck. Dale is Bryan's father. Bryan later went to work for Driven TV as a cameraman.

Just prior to Nicole's Greene County, Ill., bow-hunt in 2009, outfitter Joe Gizdic had captured this buck on film a number of times with his trail cameras.

Nicole arrowed this bad boy as he circled a decoy Pat had put out on the edge of a field.
The buck offered her an unbelievable 10-yard shot from her tree.

buck was coming straight for the waterhole.

When he got within range, we stopped him and I made a perfect heart shot at about 25 yards. He ran a short distance and went down. He was a heavy, long-tined 5-by-4 with a split brow on the left side. You could tell from his smooth rack that he had just recently rubbed off his velvet. One of the most striking things I noticed about him was his unusually long eyelashes. I guess it takes a woman to notice something like that but they really stood out. At the time, one of our pro staff members, Chad Nolte, was doing some guiding for John so he came and helped us drag my buck out to the road.

I was on an unbelievable high. I now had two big bucks on the ground in only four days of hunting. We'd only hunted three days in North Dakota and one afternoon in Minnesota, and I already had my second buck of the season. I was beginning to think there was nothing to this TV hunting!

It must have been a magical afternoon in Minnesota that day because Dale Lemke shot a beautiful trophy buck as well. Two out of the three hunters in the woods that afternoon shot big bucks. Not bad for opening day!

DECOY MAGIC IN ILLINOIS – 2009

The rut was in full swing and it was prime time in Greene County, Ill. It was mid-November 2009 and I was hunting with Tall Tine Outfitters. I should have been seeing all kinds of rutting activity but things had been unusually slow – at least in the patch of woods where I happened to be hunting.

Cameraman Mike Law and I were hunting one specific buck that our outfitter Joe Gizdic had captured on film many times with his trail cameras, but the buck wasn't cooperating. This was a very unique deer. He was a big-bodied, mature buck. From the numerous trail camera photos Joe had, he was obviously a dominant residential buck. At some point, both of his ears had been frozen off and all he had left were two small stumps where his ears had once been.

The buck also had damaged the left side of his rack. The right side was a perfect 6-point typical that hooked out at end of beam. The right G-2 had a sticker. The left side appeared to have been damaged in velvet; the main beam ended after the G-3. It hadn't been broken off. It had a hollowed out appearance, with a small cluster of points at the end, so it had obviously grown that way. The left G-3 was forked. This odd growth could have been caused from an injury.

Mike and I had hunted the property for several days and endured some really miserable cold and rainy weather. We knew our buck had been in the area.

He'd left plenty of sign, but just wouldn't show himself. I'd had a couple of close calls with several other bucks chasing does but we really had our sights set on shooting this one particular buck.

Pat also had been hunting out of state and had just returned home. He and I talked on the phone and I told him all about my several disappointing days of sitting in a tree all day long in miserably wet and cold weather with nothing to show for it. "Why don't you come home," he suggested. "We'll spend a couple of days hunting around here and then we'll go back to Illinois together when the weather is better and I'll film you."

So that's what we did. I went home. We hunted a couple of days in Minnesota and Wisconsin and then packed up the truck and drove back to Illinois. We drove all night long and got to Greene County in the early morning hours. We only slept for an hour or two at the most and then got up and headed to our stand. That morning we debated and debated about whether or not to use a decoy. Pat loves hunting over decoys and I had actually just had my first successful hunt using a decoy the year before. After that experience, I was hooked on using decoys as well. It's always so exciting to watch a buck's behavior as he comes in and reacts to a decoy.

We planned to hunt the edge of an open field to try to catch any bucks cruising from one side of the field to the other as they went from one bedding area to the next trying to locate a hot doe. When we reached our stand, we still hadn't made a decision. But Pat had brought along the decoy just in case and said, "I think I'll go ahead and put it out."

As I was getting all of our gear ready at the bottom of the tree, Pat took the decoy out and carefully set it up on the edge of the field. He sprayed it down good and came back to the tree. We got up in our stands and began a long morning vigil. It was cold and windy that day and we didn't see a thing until around 9:30 a.m. Pat just happened to look over to our right toward an area that was really thick and overgrown. Suddenly he spotted a huge buck standing near a scrape about 250 yards away. "Oh, my gosh, there he is!" he whispered.

It was the very buck I had hoped to see on my earlier hunt. He had just finished working the scrape and was starting to walk away. Since the deer was alone, Pat decided to make a loud grunt with his grunt tube to try to get his attention. Pat grunted but the buck apparently didn't hear him. He grunted again and the buck sort of glanced over in our direction. From where the buck was standing, he couldn't see the decoy. Finally Pat snort-wheezed and that's all it took. This definitely got his curiosity up and after a few seconds he started

"It was so neat to watch this buck's behavior as he approached the decoy," Nicole said. "His ears were laid back, his hair was all bristled out and he was walking stiff-legged. Talk about intense excitement!"

Check out Nicole's up-close-and-personal encounter with her Illinois buck in 2009.

coming toward us.

It just so happened that a hog-wire fence was located over to our right about 35 yards out. When the buck got to that fence, he predictably stopped. He finally spotted the decoy and immediately locked in on it. You could see his entire demeanor change as he started pacing back and forth along the fence line like an angry bull. Pat and I were frantically whispering to each other, trying to decide what to do. We knew the buck was thinking about jumping the fence, but at one

point he started looking away and appeared to lose interest in the decoy.

All of a sudden the buck focused all of his attention back on the decoy and we both knew he was going to jump the fence. Pat said, "Get ready!" The buck jumped the fence and walked straight in to a distance of about 10 yards from our tree. It was almost as if he'd been on a string. I made a perfect 10-yard shot. The buck ran out into the field about 50 yards and went down on camera. Those last few seconds were so exciting. It was so neat to watch his behavior and the way he started to posture himself at the decoy at such a close distance. His ears were laid back and he was walking stiff-legged. His hair was all bristled out and standing on end and he was ready to rumble.

Because of the buck's unusual rack, and the up-close-and-personal encounter I'd had with him, this hunt was really special. It was a memorable hunt with Pat all the way around, but the fact that we actually got the buck that I had set my sights on made it that much more special.

Nicole had hunted on the famed Hurlbert property in Buffalo County, Wis., for portions of three seasons with nothing to show for her efforts. In 2011, she made up for lost time when she arrowed this heavy-bodied old bruiser.

A BUCK TO REMEMBER IN BUFFALO COUNTY – 2011

Pat and I consider the Hurlbert property to be one of the best pieces of land in Buffalo County – if not the entire state of Wisconsin – for big whitetails. It's an unbelievable piece of land. As Pat mentioned in Chapter 11, the Hurlbert family has been managing this 5,000-acre tract for over 20 years and the whitetail age structure is phenomenal. The place is loaded with big bucks, and since it's not far from our home, we can get there easily for a morning or afternoon hunt when we're in town and not out traveling somewhere.

With that said, I had hunted this land for three years in a row and had nothing to show for my efforts. During those years I had one big-buck encounter after another, but something always seemed to happen at the last minute and I could never seem to seal the deal.

In 2009, we beat our heads against the wall hunting the property day in and day out during early season – all to no avail. We thought early season would be a great time to be in there but something always seemed to go wrong – the weather wouldn't cooperate or we just couldn't make things happen the way we hoped they would. It had rained almost continuously, and being soggy so much of the time didn't helped matters.

In 2010, the second year of hunting the Hurlbert property, it was more of the same. I hunted the entire fall and into late winter without filling my tag. We were following the landowners' strict management program and were only allowed to shoot 8-pointers, 9-pointers and extremely old bucks. That was fine with us, because on this property many of the so-called "management" bucks we could shoot were absolute monsters. I ended up going after one very old buck in particular. He was a tall, narrow 8-pointer. I saw him several times but could never get him within bow range.

One evening, I was actually filming Pat when the old-timer I was hunting came right in. He never really offered Pat a good broadside opportunity though, so Pat didn't attempt to shoot. Later that same year in December, we went to check a trail camera we had put

A number of trail camera photos had been taken of Nicole's buck shortly before she had her heart-pounding encounter.

out earlier. Pat looked down into a small ravine where he'd placed the camera and there was the buck I'd been hunting all season long lying dead in a grape thicket.

The deer had somehow gotten the left side of his main beam hooked underneath a thick grape vine. Apparently he was never able to work himself free. It must have been a horrible death. Nature can be so brutal at times. It's amazing how many freak accidents like this claim the lives of big mature bucks. So the buck I had hoped to shoot was dead and I ended up eating another tag sandwich in 2010.

In 2011, I was more than ready to see my luck change. I was determined to turn things around and make something happen on this special property. Early on, I missed a shot at a big mature 8-pointer, but we continued to hunt the property hard. We hunted several different waterholes during the early-rut period. We finally figured out that the Hurlbert property is phenomenal during the rut because there are so many big bucks running around looking for does. It's like someone turns on a light switch. During the first few days of the rut, I had several encounters with big bucks. Once again, though, I could never seem to

seal the deal.

One evening, we had three nice bucks chasing a doe near the waterhole we were hunting. Pat and I were set up near the bottom of a big ridge, and the three bucks ran that doe completely around the waterhole and back and forth across the ridge above us. We had great visibility and were totally spellbound watching them run all over that ridgetop. Naturally, we hoped one of the bucks would come down to our side of the waterhole and I might get a shot, but that never happened.

After watching those three bucks and several others, we decided to adjust our stand location. Pat thought we should be on the other side of the waterhole where most of the action was taking place. However, he knew the wind could be extremely tricky. In the bluff country of Buffalo County, thermals are very difficult to hunt. You almost need to hunt the opposite way of how you would normally hunt. For instance, if you're hunting a certain spot with an east wind, you really need to hunt that spot as though you were hunting a west wind because the thermals shift things around so much. I know that sounds crazy but it's true.

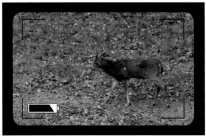

The left side of Nicole's Wisconsin warrior had two broken tines from fighting, but she was thrilled to be able to seal the deal. "To me, being able to get a big, mature buck like this into bow range is always an extraordinary accomplishment," she said.

Pat and I moved our stand to the other side of the waterhole right near the edge of a field and hunted the new location several evenings. The waterhole always seemed to come alive about an hour before dark. We saw all kinds of deer activity but I never came close to getting a shot. From trail camera photos, we knew there was an extremely old buck in the area. He was a huge, heavy 9-pointer and we estimated him to be around 9 years old. We also had photos of a number of other good bucks, but I sort of set my sights on bringing down that ancient old warrior.

Pat was very confident in the waterhole because the rut was in full swing. The weather had been fairly dry, and with the number of big bucks we'd seen out cruising for does, sooner or later we knew one of them would have to come in for a drink. Many good stand locations are strictly afternoon locations. We've made this point before: If you try to hunt these spots in the morning, you can ruin the area and ruin your chances for a good afternoon hunt. Because of early morning feeding activity, you'll often run the deer out

After some frustrating Wisconsin bow-hunts, Nicole shot this grizzled, old 9-pointer. Watch the video here!

of a good afternoon spot by trying to slip in before daylight when a lot of deer are still up and feeding or bedded nearby.

In this case, we knew we could get into the waterhole stand with minimal disturbance, so Pat said, "Let's try a morning hunt." We went in and got set up. About 9:30 a.m., Pat was watching a trail out to his right and I was looking at everything out in front of us and to the left. Suddenly Pat whispered, "Big buck!"

It was him, the ancient 9-pointer I had targeted. I

didn't realize it at the time, but he had several broken tines. Because of all the time I had put into hunting this property and all of the frustrations I had endured here over the past 2½ seasons, including many close encounters, my adrenalin was pumping overtime and my heart was beating almost out of control. All I wanted to do was get an arrow into this old bruiser. It didn't matter that a few of his tines were broken. To me, getting a big, mature buck like this into bow range would be an extraordinary accomplishment if I could pull it off.

In he came, walking along a trail. When he got within 20 yards, I came to full draw. He had a tiny bald spot right behind his shoulder about the size of a half dollar, so that was a perfect bull's-eye to aim at. I aimed for that spot and released my arrow. When the arrow hit, it didn't get much penetration. It was still sticking out as he ran off and I was immediately concerned.

He ran up the hill just out of my sight, but Pat could still see him through the viewfinder of the camera from his vantage point in the tree several feet above me. The hill the deer had run up was fairly steep. Just as I finally got him in my binoculars, he suddenly tipped forward and started tumbling downhill end over end. After I knew he was down for good, I came unglued.

It had been a frustrating three years and now I finally had a buck on the ground worthy of all that effort. He had a dark, chocolate-colored rack with massive bases, and a square blocky head and neck so typical of an old bruiser. His left brow tine and G-3 were broken. But to me he was an exceptional trophy. For sure, he was my biggest Wisconsin whitetail to date and a buck that I would not soon forget!

LATE SEASON IN IOWA – 2010

It was early January 2010 and I was hunting with well-known whitetail hunter Steve Snow in south-central Iowa. Steve and his wife are very close friends. Steve is also one of Pat's old *Driven TV* pro staff members and it's always fun to hunt with good friends. Over the years he's taken some true monsters in southeast Iowa.

I love hunting the late season in Iowa, although the weather can be brutal. I had an either-sex tag and an antlerless tag but, of course, I was hoping to shoot a good buck with my Thompson/Center Pro Hunter muzzleloader. As expected, the temperatures were bitter cold, dropping down below zero in the afternoons. In addition, at least 10 inches of snow covered the

What a way to end the season! Nicole shot this late-season Iowa beauty while hunting in deep snow over food with her Thompson/Center muzzleloader in early January 2010.

"I love hunting late season," Nicole says, "but Pat and I are always bummed when the season ends and we can't hunt anymore. Oh well, there's always next year!"

ground. In that kind of weather, you can't even stand to have your hands out of a hand muff for more than a minute or two, or your fingers will be absolutely frozen. That's just the weather you want for late season, but it certainly doesn't make it any easier.

On the first afternoon hunt, Pat and I had to walk through knee-deep snow to get to our permanent ground blind. If you've ever had to trudge through deep snow carrying all of your hunting gear as well as heavy camera equipment, you'll understand just how difficult and physically challenging it can be. We were carrying my gun, my shooting sticks, two heavy backpacks, a heavy production camera and a heavy tripod. Talk about a workout!

We were hunting over standing corn and what was left of a field of soybeans. It was a great spot and well worth the effort. Not long after we got set up, a monster 5-by-5 typical stepped out in front of the blind at about 125 yards. Holy cow! He had to be pushing 190 typical inches. This was the largest typical buck I'd ever seen. And wouldn't you know it – I was on a management hunt on this particular piece of property. I could only shoot an 8- or 9-pointer, so all I could do was gawk at that incredible buck through my Nikons and shake my head. Pat and I sat there in total awe. It was unbelievable watching him. Even though I couldn't shoot him, just seeing a buck of that size made the trip worthwhile.

We went back to camp and told Steve about what

we'd seen, and he told us he had another spot where he'd just cut the corn a few days earlier. He said the deer were literally pouring into that cut corn. We headed to the new location very early the next afternoon thinking we'd have plenty of time to set up and let things settle down before the deer started coming out to feed. Sounds like a good strategy, right? As we reached the top of a little rise about 150 yards from the permanent blind we planned to use, we peaked over into the field and it was already full of deer.

Standing right out in front of the blind was a very large 9-pointer – a shooter in every respect. Plus, since he was a 9-point he qualified as a management buck. It was only about 2:00 in the afternoon, but the deer were already on their feet and feeding because of the extreme cold. In addition to the weather, there was another reason these deer were out feeding so early. The property was extremely well managed, and Steve went to great pains to make sure that hunting pressure was minimal. These deer felt comfortable coming out in midafternoon because they had not been pressured.

I could have shot the buck from where we were hidden on the little rise, but it would have been difficult for Pat to set up the camera out in the open and get the kind of footage he needed for a good TV segment. So we decided to continue on to the blind and set up properly inside – knowing we would clear the field of deer but hoping more deer would come out later in the afternoon. We knew these deer had not been pressured all season long so we felt like the gamble was worth it.

It took less than 45 minutes for the deer to start flooding back into the field. We saw numerous does, fawns and small bucks. Then out came an absolute stud of a buck. He was an old, old buck but you could tell he still had a lot of fight left in him. He was a tall 9-pointer and had crab claws in the front which gave him a lot of character; we figured he would score in the 150s. He had five points on his left side and four on the right, and was easily 6½ years old. He came out in front of us and walked to within about 50 yards of the blind. I made a fairly easy shot with my T/C and he took off but he didn't go far.

Despite the miserably cold weather and the challenges that such weather presents late in the season, it was a memorable hunt in every way. Pat and I had seen a magnificent typical buck that was absolutely huge, and we ended the hunt by shooting an old-timer that I was very proud to put my tag on. It was now early January and for us the 2009-2010 hunting season was over. We were both bummed that we couldn't hunt anymore, but we couldn't wait until next year!

CHAPTER 13

PROVEN GROUND BLIND STRATEGIES

"You can get away with a lot in a ground blind," Pat and Nicole both say with a smile. *"And with our wild bunch, we need all the help we can get."* The Reeve family hunters love to hunt from ground blinds. Pictured from left to right are Cole, Olivia, Nicole, Isabel, Pat and Carson.

"During the past five or six seasons, Nicole and I have hunted out of pop-up ground blinds more and more each year, especially when we go to Canada," Pat says. "You can get very close for bow-hunting and the video footage is always outstanding."

Ten or 12 years ago, if you told someone you were going to hunt out of a portable ground blind to shoot a big whitetail, they'd probably call you crazy. A lot of people hunted out of permanent structures like elevated box blinds, and some hunters built brush blinds for turkeys and deer out of whatever natural material happened to be available. But very few hunters used portable ground blinds because most people believed they were not very effective for deer hunting. In those days, most bow-hunters hunted out of trees because they didn't think that deer would come close enough to a ground blind for a shot.

Boy how times have changed! Now it seems that everyone is using pop-up or portable ground blinds as part of their hunting arsenal, and many great bucks have been taken out of them in recent years. What's more, if you take a look at how many manufacturers are making ground blinds these days, you realize just how important they've become to the deer hunting industry.

Nicole and I have had great success using ground blinds for whitetails and other big-game species in recent years. We love filming out of them because the quality of the footage we get is outstanding. At ground level, the deer look more majestic, the action is more intense since you're so close, and the overall footage is much more appealing to watch. I like the excitement level that you get on the ground when you are at eye level with a big buck. You can't get that kind of in-

Pat photographed this curious buck from a ground blind while hunting over a bait pile.

your-face excitement while hunting out of a treestand.

Also, if no trees are available to hunt from in the spot you need to be, ground blinds offer a great alternative. Two of the most important keys to using ground blinds successfully are putting them in the right place, and brushing them in properly. Even though they come camouflaged, there is much you can do to make your blind blend in with its surroundings using natural vegetation. Covering a ground blind with natural vegetation like grass, reeds or tree limbs found in the immediate area can make it virtually disappear.

"As long as we have the wind in our faces, we seldom have a problem being scented by any species of big game when we're on the ground," Pat says. "We always try to set up so that the game will be in front of us and not behind us."

MAKE SURE YOU'RE TOTALLY CONCEALED

Nicole and I love to hunt food sources like corn, alfalfa or clover. We'll often set up a ground blind inside the standing corn and cover it with corn stalks. After we're finished, that blind looks like a big beaver lodge covered with corn. All you can see from the outside are two black holes where the windows are located. We always keep the front windows open for filming and bow-hunting purposes. However, we never open the windows behind us because we don't want to be silhouetted. We make sure the background behind us is totally dark. Sometimes we even wear darker clothes inside the blind to keep everything as dark as possible.

If your ground blind is set up in a good spot, you know it's just a matter of time before the deer will be feeding right out in front of you. And believe me, there's nothing more exciting than watching a big buck munch on corn 20 feet away. As a rule, when-

ever we hunt from a ground blind we try to keep the action in front of us. We want the wind to be in our faces and all of the deer we are watching out in front of the blind. You don't want the deer to get behind you and catch your wind. Sometimes we'll set up in a field facing the woods next to a hay bale or brush pile. Any kind of cover we can find, like a small bunch of trees or a little depression in the terrain might be a good place to conceal a ground blind. A setup like that is good for both filming and hunting.

As long as we have the wind in our faces, we seldom have a problem being scented. Ground blinds seem to contain scent very well. They're also a lot warmer than treestands during extremely cold weather. Where filming for TV is involved, ground blinds offer Nicole and I another great advantage. When the weather is snowy, wet, windy and generally nasty, being in a ground blind helps protect our expensive camera equipment. You can imagine what kind of wear and tear our camera gear goes through when exposed to the elements in a treestand. Keeping your camera dry is extremely important as humidity really affects cameras. If a camera gets wet, it might shut down. A lot of moisture in the air will also sometimes shut down a camera. And if it shuts down, the hunt is over. Ground blinds keep you in the game.

Nicole and I hunt in Saskatchewan every year. During the past four seasons there, we've shot nearly 100 percent of our whitetails out of ground blinds. In 2012, I shot a monster that weighed 300 pounds out of a pop-up blind. He was an old buck that was known to be very nocturnal. The outfitter had set up a ladder stand in the area where the buck had been seen and photographed, but it wouldn't accommodate two people.

So our guide, cameraman Bryan Lemke and I drove to the area one afternoon and placed a ground blind underneath a pine tree. There was a treestand in the pine above us but it wouldn't hold two people. More importantly though, there was very little cover around the area we planned to hunt and I felt like hunting out of a tree would be pretty difficult. It would be easy for the deer to pick us off in that tree. Because of the very tight hunting situation, and the fact that I was hunting

with a bow, I felt like a ground blind would be better in that situation. We brushed in the blind with pine limbs, and when we were through you couldn't even tell it was there.

We hunted out of it for several days without seeing that nocturnal buck. On the last day of the hunt, he finally came in. He glanced over at the ground blind but never batted an eye. I made a perfect double-lung shot on him with my Mathews at 20 yards. He only ran 10 yards and fell over. He was a heavy-beamed 5-by-5 with several stickers for a total of 13 scorable points. He was also the heaviest buck I have ever killed. We weighed him on a scale and he legitimately weighed 350 pounds.

Ideally, it's best to hunt out of a ground blind that has been set up for a while, at least a week if not longer, so that the deer can get accustomed to it. Sometimes you don't have that luxury and that's why it's so important to make your ground blind blend in with its surroundings. I've noticed a lot of deer seem to be a little more nervous around blinds that are not brushed-in. Unless they're preoccupied by some other distraction like a bait pile or decoy, they'll usually be a little

Pat and Nicole often spend the entire day inside a ground blind, patiently waiting for that magical moment to occur, often reading a good book, but always ready for action at a moment's notice.

Watch Pat close the deal on the trophy buck known as Pincher – from a ground blind!

When a manufactured pop-up blind isn't available, or when they have to move stand locations on the spur of the moment for one reason or another, Pat and Nicole often hunt from make-shift brush blinds built from whatever natural materials are nearby.

more suspicious of a blind that is not brushed in. On several occasions I've seen bucks circle around to the downwind side and test the wind. If a buck doesn't detect any danger, he'll usually go on about his business. But if he gets a whiff of something he doesn't like, you'll probably never see him again.

If you do decide to set up your ground blind several weeks before you plan to hunt it, make sure it's firmly staked down, especially in an open field situation. I can't tell you how many times I've recovered the pieces of torn blinds with broken and bent poles that were blown into the woods during a sudden windstorm.

THE RIGHT CHAIR IS VERY IMPORTANT

Make sure you have a good chair or stool to sit on before you get in your blind for an afternoon or an entire day. Outfitters are notorious for using noisy, uncomfortable chairs that are difficult, if not impossible to hunt from. Oftentimes they'll use metal fold-up chairs that are extremely noisy and cold to sit on

when it's below zero outside. Sitting in an uncomfortable chair where the legs are constantly sinking into the ground and throwing you off balance makes for a miserable afternoon of hunting.

A good ground blind chair should be quiet, comfortable and easy to shoot a bow or rifle from. Try your chair out before you spend hours sitting in it. Better yet, buy a folding chair that fits your needs and set it up in the backyard. Practice shooting from it. Can you come to full draw from it in a natural position without affecting your balance and anchor point? Can you effectively shoot an arrow out the window of your blind? These are important questions that need to be considered ahead of time. Make sure your ground blind chair works for you.

GREAT FOR CHILDREN

You can get away with a lot more in a ground blind than you can a treestand. That's why ground blinds are so great for kids. I've had all four of my kids in a blind with me before and never alarmed any deer. My oldest son Cole doesn't like to hunt, but he loves to go with me while I'm hunting. He loves to watch deer and he'll often take pictures of deer with his own camera.

It's so important for first-time hunters to have a positive experience, especially youngsters. If they don't, they may never want to go deer hunting again. Ground blind hunting has a way of making them want to come back and do it again. My youngest daughter Isabel loves to sit in a ground blind. She'll bring her coloring book and a backpack full of snacks and she's set for the day. Sometimes when Nicole and I have all the kids in a ground blind with us they'll bring enough food and snacks to survive for a week. We may not shoot a deer, but at least we know we're not going to

Spruce and cedar limbs always work well in front of a brush blind, and the aromatic odor from these evergreen species helps mask human scent.

Carson and Olivia Reeve pose in front of a homemade hay bale blind. Pat has taken several good bucks from hay bale blinds set up in open fields. Double Bull also makes one that looks exactly like a rolled bale of hay.

go hungry!

Where children are concerned, ground blinds are much warmer as mentioned, and they keep everyone out of the really bad weather like rain, snow or sleet. They also offer much better concealment from the deer. They're perfect for kids in so many ways because they help create such a positive outdoor experience.

When it comes to purchasing a ground blind, you definitely get what you pay for. It's worthwhile to spend a little more and buy a quality blind. I can tell you from experience that the cheaper models will not last much beyond a single season. Look for quality material that is durable. Look for good craftsmanship in the sewing and zippers. Some of those zippers made in China will drive you crazy! Look for material that is quiet in the woods and a ground blind that is stable and tight when set up. Make sure it has no flapping material that will make deer very nervous.

Many hunters like to set up ground blinds and leave them in the woods indefinitely. Others take them down and store them away at the end of a hunt or at the end of the season. There are obvious advantages in doing both. Deer do get used to seeing blinds that remain in the woods and become permanent fixtures. However, it doesn't take long for the wind and weather to do its job on manmade materials. Mice can also do a lot of damage to ground blinds that are left out. If you buy a good, quality blind and take care of it, that is, take it down after a couple of weeks of hunting, it'll last you for years to come.

USING GROUND BLINDS IN THE OPEN

As mentioned, you can get away with a lot in a ground blind. Several years ago, I was in Saskatchewan hunting velvet deer in early September. I was out one day hunting with a friend named Jimmy Hanson. We were hunting over a decoy in the middle of a large field with no cover. We had set up a Double Bull pop-up ground blind right beside a round hay bale in the middle of the field. A big buck came out, jumped the fence and started feeding several hundred yards

There is nothing more exciting than hunting on the ground using natural cover to hide in. This is whitetail hunting in its purest form!

View the amazing footage of Pat taking a huge New Mexico elk from the ground!

away. Jimmy grunted at him but he ignored the grunt. A few minutes later, he seemed to pick up some sort of scent. He looked over and saw the decoy and came marching right in.

My buddy Jimmy shot him at 15 yards. The buck never paid the least bit of attention to the ground blind. Maybe it blended in so well that it looked like a round bale. I've had that same thing happen several other times where deer didn't pay any attention to a ground blind that was set up out in the open with no cover around it at all. But sometimes they do. You never really know how they might react. Most people wouldn't even think about setting up a ground blind out in the open like that, but sometimes you have to go for broke and try something different in order to make things happen.

NATURAL GROUND BLINDS

Every once in a while, Nicole and I get into a situation where the wind is wrong for a certain treestand we planned to hunt. All of a sudden we have to set up on the ground and use natural vegetation to build a makeshift brush blind. It's not always an easy thing to do – especially if you're trying to do it in the predawn darkness. To do it right it takes some time and you usually cre-

Pat watches a group of deer only a few yards away from a natural ground blind in Canada where he and his cameraman took advantage of the available cover – spruce limbs, logs and branches – to hide behind.

ate at least some noise while getting it built.

If time allows however, you can improvise a natural ground blind using whatever natural vegetation is available; various high grasses, limbs from fallen trees, or cut limbs from whatever trees are growing in the area. Nicole and I have done everything from digging out small depressions in hillsides with shovels,

Sometimes natural blinds work better than manufactured blinds. For instance, if you are hunting on a field edge, you can tuck back into the woods a few yards and become almost invisible.

to covering ourselves up with cedar or pine limbs. Sometimes natural blinds work better than manufactured blinds because they utilize natural materials. This is especially true if you are hunting on a field edge. In that case, you can tuck back into the woods a few yards and become almost invisible.

In 2012, the wind was a big factor while we were hunting in Illinois. So Nicole and I tucked ourselves back into some hanging grape vines and built a perfect little ground blind. We backed up against a large tree and used the vines in front of us for concealment. It was a great setup. We had deer pass by within 10 to 15 yards. As long as you sit still and watch the wind, you

ought to be able to remain undetected. Sometimes deer may be moving through the woods behind you and they'll scent you and blow. In those cases there's not much you can do, but if you choose your spot carefully, most of the deer will be moving out in front of you.

In 2007, I shot a nice buck in Canada out of a natural blind I had made in some spruce trees. The TV show I was filming for wouldn't allow the use of any portable or manufactured blinds. Everything had to be natural. So I tucked back into some spruce limbs, cut a few to put in front of me and ended up shooting a beautiful 157-inch buck at very close range with my bow.

There's no question that hunting out of a natural ground blind gets you up close and personal with the deer. If you want a good adrenalin rush, try it sometime.

CONCEALING GROUND BLINDS AND STANDS

If I had to pick one key element that has contributed the most to the hunting success Nicole and I have enjoyed over the years, I would have to say that being able to remain undetected has to rank at the top. No matter where we are hunting, Nicole and I go to great pains to make sure the deer we are hunting do not see us. We are fanatics about remaining well concealed at all times. We always try to brush-in our treestands and ground blinds with leaves, branches, cornstalks or whatever other local material is available. It takes some time and effort to do this, but it really pays off.

In the early season, when the leaves are still on the trees, I'll often cut short oak limbs to place around our treestands because oaks seem to retain their leaves longer after they are cut. We'll put those branches in the grates of our stands and build sort of a "squirrel's nest" of cover around us. If oak limbs aren't available, we might use pine boughs, cedar limbs or other natural foliage. Cedar works great and also stays green for a long time. We always carry a pack of zip ties with us and use them to bundle some of the branches together, or secure them to the stand so that they stay in place. If real leaves are not available, we'll sometimes use commercial leaf products.

With two people in a tree, there is a lot more for a deer to see and a lot more camera movement, but the squirrel's nest effect that we create with tree branches allows us to get away with quite a bit. If we're hunting out of a double ladder stand, we always try to brush-in the ladder from the ground up as well, using zip ties and any natural foliage that might be available. Deer do tend to get used to ladder stands that have been out in the woods for a year or so, but if we're hunting a situation where the ladder has just been put out,

brushing it in is very important.

We do the same thing with ground blinds. We try to make them blend in with their surroundings. If we're hunting standing corn, we'll brush-in the blind with

Even if they're high in a tree, Pat and Nicole always try to use camo netting, cedar or spruce limbs, or other natural material to help break up their outlines. They know that mature bucks don't often give you a second chance.

No matter where they hunt, Pat and Nicole always go to great lengths to remain hidden at all times. They always brush-in both treestands and ground blinds with leaves, long grass, branches, cornstalks or whatever other local materials might be available.

Knowing that two people sitting in a tree with lots of bulky camera equipment often stand out like a sore thumb, Pat and Nicole take every precaution they can to remain hidden. "Always keep your movement to a minimum," Pat says.

corn stalks as mentioned earlier. If we're hunting out in the open near round bales, we'll try to camouflage the blind so that it looks like a bale of hay. Speaking of hay bales, Double Bull actually makes a blind that looks like a rolled hay bale.

Remaining concealed until the shot is made has been very important to me over the years. It doesn't matter whether I'm set up five or 25 feet off the ground. I always try to break up my outline. Height doesn't matter as much to me as being concealed. Sometimes it depends on the location. If the deer are walking up a hill behind your stand, you might be at eye level with them at some point. In that case, being totally concealed is even more important.

CHAPTER 14

THE AMAZING ALBINOS OF BUFFALO COUNTY

Albino deer are protected statewide in Wisconsin. For reasons unknown, Buffalo County seems to produce an unusual number of these amazing whitetails.

Pat was turkey hunting one spring on Tom Indrebo's property in Buffalo County when he discovered this beautiful albino fawn.

Over the course of her life, Tom and Pat followed the albino doe and documented her life with numerous photographs and extensive video footage.

Through all my years of being associated with Tom Indrebo – guiding for him and photographing deer with him in the early days – we followed a number of deer in Buffalo County, Wis. Over time, we accumulated quite a library of photos and video on some of these deer. Three of those deer that really stood out in our minds and hearts were albinos. We documented them from year to year and pretty much followed them throughout their entire lives.

For some reason Buffalo County produces an unusual number of albino deer. Albinos are protected in Wisconsin, and although some of these white deer no doubt get killed by poachers because of their unique color, many are able to survive to maturity. Except for their color, albinos are normal in every way. They do tend to have certain health problems later in life such as blindness – caused by lack of pigmentation in their eyes. Bright sunlight and the reflective light off the snow have contributed to the total blindness of many albinos. And once a deer loses its sight, its days are numbered.

A WHITE DOE

The first albino we got involved with was a beautiful little doe. I came upon her as a newborn fawn while I was turkey hunting one spring on Tom's farm. She was lying in a patch of dark leaves and her tiny white body stuck out like a sore thumb. I couldn't believe it. To me, finding an albino fawn in the woods was like winning the lottery.

We tried not to disturb her in any way. Instead, we frantically scrambled back to Tom's farmhouse to grab a couple of still cameras and a video camera. She was still in the same place when we returned and we tried to document our discovery in every way. We took pictures of her pink eyes and tiny pink hooves and it was a special treat for us to be able to record such a rare sight on film. We never did see the mother but I'm sure she was not far away.

Over the course of the next few years, we followed the life of that doe and documented it on film. Obviously she was very easy to recognize. She never traveled very far from her home range so she was usually

Don't miss this remarkable footage of the amazing albino deer of Buffalo County.

The albino doe lived to be 9 years old. Pat found her dead one spring in the area where she had spent most of her life. Over the years, she produced a number of healthy, normal fawns.

fairly easy to locate. Throughout her lifetime, she was pretty much a homebody and surprisingly never really moved a long way from her core area. Since I always assumed that most whitetails eventually venture out from their home range at certain times of the year, I was really surprised to learn that some deer confine themselves to one small area much more than others – especially in our part of the country. In other places, deer may be forced to range out because of food availability, hunting pressure or other factors that might cause them to travel away from their core areas.

We were able to follow the albino doe pretty easily through the summer and fall months, but after we had snow on the ground she was much more difficult to locate because she blended in with her surroundings so well.

Albinos have a history of poor vision. Since there is no pigment in their eyes, spending months in a snow-covered habitat probably triggers snow blindness. The eyes have no protection, and after years of being exposed to extremely bright sunlight reflected off the snow, the eyes become seriously damaged. I'm sure this was the case with her. I ended up finding her dead one spring when she was about 9½ years old. Interestingly enough, we checked to see if she'd been bred and sure enough, she had two fawns inside her. She had already given birth to a number of normal fawns each year, and I was amazed to see that she was still producing fawns at that age.

THE DOVER BUCK

The second albino we followed was a buck. We discovered him one day out on one of Tom's outlying farms. He became known as the Dover Buck. We followed him from the time he was a yearling until he was 6½ years old. As he matured, he grew a very wide rack and at one point had two short droptines. He never grew a truly giant rack but the thing that set him apart was his body size. He was enormous. In his prime, he probably had a body weight of over 300 pounds. It was always neat to photograph him because

he was such a large deer. We saw him on a frequent basis because he also pretty much stayed on one part of Tom's farm, and never seemed to venture far from his home range.

When he was 6½ years old, he started going downhill very rapidly. In the spring during antler growing time, he appeared to be as healthy as ever. But by late summer, he was blind in one eye and beginning to lose weight. In September, Tom found him at the end of a farm road one day walking in circles. His eyes had become infected and he was blind. Both eyes were clouded over and had apparently been that way for some time. Tom estimated that he had lost half his body weight, and called the Department of Natural Resources and they came out and put him out of his misery.

THE GREATEST ALBINO BUCK OF ALL TIME

The third albino deer we followed was a buck that we discovered in the same region as the albino doe. The two deer could have been related, but we had no way of proving that one way or the other. When he was a yearling, this unimpressive buck hardly had any

As a yearling, the legendary buck that would come to be known as the "Albino" had a small, non-descript rack. No one could have guessed that he would eventually grow a world-class set of antlers.

Known widely across the country as the greatest albino that ever lived, the Albino of Buffalo County eventually grew a typical rack that scored over 190 inches.

rack at all – just one short spike on one side. Maybe that's why he surprised so many people later in life. The "Albino" as he became known, surpassed everyone's wildest expectations as far as his antler growth was concerned. He eventually grew a typical rack that scored over 190 inches.

At the age of 3½, the Albino began to really blossom. A good friend of mine John Dummer, who owns the WhitetailWorld.com website, produced an excellent in-depth video on the life of the Albino titled *The Ghost Buck*. Ten years in the making, John's video documents the buck's life from 2000 to 2010. The Albino lived to be 10½.

John got some excellent video footage of the Albino as the deer matured. So did Tom Indrebo, his son Shane and John Charles, a landowner who owned property next to John Dummer. Several times during the winter John Charles was able to videotape the deer in his backyard right out of his kitchen window.

Eventually the Albino grew into a world-class typical. In 2004, the 4½-year-old deer grew a massive 5-by-6 rack. Its sheds were found the following spring and estimated to have scored just over 180 inches. In 2005, the Albino grew several non-typical points and his shed antlers later scored around 185 inches. As a 6 year old, he grew his best rack ever – a massive 5-by-5 with a split brow that scored just over 190 typical inches.

The Albino continued to grow an impressive rack for two more years. Then in 2009, he started going

The Wisconsin Department of Natural Resources was called in to put the Albino down during his 10th year after he had gone downhill and lost over half his body weight. Coyotes had bitten large chunks out of his hindquarters before he was found and humanely put out of his misery.

ALBINOS

Albinism is caused by a lack of pigment due to a recessive gene. True albino deer have pink eyes and pink hooves. Albino animals are fairly common in the wild and it is estimated that about one deer in 20,000 will be albino. Albino snakes, squirrels, rabbits, raccoons and opossums are not that uncommon to see in the wild as well. However, since they do stand out because of their color, albino prey species like squirrels and rabbits tend to be easy pickings for predators. In northern areas, albino deer are easy marks for wolves and coyotes.

An albino doe will have many normal fawns during her lifetime, but she is also capable of having an albino fawn at any time. Because of their significantly larger numbers, albino whitetails are much more common than albino mule deer.

PIEBALDS

Spotted, patched or mottled deer are known as piebalds. Often mistaken for albinos, piebalds do not have the pink eyes or hooves of a true albino. A piebald may be all white or nearly all white, or it may be spotted or blotched. Piebald deer are genetic mutations also caused by recessive genes. In addition to their odd color, piebalds usually have numerous other genetic defects like curvature of the spine, an overbite problem, poor hearing and certain internal defects. They seldom live a normal life span because of these defects. Piebalds are legal to kill in most states and are considered great trophies by many hunters.

Interestingly, much like the rare white buffalo on the western plains, white deer were considered to be spiritual, and in some cases thought to possess magical powers by various tribes of American Indians.

As a 6-year-old, the Albino grew his best rack ever, a massive main-frame 5-by-5 rack with a split brow tine.

downhill. He survived the winter but began losing considerable body weight. Having reached the age of 10 in the spring of 2010, he was just starting to grow large nubs of velvet antlers when his health apparently failed drastically. When local landowners discovered that coyotes were starting to chew large sections out of his hindquarters while he was still alive, the DNR was called in to put him down.

The Albino buck is easily the largest typical albino ever recorded in North America. Like the smaller albino buck Tom and I had documented, this deer also grew an enormous body to match his rack. Unfortunately, the Albino relocated to another piece of property during his last few years of life. Tom, Shane and John Charles continued to get occasional video footage and a few still photos of the deer on other properties, but the owner of the property on which he had relocated to would not allow anyone to film the deer or continue documenting him in any way.

John Dummer put together his excellent DVD chronicling the Albino's life from various video footage segments he shot himself, as well as from video segments and still photos shot by Tom, Shane and John Charles. He has put together an amazing record of the buck's life and he deserves a lot of credit for his

See some of the amazing video of the famous Albino buck.

efforts. You can purchase the DVD at his Whitetail-World.com website.

I started profiling the albinos and showing their story lines back in 2000 when I was producing the *Prime Time Bucks* video series for Hunter's Specialities. Unusual stories about unique occurrences in the deer woods were always very intriguing to me, and I felt that it was very important to document some of those stories on video so that hunters could enjoy them and learn from them. I continued doing story lines on the albinos when I was with *North American Whitetail Television* on the "Muzzy Moments" segments and people seemed to love them. Later still, I included stories about some of the albinos in my own productions on *Driven TV*.

CHAPTER 15

NEVER SAY NEVER

NICOLE'S LATE-SEASON MAGIC

Pat and Nicole captured these unbelievable photos of a world-class 7-by-7 while hunting in Wisconsin in 2012. Pat estimated the massive buck had a rack scoring around 204 typical inches. The buck was believed to be alive and well in 2013.

oming off a high from my 2011 hunt, I was excited to be back on the Hurlbert's property in Buffalo County during the rut in November of 2012. By now, Pat and I had learned from experience that hunting over waterholes during the rut on this land was our ace in the hole. If the weather conditions were right, that is, if it was dry and the bucks were out looking for does, hunting over one of our favorite waterholes was always going to be productive. Waterholes are like magnets at certain times of the year.

We started hunting the property hard during the first week of the rut. Right off the bat we had several encounters with bucks chasing does. It looked like it was going to be a great evening to be in the woods. Pretty soon, in came a buck I had passed up the year

Even when you're out in the woods hunting your heart out almost every day of the season like Pat and Nicole, there will be times when nothing seems to go right and tags remain unfilled.

This big Wisconsin 10-pointer is the buck Nicole set her sights on during the 2012 season. The deer was captured with the same trail camera in the same location as the monstrous 7-by-7 pictured on the first page of this chapter.

before. Now he was a big 4-year-old 10-pointer, but since I was still hunting under management rules, I wasn't sure if I could shoot him or not. As things turned out, he came fairly close to our stand but was constantly on the move, so I couldn't have gotten a shot even if he'd been a deer the owners wanted me to shoot.

We sat for a while longer and prime time was almost upon us. The leaves were extremely crunchy because it was so dry, and you could hear deer coming down the ridge at least 100 yards away. All of a sudden, a doe came in to get a drink. Before she could reach the water however, the woods absolutely exploded with activity. You would have thought someone had opened up the floodgates. The woods literally were on fire. Everywhere you looked, bucks of all sizes were running around chasing that poor little doe. There were so many deer running around I didn't know which way to look.

Finally the frenzied doe ran out in front of us and dove into a small briar thicket about 40 yards away. She tried to hunker down in those briars as best she could in an effort to make all of those bucks leave her alone. But it was not to be. The big 10-pointer I'd just seen would have none of that. He did everything he could do to get her out of those briars. He circled around her several times, then went in and started gouging her with his antlers. He was pushing against

her with his antlers trying to force her to get up.

At last she jumped up and started running toward the water. As she ran, I was horrified to see that her intestines were hanging out underneath her. She had been gouged so severely by one of the bucks chasing her that her cavity had been opened up. I wasn't sure if it had happened earlier with another buck or while she was in the briars trying to get away from the big 10-pointer.

She quickly ran into the water and started gulping it down as fast as she could. You could tell she was totally exhausted and dehydrated. The big 10 pushed her out into the deepest part of the pond and started swimming circles around her. He finally got out of the water, walked over to the edge of the woods and violently started making a scrape. She attempted to stay where she was, but about that time another smaller buck came crashing into the water and started chasing her around again.

The big 10 heard all the commotion, ran over and chased the smaller buck away. Then he started chasing after the doe again. I had never seen anything like this in my entire life. It was unbelievable. While the big buck was chasing the injured doe, smaller bucks were still running circles around us in the woods. It was nuts. Suddenly the doe took off for parts unknown and all of the bucks followed.

One minute they were all there around us, the next

they were gone. Suddenly the woods around us were dead. You could have heard a pin drop. Things were fairly quiet for the remainder of that evening. A big 8-pointer came in just before dark, but he was missing both brow tines so we decided not to shoot him. He never really presented a good shot anyway.

We hunted that waterhole a few more times during the tail end of the rut but never had any further encounters. Since we now had several commitments for out-of-state hunts in other areas, we didn't return to the property until the late season. In addition, the Wisconsin gun season was about to start and the landowners preferred that we weren't there during gun season; because they were primarily gun hunters and that was the only time they hunted.

By late season in mid-December, a lot of snow had fallen in Wisconsin and the temperatures had gotten very cold. We decided to hunt the food sources and concentrate our efforts on a cut corn field on another part of the farm. "If we can get the wind in our favor, I think we can get you a shot," Pat said. So we hung our Big Game treestands on the edge of the cornfield and prepared for some late-season action. Since we were hunting a food source, all of our hunts would be in the afternoon.

SIXTY DAYS WITHOUT A BUCK

To say that I was getting a little antsy about shooting a deer would be an understatement. I had not put a tag on a deer since mid-October while hunting in Saskatchewan, and I was starting to feel like I might never shoot a deer again. Despite numerous encounters over the past 60 days, nothing had gone right. Don't get me wrong; each time I'm out in a treestand with Pat is a special blessing whether I shoot something or not. But when you are filming for TV, there is a whole new dimension to the process of hunting. You put a lot of self-imposed pressure on yourself because

Because late-season hunting almost always involves being close to food sources, most of Pat and Nicole's late-season stand setups are geared for afternoon hunting.

This outstanding 4-by-4, obviously enjoying some Evolved Apple Crush attractant, is the same buck Nicole ended up shooting in late 2012.

Nicole's 2012 4-by-4 feeds in the background.

you feel like you have to produce a show. You still have a passion for hunting and a love for the animal that can never be altered, but there is a lot more stress and strain involved because you want to be successful.

By now, we had three big bucks on our hit list – two mature 8-pointers and one 9-pointer. All three had been photographed several times on our Eyecon trail cameras. We hunted a corn field on three separate evenings without seeing any good bucks. Since it was late in the season, we only had a limited amount of time to devote to this property because we still had a number of unfilled tags in other states. I still had a late-season Iowa muzzleloader tag to try and fill, an Illinois bow tag and my Wisconsin tag. Pat still had his Illinois bow tag, a Minnesota tag and a Wisconsin tag. In all, we had six unfilled tags. So we were trying to decide which state offered the best chance for filling one of those tags.

"I honestly think we have a great chance to get you a deer in Wisconsin," Pat said. "We have plenty of snow on the ground, it's gotten very cold and we have a great food source to hunt." So we loaded up our Polaris electric vehicle and headed for Wisconsin. The next day would be Christmas Eve. By early afternoon we were in our stands and waiting. We knew our best chance would be the last 30 minutes before dark. That's usually when the big boys start to come out.

Just as the light was starting to dwindle, I looked across the field and saw what I thought to be a large buck coming out of the woods about 500 yards away. I got Pat's attention. "I think I see a big buck across

the field," I said. He looked with his binoculars and said, "No, that buck isn't very big." Turns out, he was looking at another deer. Then he saw the buck I was looking at and said, "Oh my gosh! You're right. It's one of the big 8's!"

Even at that distance, my hearted started pounding. Unbelievably, the buck started walking across the field directly toward us. We sat there in total disbelief as he covered the entire 500 yards and walked up to within 20 yards of our treestands. A couple of does and fawns had come out and were feeding right in front of us. So here I was with my bow in hand, a 150-inch 8-pointer broadside at 20 yards in front of me and I couldn't get a shot.

We had put out some Wild Game Innovations apple attractant, and the deer were absolutely pounding it. Where was my big buck? Standing directly behind a tree at 25 yards eating apple attractant. The buck stood there for at least 10 minutes facing us with the tree protecting his vitals. All of a sudden, I saw something out of the corner of my eye. I looked over and the big 9-pointer was walking into the field. He walked in from about 150 yards away and stopped about 50 yards out – just out of range – and started feeding. Pat said, "Which one do you want to shoot?"

"The one that gives me the best shot," I answered.

I started concentrating on the 9-pointer, and Pat got the camera on him. But he was still out of range. About that time, the 8-pointer stepped out from behind the tree and stood perfectly broadside at less than 25 yards. I slowly shifted my body toward the 8-pointer as

Pat turned and got the camera back on him. Just as we were both ready, the deer stepped back behind the tree.

He remained there for what seemed like forever. In truth, it was probably at least 10 minutes. I anxiously stood that entire time ready to come to full draw the moment he offered me a shot. Then, all at once, one of the fawns suddenly spooked at some unknown object, as they are prone to do, and the entire field cleared of deer. So despite having had two of the three deer on our hit list standing in front of us at 25 yards, we ended the evening getting totally skunked.

Even though the next evening was Christmas Eve, we had to go back. We made arrangements with Pat's mom and step-dad to keep the kids for a little while that evening until we got home. After dark, we planned to hurry home and go to a Christmas Eve service with all the kids.

Soon we were back in the same tree. None of the deer had seen us the night before and we still felt very confident about hunting that spot. A doe and fawn were feeding directly in front of us at about 30 yards, and unlike the night before they seemed to be a little spooky. About an hour before dark, we looked up and saw the third buck on our hit list – another big 8-pointer – coming in to feed. This spot was unbelievable!

The buck was approaching at a rapid pace. All of a sudden he started running. He was running directly toward the food plot and the tree we were in. When he was still about 60 yards away, the doe and fawn that had been feeding in the field spooked and started running for the trees. When he saw them running, he got spooked and veered off to one side. He had been coming directly toward us, but now he circled around downwind and easily caught our scent. He blew, and in an instant was gone.

I looked at Pat and shook my head. "You've got to be kidding me," I said. In two nights of hunting we had seen all three of the bucks on our hit list and yet were unable to get a shot.

Because we'd be spending Christmas with the kids and then going to visit my parents in Illinois for a few days right after Christmas, we wouldn't have an opportunity to hunt again in Wisconsin for at least a week. We were particularly excited about spending the holidays with my parents because Pat had promised to take Carson on his very first deer hunt. Carson was still too young to hunt in Minnesota legally, but we had been able to get him a one-time apprentice tag in Illinois and Pat was planning to take him out on my Dad's 50 acres. He was one excited boy! Hopefully, he'd get a chance to shoot his first buck.

Then in early January, after visiting my parents in Illinois over the holidays, Pat and I were planning to drive down to Iowa for a few days before we headed back to Wisconsin. "You might as well try to fill your Iowa muzzleloader tag," Pat said.

LATE-SEASON MAGIC – THREE BUCKS IN FOUR DAYS OF HUNTING

So we headed down to Iowa where we planned to hunt with our good friend Chad Yates. On the second afternoon, I shot an outstanding 8-pointer with my Thompson/Center muzzleloader. Even though my buck appeared to be quite run-down from the rigors of the rut weeks earlier, he had a beautiful rack with long, white tines and a nice, large frame. I was so excited. Maybe at last I was finally beginning to break my two-month jinx. By now, we only had a few days before we had to attend the Archery Trade Association Show in Louisville, Ky. Only two days were left in the Wisconsin season so Pat said, "Let's give it one more go."

We drove all night long from Iowa so that we could get home and hunt in Wisconsin the next day. We planned to hunt the last two days of the Wisconsin season, then immediately drive to the Archery Trade Show. While we were driving home from Iowa, Pat glanced over at me with a panicked look on his face and said, "Do you realize the season is almost over and we don't have any venison in the freezer?"

It was true. We always shoot a couple of does for the freezer in late season, but things had been so crazy and fast-paced the last few weeks we had totally forgotten about it. Throughout the year, we often donate most of our venison to various Feed the Hungry programs or the HUSH Program in Iowa because the logistics of trying to bring meat back home when you're traveling from state to state can be a nightmare. And since we love venison and eat a lot of it, we depend on getting a few does in Minnesota and Wisconsin during the late season. But this year we had waited until the last minute. "If you get the opportunity, you're gonna have to shoot a doe in Wisconsin," Pat said.

As soon as we got home, we put on our camo and headed over to Buffalo County. As usual, we drove our Ranger EV over to the spot we always parked in and climbed up in the same treestand we'd hunted just before Christmas. I had a doe tag and an either-sex archery tag. As luck would have it, that afternoon I made a perfect shot on a nice doe. We never saw any bucks that afternoon. "Now at least we're not going to starve to death," Pat said jokingly.

A little known fact about Pat and I is that no matter where we're hunting, we always gut our own deer, even if we plan to donate the meat to the local food

After an extremely frustrating 60-day period in which Nicole did not fill a single tag despite many close calls, she and Pat decided to go on a late-season muzzleloader hunt in Iowa in early 2013. On the second afternoon, Nicole shot this beautiful 8-pointer with her .50-caliber Thompson/Center.

bank. Pat is a fanatic about doing it right, and so we always do it ourselves. Whenever any of the kids shoot a deer, they have to gut it themselves and help out with butchering the meat. Pat might stand nearby and give helpful hints and instructions, but they do the physical work. We feel like it's all part of their growing process, and it teaches respect for the animal. Nothing we shoot ever goes to waste.

Now we were down to the last day of the season. On the way over to Buffalo County, Pat said, "If we don't see any bucks tonight, and if you get an opportunity to shoot another doe, go ahead and fill your either-sex tag." He was right. It would be much better to fill my tag on a doe than have it go to waste. So that was our mindset as we set up to hunt that second afternoon.

After we'd been sitting awhile, a couple of does and small fawns started coming into the field. We saw no sign of any of the big bucks we were hoping to see. Pat said, "Well what do you think?"

"I don't know," I answered. "Maybe the bucks are on a different pattern now. Maybe I should go ahead and shoot another doe."

"That sounds good to me," Pat said.

A few minutes later, one of the does stepped into range and I came to full draw on her. She had been standing perfectly broadside with her head down feeding, but just as I was about to release my arrow she shifted her body so that she was facing toward me. I couldn't shoot. I had to let down. Just as I let down – with the idea of waiting for her to turn broadside again – I looked up and saw one of the big 8-pointers we were after coming down the hill into the field. I couldn't believe it! He was a brute, and he was coming in hard like there was no tomorrow. What's more, he was coming right to us!

I waited until he got within 25 yards. I carefully aimed and released the arrow that originally had been intended for the doe. It was a good shot. He ran about 50 or 60 yards and piled up. He had a beautiful dark-colored rack with bladed tines. We figured he was 5½ years old. He also had a gorgeous cape with white markings around his eyes and throat patch. He was very distinguished looking and I was very proud. After the shot, I was so excited I almost fell out of the tree. It had been such a long, hard season and I was so relieved. It felt extremely good to know we had been down to the wire and had finally pulled it off. I couldn't believe it!

So Pat and I were planning to leave very early the next morning for the Archery Trade Show in Louisville. But we ended up dealing with my buck for the next few hours that night, filming recoveries, a very time-consuming process, and getting him out of the woods. Since we also wanted good daylight photos of him, we spent several hours the next morning taking some good still photos. After we were through, we hung my buck in the cooler and got cleaned up. I quickly threw some of my dress clothes together for

Witness Nicole breaking a streak of bad luck with this beautiful Wisconsin buck.

With only two days left in the Wisconsin season, Pat and Nicole rushed over to Buffalo County upon returning from Iowa to try to fill Nicole's unused Wisconsin tag. On the last day of the season, Nicole shot this outstanding main-frame 4-by-4 with bladed tines and a sticker on its left burr.

the trade show and we got ready to head to Kentucky.

For all practical purposes, my hunting was over for the year, or at least it should have been. I had not shot a buck from mid-October to the beginning of January, but now in the span of several days, I had two fine late-season bucks to my credit. Suddenly Pat had a brainstorm. Always looking for every opportunity, always the driven deer hunter, always thinking about ways he could make the show better, he said, "Since we'll be driving through Illinois on our way to and from Kentucky, and since we both still have either-sex Illinois archery tags, why don't we pack our hunting gear. We'll have one afternoon to hunt in Illinois on the way home before the season closes."

We'd be hunting with our good friends Darren and Sherri Martin on their farm in Schuyler County. They encouraged us to come, but made it clear that it would not be easy to shoot a big buck. For one thing, many of the mature bucks on their property had already shed their antlers. "If you can find a good buck that still has both of his antlers, have at it!" they told us. So despite the odds, we decided to go for it.

I'd be hunting with our full-time cameraman Bryan Lemke and Pat had cameraman Dan Meyers with him. Brian and I planned to hunt out of a permanent ground blind on the edge of a food plot where Darren had seen a really nice buck. Darren had actually shot a monster buck with his Barnett crossbow in that same food plot several weeks earlier. Pat and I had seen the buck he shot a month or so earlier. Darren's trophy turned out to be an awesome 10-pointer that grossed 168 inches. On the afternoon he killed his big deer, he'd seen another big buck come out to feed in the same field.

This long-tined 4-by-4 had been on their hit list all season long, and Nicole had several close encounters with the buck without being able to get a shot. On the last day of the Wisconsin archery season, everything suddenly came together!

After Nicole was able to shoot two great bucks at the end of the 2012-2013 season, she and Pat headed to the Archery Trade Association Show in Louisville, Ky., where they attended a cook-off competition with Seth McGinn of Can Cooker, one of their TV sponsors.

Pat checks out some camera equipment with his good friends at Campbell Cameras, innovators and suppliers of quality outdoor video equipment.

During the past six seasons, Pat and Nicole have made an amazing team. They've hunted together all over the world, and have consistently taken trophy whitetail bucks across the U.S. and Canada. Nicole will tell you that the Driven Team is the best hunting team in the business!

On the way home from the ATA show in Kentucky, Pat and Nicole were able to stop in Illinois and make one quick afternoon hunt on property in Schuyler County belonging to their special friends Darren and Sherri Martin. Wouldn't you know it? Nicole tagged this 4-by-4 beauty with her Barnett crossbow.

This was the first season that Illinois had made it legal to hunt with a crossbow after the second gun season using your regular archery tag, so I decided to use a crossbow like Darren had done. I had my pink Barnett crossbow dialed in to about 60 yards, and knew it would be lethal at anything under that distance.

We saw quite a few does and fawns out feeding that night. There were lots of brassicas in the mixed food plot we were hunting and the deer were tearing up the turnips. Suddenly we saw a big buck – *the* buck as it turned out that Darren had seen earlier – and he was coming in our direction. He was a large 8-pointer with a split G-3 on his right side, and it was a miracle he was still carrying antlers. The weather was bitter and nasty that afternoon, cold with mixed sleet and rain. Conditions were perfect for deer to be moving, but not so great to be out in the elements. Fortunately I was hunting from a Shadow Hunter permanent ground blind. When he got within 50 yards, he stopped and turned broadside. I made a perfect shot with my crossbow. He ran just out of the field and went down in the edge of the woods.

Check out the great footage of Nicole's late-season Illinois crossbow buck.

I was in shock. I had taken three big bucks in four days of hunting in three different states – all in early January 2013. I had not taken a single buck in all of November or December despite monumental efforts and numerous close calls, and now it looked almost as easy as falling off a log. I was on cloud nine, but I knew better. It just goes to show what perseverance can do. It also shows what it means to be truly driven. If you put in your time, remain dedicated and take advantage of every opportunity, eventually it's going to pay off.

CHAPTER 16

COMING FULL CIRCLE
MAKING IT A FAMILY AFFAIR

This wonderful photo depicts the entire Reeve family gathered around a beautiful 10-point buck taken by Olivia in 2010. Smiling faces from left to right are Isabel, Nicole, Olivia, Cole, Pat and Carson.

When it comes to hunting and shooting, Carson, left, is a chip off the old block. Cole, right, loves the outdoors and loves to fish but he's not into hunting as much as the other three Reeve children.

Carson, top, and Cole, bottom, love to shoot their bows and practice with their dad.

Four years ago, Nicole and I bought some land just outside of town so that my four kids would have a place to go and do a lot of the outdoor activities we try to encourage. We built a large storage building with living quarters on one end so that we'd have a place to store all of our equipment. The "shed," as we call it, has really become the family hangout.

In the summer of 2012, Nicole and I held our wedding reception at the shed and it worked out very well. It was large enough for all of our friends and we had a great time. Eventually we plan to build a house on the property. As you might imagine, our family spends a lot of time out there. We hunt on the property, look for sheds, plant food plots, go snowmobiling and share special times together. We have a swimming pond out front and have cookouts in the summertime. As of the spring of 2013, Isabel was 7, Carson was 9, Cole was 12 and Olivia was 16.

I think that three out of the four children are going to be hunters. Cole loves the outdoors, but he'd rather save an animal's life than kill it and we respect him for that. He loves to catch frogs, he enjoys fishing and he loves to look for sheds with the family. Of all my kids, though, Carson is the most like me. He lives to be outside hunting anything he can, shooting or trapping gophers. My mom said it best. Speaking of Carson, she said, "I've had the best pleasure in my life watching my son grow up twice."

It's always been very important for me to make sure the kids are involved in nature in some way; trapping, riding four-wheelers, shooting bows, mushroom hunting, riding snowmobiles in the winter, going on family

Since the Driven TV team now contains six charter members, the adventures that await this dynamic family are unlimited! "You ain't seen nothin' yet," Nicole says with a broad smile.

shed-hunting adventures or just exploring the woods and roaming around the property. That's been a huge focus for both Nicole and I. We certainly don't force it on them, but we make sure the opportunity is there for them to participate. Because of that, I think they've all grown up with a real appreciation for nature.

When Nicole and I were growing up, going to deer camp was as traditional as apple pie; everyone did it in our era. Learning how to hunt, handle a firearm safely and have respect for nature taught us many important values. But now things have changed so much. Sadly, it's not that way any more with most children. The kind of values we learned going to deer camp are not being taught to many of today's kids. That's why so many kids are misdirected and confused.

In the four short years we've owned the property, we've already made a lifetime of memories. In Minnesota you have to be 12 to legally hunt deer, so Carson and Isabel still have a few years to go before they can hunt legally. But there's no way Nicole and I are going to go hunting without them. When we're home, they're going with us; it's that simple. You're not going to stop them. If we were to leave them at home, I

think they'd both throw a fit, just like Nicole did when she was younger. They are both totally eaten up with the hunting bug!

So they go with us whenever we're hunting close to home and we always have a great time. Olivia was able to turkey hunt legally before she could deer hunt. She shot her first turkey at age 9. I think our hunting experiences together have helped cement a much stronger father/daughter relationship. She's growing up awfully fast, and she has a lot of interests, but she loves to deer hunt and it's been a big part of her life. If Nicole and I can build a solid foundation with all of our kids through sharing the outdoors, I feel like our family will be much stronger and much closer in the long run.

Carson shot his first squirrel, a big black squirrel, at age 7. He cherishes the memories and photos of our squirrel hunt so much. You would have thought he had killed a B&C buck! It meant everything to him. He's having that squirrel mounted with money he saved up himself.

We don't want our kids to think they have to shoot a deer each season and be upset if they don't. We want them to cherish the memory and enjoy doing it. Last

Carson lives to go to the woods with his dad. His grandmother says he is a carbon copy of his father.

Whenever Pat and Nicole go hunting anywhere around home, one or more of the kids are always in the blind with them.

Both girls are budding hunters. Olivia, right, has already taken several nice deer. In the fall of 2013, she traveled to New Mexico with Pat and Nicole where she shot her first trophy bull elk.

year, Olivia never filled her deer tag, after several years of getting a deer each year, but she had a great time just being out in the woods.

Being away from my kids so much for extended periods of time is tough. But that's the nature of my job, and a big part of my job as a parent is a balancing act. During the last couple of years alone, Nicole and I have missed seeing many important events in the lives of our kids. It seems like there's always a price to pay with any successful endeavor. In my case, it's the family. We feel extremely fortunate to do what we do, but it's never been easy.

So we've tried extra hard to be there for the kids whenever we can. The minute we get home from a trip, we immediately jump into the parents' role and take care of the kids because that's the way we want it. In that respect, Nicole has been a great step-mom or secondary parent. She loves our kids and they love

her. What she has been able to do with them is amazing. But then, she's an amazing woman!

OLIVIA'S QUEST FOR "FORKIE"

As soon as she was legally able to hunt in Minnesota at age 12, Olivia shot her first deer, a doe, while hunting with my good friend John Redmond, owner of Fair Chase Outfitters. She fully understood why shooting a doe was important and she regarded it as a real trophy. And it was! I showed her how to field-dress her first deer and now she is expected to do it herself. She also helps out with the annual butchering jobs. Nicole and I always shoot at least several does for the freezer each year and we always butcher our own meat.

Olivia first got interested in a buck she named Forkie in early 2009. While out shed hunting with the family in March, she found one of his sheds. It was the left side and it had a forked G-2, thus his name. The

*Pat couldn't be prouder of his two daughters, Isabel, left and Olivia, right.
Both girls love the outdoors and enjoy many different outdoor activities.*

Pat and Nicole make every effort to include all of the children in their varied outdoor and filming activities.

Olivia proudly poses with a fine turkey gobbler. She shot her first turkey when she was 9.

"Carson is a hunting machine," Pat says proudly as his son holds up a black fox squirrel.
Carson saved his allowance to have the squirrel mounted.

Olivia proudly poses with one of several does she has taken. All of the Reeve children help out with the skinning and butchering chores each year.

9/22/2010 2:24 AM

This is one of several trail camera photos taken of Forkie, a buck that Olivia hunted for several years.

young buck was not yet a shooter but he was definitely a buck to keep an eye on for the future. We got lots of trail camera photos of him in velvet later that year as a 2½ year old. He was definitely a buck that I hoped Olivia might get a chance at the following season.

The next year, 2010, we continued to get lots of trail camera photos of Forkie. He was now 3½ and had a beautiful 5-by-4 rack with forked G-2s. We knew he was mostly nocturnal from the trail camera photos we were getting, but Olivia nevertheless hunted him all season long. By now, she had her heart set on getting him. Nicole and I wanted her to be successful as much as she did.

By the time he was 3½ years old, Forkie was a beautiful buck with some outstanding headgear. Olivia made an all-out effort to hunt him during the 2011 season.

However, the season quickly slipped by and finally we were down to the last day. I advised Olivia to consider shooting another deer if the opportunity presented itself, and late in the afternoon a beautiful 10-pointer came into our food plot. Olivia shot him with her T/C muzzleloader. Forkie had never shown himself during daylight hours. Although she was very proud of her outstanding 10-pointer, Olivia was a little disappointed that she had never even gotten a glimpse of Forkie.

In March 2011, on an overcast, rainy day perfect for shed hunting, we all headed out to look for Forkie's sheds in a patch of woods where we knew he had spent much of his time. We knew he had survived the season through recent trail camera photos. After several hours of searching the woods in the partially melted snow, Olivia found his left side. As everyone was standing around congratulating her, she looked over and saw his right side lying on the ground a few yards away. Finding both his sheds energized Olivia even more. That summer she helped me plant food plots and we did everything we could think of to attract Forkie to our property. Come the 2011 hunting season, Olivia planned to make an all-out effort to get him.

That summer we got our first trail camera photo of Forkie on Aug. 28. By now he had grown into a sizable 4½-year-old brute. His rack was much larger and had a lot more mass. Olivia hunted him as much as she could in the early season. Unfortunately, Nicole and I hunted out of state much of the season and didn't get home until late November. So Olivia wasn't able to hunt Forkie as much as she had hoped to during the Minnesota firearm season.

Upon arriving home, we immediately checked our trail cameras and discovered that a number of pictures had been taken of Forkie through Nov. 10. After that, there was nothing. Nicole and I were thinking the worst; that the deer had probably been shot by some-

One of the many trail camera photos taken of Forkie at age 4½.

Although Olivia had set her sights on trying to shoot Forkie during the 2010 season, she ended up taking this outstanding 10-pointer on the last day of the season because Forkie never showed up.

one else. Then, on Nov. 20, there he was in a nighttime photo. Knowing he was alive was good news. However, as I studied the photo I got a lump in my throat. Forkie had been shot in his lower left back leg. It looked to be a very serious wound. When Nicole and I delivered the sad news to Olivia, she was crushed.

Now, I figured her only chance was to try to get him during muzzleloader season in late November or early December before the coyotes got him. Olivia hunted him for nearly a week without seeing a trace of the deer. Then, on Dec. 2, a new trail camera photo taken at night revealed one of my biggest fears. Forkie had prematurely shed both antlers due to the stress and trauma of his leg wound. Olivia's hunt for him was over.

"When Dad told me the news my heart sank," Olivia said. "I was glad he was alive but I knew he wasn't out of the woods because Dad said the coyotes still might get him."

On the last day of muzzleloader season, Olivia shot a doe for the freezer to fill her tag. We kept getting trail camera photos of Forkie through Dec. 30. Then he simply vanished. In March 2012, the family started looking for his sheds. "I searched and searched but found nothing," Olivia said. Then, a few weeks later when the family was out mushroom hunting, Olivia stumbled onto both of Forkie's sheds. At least now she had two complete sets of his antlers.

Watch the exciting video of Olivia's first buck – a dandy 10-pointer!

An elated Olivia Reeve shows off both of Forkie's sheds she found in the spring of 2011 while mushroom hunting with the family.

Neighbors several miles away reported seeing a big buck with a forked right side and a big club on the left side, indicating some type of injury.

They also reported the lower portion of the buck's back left leg was missing. Then, early in the 2012 season we got word that one of our neighbors had in fact killed Forkie. He had survived his leg wound after all, only to be killed the next season. Typical of bucks that have had serious leg wounds, one side of his rack contained a cluster of abnormal points, while the other side was more normal with several splits and sticker points.

Certainly Olivia was sad to hear about Forkie's demise, but she has some great memories to look back on. And because of those memories Forkie will always live on in her mind. Her hunt for this buck was both

memorable and bittersweet, but her quest for Forkie taught her many valuable lessons in life and gave her a passion for deer hunting that I hope will be with her forever. Olivia never did fill her buck tag in 2012, but she enjoyed the season hunting with Nicole and I nevertheless. And she helped us butcher the meat from the does we shot.

CARSON'S FIRST BUCK, ILLINOIS 2012

Carson is our natural-born hunter in the family. He takes after me. He'll hunt anything – squirrels, gophers, pigeons, frogs, raccoons – you name it. He just loves to be outside with a gun or bow in his hand. He'd seen lots of other kids shoot deer on TV and started working on me to take him deer hunting. So in

Much to Olivia's distress, trail camera photos taken in late November and early December 2011 revealed that Forkie had been shot in the back leg. A short time later the buck shed his antlers prematurely as a result of the injury.

the summer of 2012 when he was 9 years old I made a promise to him. "If you study hard and make all 'A's, I'll take you deer hunting over Christmas vacation."

"All 'A's?" Carson argued. "That's not fair."

"Yep, all 'A's," I insisted.

"Okay," Carson said.

I thought I was safe. I never thought he'd do it but he did. He really buckled down and when his report card came he'd made all 'A's. So Nicole and I decided to take him with us to Illinois over the Christmas holidays while we were visiting her folks. In Minnesota you have to be 12 years old to deer hunt legally, but in Illinois we were able to get Carson a one-time apprentice license. At only age 9, Carson wasn't yet big enough to pull a 40-pound bow, so we let him shoot a Barnett crossbow on his first deer hunt. Crossbows are great for young kids. There is no recoil and no loud bang. They're easy to manage and deadly accurate. Carson started practicing long before our hunt and he was very efficient at 40 yards. Nicole has made lethal shots at over 50 yards with her crossbow.

I didn't want Carson to feel any kind of pressure. "Shoot whatever you want," I told him. "It doesn't have to be a giant buck. Shoot a doe or spike or anything you want. Just enjoy the hunt."

It had snowed heavily the day before we arrived at the Jones property in southern Illinois. On our first afternoon, we went out to a portable ground blind. The weather was not very cooperative. We saw a few does late in the afternoon but our shooting light was beginning to fade and Carson never really had a good shooting opportunity.

On the second afternoon, we went to a Big Game permanent ground blind overlooking a field. Several does came out in the field and we watched them for a while. Fortunately, none of them ever got within crossbow range. After sitting awhile longer, Carson said, "Dad, here comes a big deer!" It was a beautiful 8-pointer. He came out into the food plot we were watching and started feeding, but was well out of range. Carson got very nervous and antsy. That was the deer he wanted to shoot. Since I was running a camera so that we could get his first buck on film, he had to man the crossbow on his own.

All at once the buck started walking right toward us. Carson steadied his crossbow on a set of Bog-Pod shooting sticks and started aiming. He aimed very carefully and flipped off the safety. He squeezed the trigger and shot that buck right through the heart. It was a perfect shot and he was really excited! Seeing his face light up and seeing that big smile made things really come full circle. It was a special hunt and a special memory. Hunting has taught Carson a lot of important values at a young age. I look forward to many more hunts like that with him and all of my children!

LAST WORD FROM PAT

I see our world of hunting as we know it changing so rapidly. What will the future hold? I hope my kids will always understand hunting and understand what an important tradition it is. I hope they'll always have a passion for the sport. It's been a way of life for Nicole and I, as well as for my dad, my granddad and her dad. A year or so ago we took the kids out and shot some squirrels. Then we brought them home, cleaned them, cooked them and ate them for dinner. Everyone thought they were very good. We want to make sure the kids understand how important it is to eat what you shoot.

But, we also want them to have an appreciation for nature in general. Watching a sunrise, observing an eagle soaring in the sky – those are things I want them to cherish. I want them to remember the memories we build together, and cherish them as well. I want them to carry on the legacy and hunt for the right reasons. *Stewardship, respect,* and *appreciation* are three words I'd like my kids to live by long after I'm gone.

To me, having a video record of a hunt means capturing memories of the kids that can be passed on for future generations. I'd give anything if I had videos of my grandfather and father hunting back in the old days. That's one of the reasons I do what I do. I want to re-

Carson's first buck ever was taken in Illinois in December 2012! The old warrior was found to be 6½ years old. Sheds from the buck were found on Jim Jones' property.

cord those events now for people to enjoy in the future. That's one of the most important aspects of what we do.

In addition to being able to share our passion for hunting with the kids, one of the most rewarding things I've witnessed has been to read some of the fan letters Nicole receives, and see the response she gets at shows from young girls who are getting involved in hunting with their families. Because they have mentors like Vicki Cianciarulo, Kandi Kisky and Nicole, these young girls are now becoming passionate hunters. The same is true with their mothers and grandmothers. They are the future of hunting.

We want our kids to know there's more to hunting than just going out and shooting something. And now, thank goodness, it's become more of a year-round sport. We hunt sheds in the spring. We plant trees. We build waterholes. We plant food plots in the summer. Much of what we do benefits other wildlife tremendously. We try to teach the kids to put in more than you take out. When they see the fruits of their labor, it really does take things to a whole new level.

When we first bought our property, we put

Carson shot his outstanding buck with a Barnett crossbow.

A proud young Carson poses with his adopted grandfather, Jim Jones, Nicole's father.

Long before his unforgettable 2012 hunt, Carson spent considerable time learning how to shoot a crossbow with the best teacher in the world – his dad!

Archery has long played an important role in the lives of Pat and Nicole, and it hasn't taken much effort to pass their love for the sport on to the children. Here Carson high-fives his dad after a great grouping with his Mathews Genesis bow.

out dozens of bluebird houses. We also planted several varieties of trees. Carson got hooked on trapping gophers. Trapping gophers is on his "top three" list of favorite things to do in the world! That was mine when I was his age too. It makes me so proud. We're lucky to live in a rural area where kids can still do rural things like that.

When I was young, I remember taking a new shotgun to school to show my friends. Those days are gone forever and it's a shame that our world has changed so much. But it is what it is and we can't change what has happened. However, we can get our kids involved in the outdoors and teach them values that will stay with them throughout their lives.

Some people think Nicole and I are crazy to spend so much time out in the elements. In order to do what we do, though, we've got to be willing to sit in a freezing cold treestand hour after hour, day after day. It takes a lot of energy, determination and willpower. That's why it's a way of life for us and not just an occupation. That's why we're so passionate about what we do. To Nicole and I, there's a lot more to what we do than just the hunting aspect. As we've both said before – it's about the people we meet, the experiences we share and the memories we make.

Isabel, the youngest of Pat's four children, is also a chip off the old block. She loves to hunt for sheds and join the family on any type of outdoor outing.

Watch Carson get his first buck – a great Illinois 8-pointer!

Pat and Nicole tied the knot on June 23, 2012. The wedding party, composed of friends and family, had a lot of fun on the big day. The reception was held on Pat and Nicole's 30-acre farm at the "Shack," the recently constructed building and guest house that was finished just before the wedding.

This book has come to a close but the next chapter in our book of life has yet to be written. What will be in that next chapter? Another big buck for Nicole? A trophy buck for one of the kids? An exciting new adventure to a place we've never been before? I sincerely hope it'll include all of those things. But who can really say what the future will hold? That unknown factor is one of the things that makes life even more exciting.

On a day-to-day basis, we don't really know what we'll be doing in two months or six months or two years. We don't even know what next season will hold for us. But we do know that we'll be doing everything within our power to keep doing what we've always done and keep having fun with the kids. It's the life we love and the only life we know. And while we're out there doing it, we'll always strive to improve on what we've done in the past. To us, that's the most important thing we can do.

I suppose we'll just keep on doing what we love and let the next chapter write itself. In the meantime, we hope you've been able to get a little insight into how we hunt and what we do. Life should always be an adventure, so we hope you'll go out and find a few of your own. That's what being driven is all about!